Modern Masters of Religious Education

Contributors

Johannes Hofinger

Findley B. Edge

Randolph Crump Miller

D. Campbell Wyckoff

John H. Westerhoff III

Howard Grimes

C. Ellis Nelson

Harold William Burgess

Donald M. Joy

Eugene F. Hemrick

John H. Peatling

James Michael Lee

MODERN MASTERS OF RELIGIOUS EDUCATION

edited by

MARLENE MAYR

Religious Education Press
Birmingham, Alabama

BV
1470.2
.M63
1983

Library of Congress Cataloging in Publication Data
Main entry under title:

Modern masters of religious education.

   Contents: Introduction / Marlene Mayr — The catechetical Sputnik / Johannes Hofinger — A search for authenticity / Findley B. Edge — [etc.]
   1. Educators, Christian—United States—Biography.
I. Mayr, Marlene.
BV1470.2.M63   1983   209'.2'2 [B]   82-25009
ISBN 0-89135-033-0

Religious Education Press, Inc.
1531 Wellington Road
Birmingham, Alabama 35209
10 9 8 7 6 5 4 3 2

Religious Education Press publishes books exclusively in religious education and in areas closely related to religious education. It is committed to enhancing and professionalizing religious education through the publication of serious, significant, and scholarly works.

PUBLISHER TO THE PROFESSION

Contents

Introduction

When I first became involved in North American religious education a few years ago, I was fascinated by the different persons and theories in this field. Now, some years later, I am still interested in these people and these theories.

In talking to religious educators here and there, I have discovered that they too are similarly interested in the major figures and theories in the field. Hence I thought it might be a worthwhile project to edit a book in which some of the most influential and important religious education leaders would have the opportunity of *telling their personal histories as these histories relate to the forging and hammering out of their present positions.*

The purpose of this book is twofold. First, it aims to reveal where the contributors have come from in terms of their current theories or viewpoints. Second, it endeavors to help religious educators in the field gain new hope and insights for their own religious education activity by seeing how important leaders in the field have developed professionally.

In my original letter inviting major religious education leaders to contribute an essay to this book, I specifically asked each one to have as the content axis of his or her chapter those events, persons, situations, books, influences, and so forth, which have significantly affected his or her own present theoretical perspective and practical stance in religious education. I further stated that these events, persons, situations, books, influences, and the like, may embrace any time span the contributor might decide upon. My goal in all of this was to motivate the contributors to make their essays highly personal. Thus my intent was to make each essay the personal story of that contributor's life—not his or her life in general but instead those realities which have significantly influenced the contributor to take the intellectual, affective, and existential stance to religious education which he or she presently has. In short, I wished this book not be so much a collection of overall personal journeys but instead a set of overall professional journeys as informed and permeated by personal journeys.

Because this book is a compilation of the professional journeys of twelve outstanding and diverse religious education leaders, it is therefore an overview of the most influential religious education theories and thinking in the contemporary era. The professional journeys of the religious education leaders are necessarily and intimately interwoven with their theoretical views. The essays are basic and applied theory on the hoof, so to speak. To put it a little differently, the essays in this volume represent a highly personalistic way of examining the structure and dynamics of the theories and the thinking of each of the religious education leaders represented in this volume. Consequently, individuals wishing to better understand the main currents and principal theories of post World War II American religious education will, I hope, gain much by reading this volume. I truly believe that one of the most significant contributions which this volume can make to the field is that it constitutes, in actual point of fact, a very human overview of, and a deep personalistic revelation into essential theory in contemporary religious education.

Now that all the essays are in and the manuscript is ready to be sent off to the printer, I can state with great satisfaction that I am delighted by the caliber, candor, and diversity of the essays in this book. I am truly honored to be the editor of the professional autobiographies contained in this volume.

It seems to me that these essays, containing as they do an enormous range of Christian backgrounds and experiences, are not only highly illuminative for the field of religious education itself, but also are singularly helpful to historians and others seeking to lay hold of that extraordinarily important but usually elusive and hidden vital strain in American church history, namely the living personal struggles and here-and-now situational exigencies which more often than not are far more influential and decisive in the church's life than more visible events like the number of new edifices built each year or the names of important ecclesiastical administrators. Indeed, this present volume presents a rich and intimate tapestry of twentieth-century American Christianity as seen from the inside, so to speak.

Readers of this book are entitled to know my basic criteria for inviting the authors whose fine essays appear in this volume. In general, I had five principal criteria for selection. First of all, I restricted my focus to the Christian sector of religious education. I did this not because of any lack of appreciation of non-Christian religious education, but because

Christian religious education is the field in which I have been most involved in recent years. Besides, restricting the scope of the book to the Christian sphere made the project more manageable in terms of size. Second, I confined my range to those religious education leaders whose primary influence lay in the period following the Second World War. There are other volumes such as *Pioneers of Religious Education* edited by Boardman W. Kathan which deal principally with the lives of religious education leaders whose main influence lay in the first half of this century. Third, I narrowed my scope to persons who at the time of my initial invitation (spring, 1981) had spent at least ten years in positions of professional leadership and influence in Christian religious education. My intent here was to present religious education leaders whose work had stood the test of time and whose influence was perduring, rather than to offer religious educators who might be instant meteors lighting up the religious education sky for a few years and then disappearing in name and influence. Fourth, I limited my attention to those religious education specialists who have tended in one way or another to be pioneering or innovative in the field as contrasted to those many fine religious educators who are principally derivative thinkers or primarily disciples. Fifth, and by far the most difficult for me, was to invite those religious education leaders whom I and others with whom I talked believed to be the most influential persons in the theory and practice of religious education in our time—highly influential in the entire Christian church at large, or in some cases highly influential in a particular denomination as that denomination impacts upon the whole of Christianity. This criterion is, of course, tinged with a certain amount of personal and group subjectivity. I attempted to minimize this inevitable subjectivity by certain more-or-less "objective" measures such as by seeing which religious education leaders frequently were mentioned (positively or negatively) in the professional literature, locating the dynamic thread of relationship between current thinking and practice on the one hand and previous statements of position enunciated by key religious education leaders on the other hand, and so forth. Notwithstanding, the fifth criterion does contain, as I readily admit, a certain inevitable strain of subjectivity.

Each of the distinguished religious education leaders whose autobiographies are included in this volume has exerted considerable influence on the field. Johannes Hofinger has been a major force in bringing about a change from the former Baltimore Catechism mentality in catechetics to a mentality imbued with spirit of kerygmatic theology. Findley Edge has been singularly effective in bringing about a vital *apperatura* in the way in which Baptists think about and do Christian education. Randolph Crump Miller, quite possibly the most important Protestant religious educator in the postwar period to date, brought about a major shift in the field by making theology the center and goal of Christian education. D. Campbell Wyckoff has surely been the most potent voice in our time on the issue of the structure and form of the Christian education curriculum. John Westerhoff has undoubtedly been one of the two or three most exciting and forward-looking figures on the American religious education scene since his first important tract was published in 1970. Howard Grimes has been a true pioneer in getting religious educators to appreciate that religious education is not so much a separate form of ministry as it is the work of the whole church. Ellis Nelson has been the person primarily responsible for helping religious educators to view the faith-journey in the religious education process from the exquisite combination of socialization theory, biblical truth, and congregational reality. Harold Burgess not only has significantly changed the complexion of the Christian education face of the small Protestant denomination of which he is a leading member, but also has provided the field with a seminal and widely-used category system for building a vibrant and effective religious education program. Donald Joy has done pioneering fundamental work both on the shape of evangelical Protestant Christian education curricula and on the empirical foundations for moral development in a Christian vein. Eugene Hemrick has affected a quiet yet major revolution in catechetics through empirical studies of various facets of the American catechetical scene— studies which, before Hemrick's arrival in Washington, were generally looked upon with considerable skepticism and often outright hostility by catechetical officials and other Catholic leaders. John Peatling has been probably the most influential voice in promoting sophisticated and ongoing empirical research in postwar American religious education. James Michael Lee, perhaps the only religious educator in this period to present a well-developed comprehensive and systematic macrotheory of religious education, is also the originator of the very influential social-science approach to religious instruction.

The ordering of the chapters is patterned after the overall typology presented in Harold William Burgess's book *An Invitation to Religious Education*. This typology is not only the most widely-used in religious education, but also is ideally suited to this present volume. The first two chapters exemplify the traditional theological approach, with Hofinger embodying the Catholic sector of this approach and Edge ably enfleshing the Protestant sector. Though Edge's essay clearly falls within the purview of the traditional theological approach, still some subtle shadings toward the contemporary theological approach can be discerned. The chapters by Miller, Wyckoff, Westerhoff, and Grimes are representative of the richness and diversity of the contemporary theological approach to religious education. In Grimes's sensitive chapter there is a slight swing toward the social-science approach, though Grimes still unambigiously adheres to the contemporary theological position. Ellis Nelson's essay is a bridge chapter between the varieties of theological approaches and the social-science approach. The latter is ably bodied forth in the essays by Burgess, Joy, Hemrick, Peatling, and Lee. I was unable to locate any highly influential postwar religious educator who represents the fourth segment of the overall Burgess typology, namely the social-culture theological approach.

There is a certain natural though unintentional historical cycle to the chapters in this book. For example, the author of the first chapter and one of the oldest contributors in terms of chronological age baptized both children of the concluding chapter's author, who is one of the youngest contributors in terms of chronological age.

Quite a few enlightening features emerge from this book's rich tapestry of essays. On the heartening side, the essays of some contributors whose corpus of writings are very scientific are among the most passionate and personalistic in this entire volume. On the disheartening side, only two of the contributors are laypersons—and one of these presently has a foot in the sanctuary, so to speak.

Books consisting of contributed essays are often criticized by some reviewers for being "uneven." Well, let me state right now that this book is very uneven. It is uneven with respect to chapter length, with respect to the degree to which a contributor's personal life intersects his profession, with respect to sparkle and inherent interest, with respect to the backgrounds of the authors, and the like. If this book were not uneven, then it would not be the book I intended. Scientific books must by their very nature be even. But books which treat of human growth and development in a highly personalistic way must necessarily be extraordinarily uneven, because human life is uneven. To attempt to make the contributions of this book "even" would be to flatten this book to a state where all the vitality and life would be squeezed out. I did everything I could to give the authors complete freedom; even the three guidelines I suggested in my letters to them were only loose suggestions which could be followed or not depending on each author's own perception of his professional journey. The author of the shortest chapter, for example, frequently speaks in scintillating one-liners. When he submitted his chapter, he asked me if I wanted him to make it longer. I responded that he should write whatever length he deemed appropriate to the professional story he wished to tell. The author of the longest chapter almost invariably writes very lengthy books. This volume's most personalistic and passionate essays are just as precious to the book (and to me) as are the essays of the authors who tell their journeys in a more detached and objective fashion.

Editing a book like this is a dangerous undertaking in that few readers will be totally satisfied with the persons whom I invited to be contributors. Inevitably a reader will say: "Why was my favorite religious education leader left out of this collection?", or "How in the world did she invite *that* individual to contribute an essay?" As I mentioned earlier in this Introduction, I did have certain criteria to guide my selection; however, in the final analysis, the selection was what Americans like to term "a judgment call." I only hope that many, and possibly most religious educators will go along with my judgment calls.

This volume does not pretend to be complete. Without doubt there are outstanding religious education leaders who, by dint of oversight on my part or by reasons of size limitations of this book, are not included. Surely this volume is poorer because of the absence of these individuals. I should note, however, that not every person whom I invited accepted my invitation. For example, the man whom I consider the nation's most important theorist and researcher on adult religious education was unable to contribute because he was then recovering from serious surgery. I invited three women to contribute—not because they are women, but because they have made what I and others believe to be outstanding pioneering contributions to the field. (As a woman, I deeply resent the blatant sexism of some pushy females and especially of some insecure males who contend that women should be represented in public forums not because they have made outstanding contributions but rather simply because they are females). Two ladies declined my invitation because they were so swamped with previous commitments that they simply had no time to write an essay for this book. In the third instance, I came to

the conviction rightly or wrongly that the lady was interested in receiving a greater financial remuneration for her contribution than a volume
of this nature could possibly afford; hence with sadness I withdrew my
invitation to her. The only genuinely unusual case I encountered was
that of an outstanding and highly influential religious education leader
who originally accepted my invitation to contribute. He asked to see the
names of the other contributors, pointedly noting that their identities
might possibly influence what he would write. When he learned who
his fellow contributors were, he withdrew from the project on political
grounds, asserting that certain kinds of religious educators whom he
believed should be included were not represented. In one sense, I truly
regret that this man's professional journey is missing from this volume.
However, in another sense I am relieved that his essay is missing in that I
want this book to be a set of professional odysseys, not a series of political
statements masquerading as professional odysseys. I want this book to be
a collection of professional histories told as honestly and as authentically
as possible in terms of how these histories occurred; I do not want these
professional histories to be doctored or otherwise slanted in order to
further the autobiographers' current political views. Furthermore, I
totally oppose efforts to politicize this volume in terms of whether a
contributor feels politically aligned or not to the other contributors,
whether the range of essays is acceptable to a contributor's political views
of what that range should comprise, and so forth. Politics tends to exert a
corrupting influence on whatever it touches, and I do not wish to have
this corrupting influence seep into this book, much less engulf it. After
all, the readers of this volume are entitled to inside, intimate, and
authentic accounts of the authors' professional journeys. Readers looking for a set of political manifestos will have to go elsewhere.

Just a few days ago we at Religious Education Press received a lengthy
letter from a person who will shortly be writing a book for us. At one
point in his letter he remarked that he believes that the field of religious
education is so competitive at the present time that religious education
professors and experts find one another a threat rather than a source of
potential help and collegiality. I have attended several national religious
education conventions and from what I was able to judge from what I
experienced there, this future REP author might have a point. One of
the hopes I have for this volume is that it will stimulate religious education leaders as well as religious educators in the field to work together
more collegially even if their views are widely diverse. It is especially

Chapter 1

The Catechetical Sputnik

Johannes Hofinger

Of all the numerous essays I have written, this present one is, as far as I remember, the only one which I decided to author not because of its appealing topic, but in order to comply with the insistent invitation of a good friend. This simple fact seems to demonstrate convincingly that in my literary work I enjoyed great freedom and that I did not hesitate to use it. My writings reflect my personal interests and my personal choices.

How I Learned To Appreciate Family Education

In later years I often advised my students to reflect on their own upbringing, and to learn from such reflections for their work in religious education. Quite early in life I had discovered for myself the great benefit of an impartial reflection on the education I had received at home and in school. The very fact that my own education to a Christian life was healthy, effective, and devoid of any deeply disturbing experience, although not without the unavoidable mistakes and problems, made an objective evaluation rather easy and helpful.

Long before I learned from books about the formative power of Christian family life, I had experienced this blessed power in my own religious growth. This experience was for me of very special importance. As a student I became an aggressive bookworm who preferred interesting books, particularly on history, to any kind of sport. Later I became an enthusiastic teacher with all the qualities of a genuine *Schulfuchs* (school fox) as we call it in German. Without the unforgettable experience of my own finding God within the family, I would have in the process surely succumbed to the danger of overrating school and scholarly teaching in the field of religious education.

Both of my parents came from deeply religious families of best Tyrolian tradition. We were all healthily proud of our "holy land Tyrol," as it had been called in those days. And it really deserved it. Three brothers of my father were diocesan priests. All three were men of deep faith and manifest integrity of life, but without a particular gift of communication with us four boys. By far the poorest in this regard was the eldest among them, a teacher of history in the minor seminary with the title of "professor." He was the typical professor of the old style. Notwithstanding a sincere admiration for his learning and unquestioned acknowledgment of his fairness and impartiality, I resolved in my high-school years that I would never become a teacher of this kind.

These uncles usually spent their summer vacation with our family. I learned most from them by being allowed to participate respectfully in their evening conversation with my father. This was talk of mature men and Christians who shared their views, insights, and convictions about the exigencies and events of their times.

My father, too, had some difficulties in communicating with us during childhood. He would never play with us except for some rare chess parties after we had reached teenage. He obviously loved us and was noticeably proud of us, especially of our success in school. We were clearly aware that he expected us to get superior grades in all subjects. And we did. His wholesome ambition based on real achievement was infectious. Of his four sons (we had no sisters), I was the third and in many ways the one most similar to him in the whole make-up of our personality. What induced me to lifelong work in the field of catechetics was not any special attraction to the little ones or a natural facility of communication with them, but the religious conviction of the importance of religious education. My own predisposition prevented me from any over-emphasis on the catechesis of children and inclined me to procure for the catechesis of adolescents and adults its due place.

We brothers respected father and loved him sincerely, although in a more restrained way. We were clearly aware of his fatherly care for us and accepted his uncontested authority. We admired his manly character and his professional efficiency as businessman and provincial politician. Without noticing it, we learned from his remarkable common sense, his realistic approach to life, and his exemplary dedication to his duties in family and civic community. He was open to new ideas. At the beginning of this century he brought electric lights into our town.

There, our family had the first electric stove, the first electric washer, and also, I think, the first typewriter in father's office and the first cash register in our shop. Such openness to the new went hand in hand with aversion to exaggeration. Father preferred, on principle, the sound middle line. He was in danger of underrating the emotional aspect of life. Of all his children I may have received the most enduring influence from him for my basic attitudes to work and life.

Before I was three years old, my mother died in fulfilling her duties as mother. The eight years of her life with father must have come close to the ideal of a happy Christian marriage. I only know about this from my father and many others. Personally, I have only some vague re-membrances of my mother. Yet the high respect which people showed when speaking of her was a great encouragement for me and a strong impulse to follow her example.

Father married again. My stepmother, a devout Christian, loved me and I loved her. But her educational influence was far surpassed by that of our governess. We called her "Gredei" (Margaret). She came from a farming family. In the primitive one-class school of a mountain village, she had received her rudimentary education which she later deepened by some selected reading. She never became a learned person, but, as everyone admitted, she was an outstanding Christian and a born educa-tor who loved us four boys with a truly motherly love, and with a wonderful understanding of the characteristics of healthy boys. Our education was genuinely masculine. More than anything else, my ever-growing admiration for Gredei's personality and my deep love for her prevented me from turning into a poor chauvinist in the one-sided masculine atmosphere of our family.

In the whole process of religious growth, so many influences work together that any attempt to single out a predominant one must be made with due emphasis on its interplay with the others. With this in mind, I dare to say that of all persons I have met in life Gredei was the one who influenced me best and deepest in my religious growth. My later studies in religious education only confirmed my early conviction of her superi-or gifts for religious education. What I learned from her about Christian living also applied to my catechetical work. She gave me an object lesson I could never forget and from which I profited greatly in later catechetical studies.

My own religious experience in early life made me forever skeptical of all trends in religious education which unduly insist on much theoretical knowledge of the educator. My historical studies of later years only confirmed my reservations. Why have we, until now, not made more solid historical studies about acknowledged great examples of successful religious education in the past in order to learn from them for our times?

One major deficiency of our education at home was a total lack of timely information about the facts of life. Even Gredei failed in this important matter. It was a regrettable mistake, but since the basic principles and attitudes of an authentic Christian life had been developed early and solidly in our lives, this omission was not disastrous. When the right time came and nobody spoke to us, God helped with the right books. In Catholic books of those days you could not, of course, find the necessary information. So I helped myself with Protestant books. That was my first wholesome "ecumenical" experience.

The religious education within the family was complemented by the work of the school. My best religion teachers were a sister and a lay teacher. In Austria of old, priests were supposed to give the catechism class in the school. Thanks be to God they did not apply this outdated law to the lower grades. When I entered elementary school in 1911, the catechetical renewal had just started in my home country. Sister Blasia, a Daughter of Charity, then already of advanced age I am quite sure, had read almost nothing on renewed catechetics. But motivated by deep faith and motherly love, she found the right way herself. I think that even today religion teachers of grade one could learn from her teaching of religion in which she used, intensively and properly, stories and pictures. In second grade, a lay teacher, Miss Tschofen gave us excellent preparation for First Communion. We learned a lot with these two teachers, but it would be quite wrong to say their religion class was geared to transmitting doctrine. They formed our hearts.

Honesty obliges me to admit that the worst catechist I had in the elementary grades was our pastor, a doctor of theology. His study of theology did not make him a great catechist. As dean he had to examine the religion classes of his deanery. I fear that he could offer very little advice and support to other religion teachers. Later on in my teenage years, I used his theology library for my studies. I respected him as a good and learned priest and even chose him as my confessor, but reflection on his catechism class taught me above all what should be avoided in teaching religion.

Happy Years in the Seminary

At age eleven i entered the minor seminary, the Borromaeum in Salzburg, with its excellent high school of the humanist type. The Austrian
high-school education takes eight years. The first four years are the
equivalent of the American junior high, and the last four years, that of a
junior college. A humanist high school was supposed to train an intellectual elite. Only a small minority of the youth aspired to this kind of
education. Of those who tried, a considerable number were eliminated
in the first years, since they could not meet the strict demands of the
school, especially with regard to Latin, Greek, and mathematics. But in
our high school, my uncle, the "professor," also dismissed many students with low grades in history and geography.

In this way our minor seminary provided the Archdiocese of Salzburg
with a clergy of high academic standards. As a student I accepted our
school education as a matter of course and was proud of it. Only later in
life did I become aware of the problem it raised for the formation of
future teachers of religion. Priests who came from this type of academic
study were often inclined to follow an intellectualistic approach in
religious education. The pastor of my home town, the learned doctor of
theology, was an example of this. Of my three priestly uncles, the two
older ones excelled academically, but not in religious education. The
third one was academically inferior to his brothers, but he became a
superior teacher of religion in elementary and high school. Such facts
point to a problem, but of course they do not prove that the right
solution is the lowering of academic standards.

All the main subjects of the seminary high school were taught by
priests, most of them with doctorates in their particular subjects. We
respected them as priests and teachers, as they deserved. I would have
liked more personal contact with them beyond the encounter in class.
Throughout all eight years of high school, our home-room teacher was
the teacher of Latin and Greek. Wisely he did not burden us unduly
with Latin and Greek grammar, but conveyed to us a true understanding
and appreciation of classical literature and humanist culture. He was a
real humanist in the best sense of the word, with a special gift for
opening our minds in an authentic Christian way to human values and
situations. From him I learned first and best how religion can be taught
effectively and unobtrusively with a secular subject, provided the teacher sees his subject and task in the light of faith.

Professor Brändstatter's teaching contrasted noticeably with that of Professor Feichtner who taught us religion. He, too, was a learned man and worthy priest. He was an excellent musician and, as director of music, secured for our seminary high school the superior standard of musical performance one would rightly expect from the seminary of Salzburg, a center of classical music. His classes of religion were carefully prepared, clear and solid, but not inspiring. They lacked the indispensable kerygmatic dimension. What he presented was good theology, but it was not enough the message of life we teenagers needed. I still remember that even as a student I became aware of this limitation and regretted it, since I knew of his good will and was conscious of our need. What I found lacking, in fact, prepared me to later insist on a truly kerygmatic catechesis.

Nobody expected a mature priestly vocation from children who enter a preparatory seminary at eleven years of age. We were only supposed to have the desire to become priests, and to find out what such a vocation would really imply and how it would fit us. But like many of my fellow students I was then already determined to prepare myself for priesthood. I knew very well that my whole family, and most especially Gredei, had noticed with great joy for a long time my sincere desire to become a priest. In retrospect, I appreciate the complete freedom I was given in choosing my vocation. I felt truly at home in the priestly atmosphere of the minor seminary and could hardly understand some fellow students who felt homesick after each vacation.

In the time of adolescence, for a period of about one year, there was a crisis, not so much with regard to my priestly vocation but with regard to seminary life. As soon as my father noticed it, he was ready immediately to take me out of the seminary. His only remark was that he expected me to be thankful for what I had received in the first four years of seminary education. That I sincerely promised.

During the following summer vacation, I was supposed to look for a place to stay in the town of Hall, near Innsbruck, where I wanted to attend a renowned high school of the Franciscans as a day student. But I did nothing. At the end of the vacation I made a pilgrimage to Maria Kirchenthal, a shrine of the Blessed Mother, hidden in a ravine and surrounded by the precipitous mountains of the Northern Tyrolian Alps. There I decided to return to the seminary. Because I had formally given notice of my leaving at the end of the preceding academic year, my superiors must have been surprised when I showed up again. They accepted me without difficulty, although I had a reputation as a rather unruly seminarian.

Soon after I experienced a profound interior renewal which gave me a mature understanding and a joyful acceptance of Christian life and of my priestly vocation. The following years in the seminary I have always considered as the most happy, most decisive, and most fruitful years of my life. I was then not yet sixteen years old and obviously still immature in many respects, but with God's grace I reached a depth of insight and commitment which gave me the definitive orientation for the rest of my life.

From then on I became deeply aware of the necessity of a thorough ongoing renewal not only in my own life, but also in the world around me. We were in the first years after World War I, a time of profound reorientation in church and society. My interest in history concentrated on periods of religious renewal within the Christian community. Also, I became deeply involved in the life of the seminary. The time of negative criticism and revolt was over. With good friends of the same religious outlook, I now wanted to contribute positively to a renewal of our seminary from within, beginning with ourselves. Like Saul of Tarsus, I, too, needed some time to convince my superiors and my classmates that my conversion was sincere and lasting. Fortunately, I stood the test.

From the time of my conversion experience, I felt a clear call and a powerful urge to communicate my own new outlook on life to others. More than once I burdened my classmates with my new apostolic zeal. I had not yet learned to distinguish a true apostolate from proselytism. At that time I did not think in particular of later work in the field of catechetics, but my new apostolic attitude prepared me for future cate- chetical activity and, in fact, decided the basic approach of my later catechetical work.

I wanted to become above all a zealous priest, and I already had the perception that my proper place for priestly work would not be in parish work but some teaching position and work with young people. I would describe myself as a born teacher. But from the time of my turning to God as a teenager, I was determined to make any teaching about God, the world, and life a means for a personal encounter with God. I did not yet know the term *kerygmatic* but what I had in mind was clearly in the line of kerygmatic theology and catechesis. In those days I probably would have used the word *spiritual*. In later years my audiences and the readers of my books might have understood me better if I had used the word *spiritual* for the strange Greek term *kerygmatic* in describing the right approach to catechetics.

It was not yet time, during my teen years, for any professional study of the process of religious education and of spiritual growth. Yet from my own experience and from my work with others, I knew of the central place which true prayer has in any genuine encounter with God. Since then, helping others to find God in life has meant to me, above all, helping them to find God in authentic prayer. Without thinking of catechetics as such, I had been immunized forever against any approach which does not give prayer its proper place in religious education.

As a teenager, of course, I still had a rather simplistic understanding of religious education and every other kind of apostolic work. But later studies and experiences of life only confirmed the basic insight of those happy years: To be a true and happy "apostle"—to speak in the language of those days—requires, besides God's grace, above all a deep and authentic religious experience. Such a profound experience and a burning desire to communicate it to someone else will quite easily find a way of communication. But knowledge of the dynamics of communication does not by itself generate any genuine religious experience.

The second part of my stay at the minor seminary was blessed with a number of very beautiful friendships with fellow students and also with the priest who was in charge of our spiritual formation, Dr. Anton Schmid. He was professor of moral theology at the University of Salzburg. As moderator of the Marian sodality, he gave us excellent weekly spiritual conferences. In the time of my conversion he had helped me in a masterful way. Since then I was aware of his deep personal love. My friendship with him naturally had the character of a son-father relationship, and just by this, it mightily contributed to finding a relationship with God the Father in terms of a filial friendship. Because of my own happy experiences of teenage, in my educational work I have always firmly believed in the tremendous formative power of true friendship and in the possibility of genuine friendship between teacher and student. And from my own experience I also believed in the blessings of a sound, but rather intensive spiritual direction.

After my humanistic studies in Salzburg, the archbishop offered me a place in the famed Collegio Germanico, the national German College in Rome. Known as the "Germanicum," this institution is the model of the many national colleges (or better, national seminaries) in Rome, where students from various nations prepare themselves for the priesthood. Founded in 1552 by St. Ignatius of Loyola, the Germanicum is the oldest of the national colleges and served as a model for the Council of Trent's decree on seminaries. When I came to Rome in 1924, seminary life still followed the program of priestly formation as outlined by the Council of Trent (1563) and further developed in the following centuries. Of course, this is not the place for a discussion of the educational value of Tridentine seminaries. But gratitude and honesty oblige me to say that I remember the year of my studies in Rome with joy and, like the vast majority of my fellow students of then, I am deeply convinced the style of our seminary life prepared us well for our priestly life to come. I must add also that the Germanicum presented the Tridentine model at its best and that 1924 differed considerably from 1982.

The seminarians of the Germanicum do their philosophical and theological studies at the Gregorian University. During the first year of my philosophical studies, I decided to enter the order of my teachers, the Jesuits. They were in charge of both the Gregorian University and the Germanicum. I had thought of becoming a Jesuit before I went to Rome, but I knew them only from books and looked for an opportunity to see their members and work more closely in the reality of life. In Rome I looked at them with a positive, but nonetheless critical, attitude. In my decision to join them, the personal example and sound spirituality of the Jesuits who lived with us in the Germanicum had a conclusive impact. I could surely not say the same about the philosophical lectures of the Gregorian University. Now, almost sixty years later, I would rate them even considerably lower than I did then. But it would be unfair and incorrect to infer from this evaluation of my first year of philosophical studies that there was a low standard at the Gregorian University as a whole at that time. Father Paul Geny, our main professor during the first year of philosophy, died in a tragic accident before I left Rome. I shall keep forever my admiration of his priestly character and apostolic zeal. But soon after I had left Rome, I became aware of the limitations of his narrow Thomism, without however becoming in any way biased against a sound Scholastic approach to philosophy and theology.

When I decided to join the Jesuit Order, I was clearly aware of their intensive engagement in religious education and theological studies. Yet I don't think this had any considerable influence on my decision. What attracted me convincingly was the apostolic spirituality of the Jesuits and their style of life. The decisive question was not what I wanted to achieve in life, but what I wanted to become myself. I was much more concerned with my own education than with the education of others.

The Long Years of Jesuit Formation

Since their establishment, the Jesuits have always believed in the importance of a long and thorough formation before a person could properly engage in any kind of priestly apostolate, especially in the field of religious education. From the beginning, also, they have tried to keep a balance of solid spiritual and professional training in this long process of formation. The true Jesuit firmly believes a sound self-education to be the best preparation for the education of others, young and old alike.

Now, in retrospect, I remember with joyful gratitude the years of my own formation within the order. I did not find them long and tiring. I was simply convinced this was the only right way to attain the desired goal. By this I don't mean to imply in any way that everything was perfect in the Jesuit formation of those days. I only want to say it was surely good enough to remember it above all with lasting deep gratitude, and then to learn from its mistakes—without any harmful resentment— for an even better education of others.

After two happy years of novitiate, I was sent to the Berchmans College at Pullach, near Munich, to complete my philosophical studies. With youthful enthusiasm I plunged into the depths of philosophical speculation, especially in the second year of my stay at Pullach when we studied theodicy, the philosophical knowledge about God, under Father Maximilian Rast. I still remember his disappointment when years later he heard that the "metaphysician" I was with him had fallen so far and had concentrated on such an earthly, superficial subject as catechetics. His inadequate evaluation of catechetics did not disturb my thankful remembrance of my philosophical period of life. I am convinced these philosophical studies helped my catechetical work of later years. It may be that, without noticing, I remained sometimes too much the metaphysician even in the field of religious education.

Between the philosophical and theological studies, young Jesuits usually teach for some years at a Jesuit high school, or work there as prefects of discipline in close contact with high-school students. My assignment was primarily teaching Latin and German at the Jesuit High

School of the Freinberg, near Linz, in Austria. At that time it was what we called an "Apostolic School"—a minor seminary for boys who felt a vocation for apostolic life as religious or diocesan priests. The rector of the seminary was Father Richard Karlinger, a first-class educator of the best Jesuit tradition, with great love and understanding of the students and the young Jesuit teachers. I learned much from him in the three years I taught under his direction.

Although I did not teach religion, my experience as high-school teacher was a momentous opening towards religious education. I had great concern for teaching my subjects properly and successfully. The academic success of my students meant very much to me; I would say now it definitely meant too much. But I saw the whole work as real education; I wanted to form persons. My position as homeroom teacher offered many opportunities for educational and religious guidance and support. In the high school of Freinberg, I became—and have remained—an enthusiastic teacher. Naturally, I was in danger of over-emphasizing the instructional dimension in the whole process of education. But instinctively I felt I had to overcome this danger by a concern for a personal encounter with God through prayer.

Very early in my career as teacher my reflection on the whole process of instructional communication made me see teaching as a noble service by which the teacher facilitates the learning of the student. The faculty of Freinberg excelled in this spirit of educational service.

The seminary high school of Salzburg surpassed the seminary high school of Freinberg considerably in the academic standard of its faculty. But Freinberg surpassed Salzburg in terms of its great concern for the academic progress and character formation of the students, and therefore achieved better educational results. From this comparison of the two high schools so dear to me I learned an important lesson for my educational theory.

A Decisive Encounter of Life

The three exciting years at Freinberg passed all too fast. In the fall of 1932 I started my theological studies at the University of Innsbruck where the Jesuits are in charge of the department of theology. Before the beginning of the academic year, I had been appointed to help Father Josef Jungmann in my spare time, in his work as editor of the *Zeitschrift für Katholische Theologie*, one of the leading theological reviews in German-speaking countries. Father Jungman was its editor for thirty-nine years and contributed decisively to its high theological standard. My work for him consisted primarily in proofreading the galleys for each issue of the review. It had as such no special formative value, but it brought me in close personal contact with this outstanding man who influenced my theological and pedagogical thinking more than anyone else.

The collaboration with Father Jungmann was pleasant, but not exciting; the personal contact with him was much more inspiring than fascinating. In the course of the years there developed between us a wonderful friendship in which I was always the one who primarily received. I had the impression he felt I understood him well and considered me as the main inheritor, popularizer, and developer of his catechetical thought. One of the last letters before his death was a letter to me in which he said that, almost blind, he still tried with the help of a powerful magnifier to read my latest book.

I learned most from Father Jungmann through our frequent conversations and later through letters. His writings obviously further deepened what I had already learned in private conversation. During the years of my theological studies, Father Gatterer taught pastoral theology and catechetics. Father Jungmann taught liturgy, but he also directed a catechetical seminar. He was an outstanding moderator of catechetical and liturgical seminars.

Shortly after the beginning of my theological studies, Father Jungmann assigned to me as a topic of investigation and presentation in his catechetical seminar, the aim of religious education according to the catechetical school of Munich and Vienna. I must admit I have forgotten the exact formulation of the theme, but I do remember Father Jungmann gave me great freedom in approaching and treating my topic. Like the early leaders of the catechetical renewal, at that time I still saw catechesis far too much as "teaching" and not enough as education. I also clearly remember Father Jungmann's reservation with regard to my views of that time, but he respected my academic freedom. This broadness of mind stimulated my desire for more intensive involvement in catechetical studies and closer collaboration with him on a deeper level.

At the beginning of the second year of my theological studies, my superiors let me know that I should prepare myself for an academic career in the field of theology and, therefore, for obtaining a doctorate in theology. In those days candidates for a theological doctorate started very early in the planning of and working on their doctoral thesis. For this I had to find a suitable mentor, and my unquestionable preference was Father Jungmann. First, he recommended an investigation of the origin and special character of the catechisms of Sagan in Silesia which, toward the end of the eighteenth century, had an important role in religious education in Germany and Austria.

The theme perfectly suited my historical and pedagogical interests. I started my research with youthful ardor and devoted myself to it so conscientiously in the following years that there was some detriment to the rest of my theological studies. My mentor followed the work with obvious personal interest and valuable advice without ever imposing his views. Soon he encouraged me to widen the field of my investigation, to study in more detail the development of catechisms in German-speaking regions since the Catholic reform of the sixteenth century, and to extend my research into the nineteenth century.

I accepted his suggestion, and at the end of the four years' course of theology I had my dissertation almost ready for the press. In 1937 it was published as *Geschichte des Katechismus in Oesterreich seit Petrus Canisius mit Berücksichtigung der gesamtdeutschen Katechismusentwicklung*. The glory of the book lasted only a short time. In March 1939 Hitler annexed Austria, and sometime afterward the Nazis ordered the book to be "pulped." When I wrote the book I had no intention of hinting at the Nazi regime in Germany. It may be that I indicated disapproval of undue interference by the state in the catechetical task of the church when I referred to such interferences in Austria during the eighteenth century.

To enable me to make a very thorough research of catechetical history, Father Jungmann, as director of the catechetical seminar and its library, even financed two trips to monasteries and other places where ancient catechetical material could be found. To compensate for this most helpful and encouraging benefit, he commissioned me to buy valuable catechisms of the past for his catechetical seminar. As a result, he acquired the richest and most select collection of ancient catechisms and other catechetical material in all of Austria and Germany. He considered it, henceforth, the jewel of his first-class library.

For me, Father Jungmann was the model of a Christian scholar, teacher, and author who, with deep faith, devoted all his time and strength to his scientific task. He excelled by discipline, accuracy, and masterful arrangement of the details for proving pertinent insights. The following instance may illustrate our mutual relationship and his own way of life. When I started to work on my dissertation, he told me: "In your research you will soon make interesting discoveries and want to continue your study into the night. I would advise you to determine a given hour when you stop your reading and writing. In the morning, you may start at any time you like—even at 2:00 a.m. That will never become a harmful passion." I followed his advice and very soon discovered it required some sacrifices, but brought wisdom, strength, and order into my scientific life.

My dissertation dealt specifically with the Catholic catechisms. However, I also had to study the main Protestant catechisms. One of them was the catechism of Heidelberg, the most outstanding Calvinist catechism of Germany in the sixteenth century. I had ordered an early copy of it from a German university. When it arrived I took the booklet and read the short preface. It presented God's plan of salvation so beautifully I could not help weeping. I did not feel ashamed of these tears. I have studied many Catholic catechisms, but I cannot remember that I ever wept. Although, as a faithful Catholic, I could not accept particular doctrines of the booklet, sincerity obliges me to admit the catechism of Heidelberg presented the central message of God's love better than many Catholic catechisms. Many years had to pass before I realized the full ecumenical significance of my encounter with the catechism of Heidelberg.

I think I was never in danger of being unduly dependent on any textbook in my own teaching, but pedagogical realism kept me ever conscious of the importance of a good textbook for students and the average teacher alike. This is especially true if the Christian life to which we lead in religious education is, by its nature, the answer to a call God presents to us in historical revelation.

My historical studies only deepened my conviction of the real need for a common textbook of religious instruction. Such a textbook was usually called a catechism. Historical evidence convinced me that the first catechism which hit the mark and had a very wide circulation was the small catechism of Martin Luther. True, the Catholics had some booklets of this kind before Luther; I myself discovered some new ones. But only the catechisms of Peter Canisius, the first German Jesuit, offered a Catholic solution to the demands of those times.

My dissertation on the history of the catechisms in Germany and

Austria was intended as a contribution to the development of a timely common religion textbook, a project which then was being discussed heatedly in both countries. My historical studies were inspired by the conviction I shared with Father Jungmann that history can provide valuable lessons for the progress of religious education—that we can and must learn from the attempts, achievements, and failures of the past.

One of the lessons I learned from my research was the harm done by uncontrolled particularism and subjectivism in the field of religious education. The catechisms of Sagan and the catechisms originating from them which were produced and prescribed for all of Austria were not perfect. Yet the conformity of religious education which they secured was a remarkable achievement compared with the catechetical jumble which characterized much of the eighteenth century.

I do have an aversion to any interference by the state in the pastoral life of the church. However, I would not deny the Austrian government of old had a sincere interest in solid religious education and contributed very much to its general progress by forceful insistence on a better formation of the teachers, along with an effective supervision of their work by capable and dedicated school inspectors. The church should have learned much more from the modern state in its relationship with its own teachers and schools. At the time of my doctorial studies I felt it hadn't, and what I observed later in many countries, including the United States, has confirmed this opinion.

With Father Jungmann, I always shared concern for correct doctrine in the whole process of religious instruction. According to Catholic understanding, religious education is education to a life of faith, and faith is man's answer to God's life-giving word as it comes to us from the apostles through the service of the church. Yet concern for correct doctrine must not make us blind to other essential aspects of religious education. And it also must not be confused with unhealthy catechetical scholasticism.

This I wanted to show with the Austrian catechism of 1806 on which, because of its particular importance, I focused the historical research and catechetical analysis of my dissertation. One-sided concern for correct doctrine, combined with failure to understand the difference between catechetical and scholastic presentation of the Christian message, produced a catechism which lacked much of the promising catechetical qualities of the first catechisms of Sagan. My close examination of the Austrian catechism showed convincingly that it is the first outstanding representative of a scholastic catechism, the type of catechism which admittedly reached its final "perfection" in the catechisms of Josef Deharbe, S.J.

My dissertation was in some way an historical illustration of what Father Jungmann, just the year before, had masterfully explained in his most important catechetical book: *Die Frohbotschaft und unsere Glaubensverkündigung*. It is one of the deepest and most influential books of the twentieth century on religious education. No other single book did as much to pave the way for the comprehensive pastoral renewal as intended and delineated by Vatican Council II. Religious instruction is for Father Jungmann, above all, motivation and guidance to an authentic Christian life. In the process of instruction, content and method must go harmoniously together, but content is even more important than method, although never a substitute for it. The transmission of God's plan of salvation is not the whole of religious education and, of course, not an end in itself. That Father Jungmann always considered a mature Christian life as the real aim of all catechetical activity is obvious from an unbiased study of his writings. But to reach this goal, God's loving plan for man must be properly presented to those who are supposed to accept and to live it. In his presentation, which Father Jungmann pertinently calls *Glaubensverkündigung* (proclamation of faith), it is not enough to provide a correct exposition of Christian doctrine. God's main intention in all of his speaking to man in general, and in particular his plan of salvation with regard to the audience being addressed, must become the operative principle for the adequate selection, arrangement, and presentation of the catechetical content. What God had intended as Good News must be faithfully transmitted as Good News. From the catechesis of the apostolic and early church we learn, above all, concentration on the substance of the Christian message. It is the wonderful gospel of God's saving love, with its center in Jesus Christ, our Lord and Savior.

These basic insights of Father Jungmann's book express my own catechetical creed. His book was enthusiastically accepted by the promoters of pastoral renewal. But it also has been passionately opposed by others, including some important ecclesial leaders. Within a year after its publication it had to be withdrawn from the market to avoid further complications. The original German text was never published again. Thus, it was a great joy to Father Jungmann when, in 1962, we published a good English translation by Father William Huesman, S.J., together with four essays which elucidated the book's tremendous impact on the pastoral, liturgical, and catechetical renewal of those times. I was general editor of the book, which appeared under the significant title *Good News—Yesterday and Today*.

Call to the Missions

In 1937 missionaries were urgently needed to volunteer for the work of Austrian Jesuits in China. I applied, was accepted, and left for China. Years later Father Jungmann told me he had earnestly considered objecting to my missionary assignment and asking for my appointment as his assistant and eventual successor, but his respect of my missionary vocation let him stand off.

After two years of studying Chinese in Peking, I joined the St. Joseph's Seminary as professor of dogmatic, or, as it is often called, systematic theology. It remained my main subject all the years I taught in the seminary, first in Sienshien, Hopeh; then in Kingshien, Hopeh; and finally, after we had left China with our seminarians, in Manila (1949–1958). These were only the principal places where our seminary found a home in the unsettled conditions of the Japanese war and the following Communist unrest. Besides dogmatic theology, I also taught catechetics whenever courses on catechetics were given.

My professorship of dogmatic theology offered an ideal opportunity for realizing what Father Jungmann regarded as an adequate preparation of seminarians for their future catechetical work as priests. The usual seminary course had badly neglected the kerygmatic aspect of theology. It may have succeeded in a rational penetration of the Word of God, but it did not satisfactorily prepare for an adequate presentation of the gospel.

Soon after the publication of his *"Frohbotschaft,"* Father Jungmann published in his review articles by some young Jesuit professors advocating the development of two different kinds of theology: one basically theoretical, and the other basically practical. Everyone would agree there is a considerable difference between a postgraduate course for those who specialize in theological research and the common seminary course of theology. But this does not mean two different kinds of theology with different formal objects. Father Jungmann's support of a separate kerygmatic theology is quite understandable when viewed with the background of the special way systematic theology was then commonly taught in Catholic seminaries. The scholastic approach of those times lacked the indispensable kerygmatic dimension. But the remedy cannot be found in a separate kerygmatic theology. The support Father Jungmann gave for some time to such a solution positively hurt his cause in the critical years of the late 1930s and early 1940s.

In my last discussion with Father Jungmann before I left for China, I mentioned that, in my opinion, all theology needs a kerygmatic orientation. Later Father Karl Rahner expressed the same view when he said that any form of theology that takes its task seriously is kerygmatic in character. I have sincerely tried to follow this principle in my theological teaching. For doing this in a way well adapted to my students, I found remarkable help in the textbook of dogmatic theology which a former student at Innsbruck, Dr. Maurus Heinrichs, O.F.M., had prepared for seminarians in China. To my knowledge, his four-volume work, *Theses Theologiae Dogmaticae* (1941) was the first attempt at a kerygmatically oriented dogmatic theology for seminarians in the missions. I will keep forever a pleasant, thankful remembrance of my meetings with Father Heinrichs in China and later in Japan. I cannot remember anyone else by whom I felt so well understood and encouraged with regard to teaching theology in a missionary seminary.

From the beginning of my academic career, I have combined intensive literary activity with teaching. My numerous articles appeared first in missionary reviews in China, then for many years in theological, catechetical, and liturgical reviews of Europe. Since 1954 my articles have appeared also in similar publications in the United States, and since 1970 some articles have been published in Latin America. Almost all of my books are a revised edition and planned combination of former articles.

The first and most important series of articles I produced during my twelve years in China (1937–1949), published in 1940 by the *Collectanea Commissionis Synodalis* of Peking, dealt with the important problem of the right arrangement of the catechetical material. I tried to demonstrate the significance of a proper arrangement of the catechetical material for a better understanding of the central idea and nature of the catechetical content. The leading catechisms of the nineteenth and the first part of the twentieth century arranged the material according to the guiding question: What must man do to reach salvation? In this way the Christian message became a system of obligations and lost its character of a real gospel. A gospel is, by its nature, a message of values. Therefore, the catechetical material must be arranged as a system of values which challenge man to a new life. Following the famous catechism of the Council of Trent (1565), often called the Roman Catechism (*Catechismus Romanus*), I recommended that God's overwhelming love should be presented first with the sections on the Creed and the sacraments. This challenges man to a new life of love. Then the following sections on commandments and prayer deal with this new life of love.

Father Jungmann immediately noticed the special significance my reflections had for the work on a new catechism in Germany. In his characteristic sense of humble collaboration, he took the pains to provide a substantial German summary of my Latin articles for the *Katechetische Blätter* (1941), a leading German catechetical journal.

In the summer of 1945, our bishop encouraged me to arrange a workshop for some of my best students and to study with them the problem of adult catechesis as we encountered it in our mission of Kinghsien, Hopeh. Each missionary was entrusted with the pastoral care of many small mission stations, which he could visit only a few times a year. This required special concentration on the core of the Christian message, so that the Christians who lived in these little communities would find the necessary support for a solid Christian life, founded on the central truths of Christian faith. The fruit of our workshop was a short text which, under the heading *Our Good News*, presented the main themes of Christian religion as the joyful tidings of God's love. The bishop insisted on its immediate publication in Latin and Chinese. Only ten years later it appeared, with the necessary revisions, in English, as the main section of my book *The Art of Teaching Christian Doctrine*.

I was always aware that religious education requires much more than the communication of doctrinal content. But theoretical reflection as well as close contact with the real catechetical life convinced me ever more of the paramount importance of conveying to the religious educator a genuine existential understanding of Christian religion which he can then share in the process of religious education. Only in this way can it come to an authentic "Sharing the Light of Faith," to use the pertinent expression by which the bishops of the United States characterize catechesis in the National Catechetical Directory of 1979. As for myself, I never had any doubt my personal contribution to religious education, if any, should be in the sector of the content of catechesis, with special emphasis on the proper doctrinal and spiritual formation of the religious educator.

Serving the Nations

In 1947 the Communists forced us to transfer our seminary from King-hsien to Peking, which was still in the hands of the Nationalists. Then in January of 1949 we had to move again. When the Red Army surrounded Peking, the staff and students of the seminary left for Shanghai in the very last civil airplane, an aircraft of a Protestant mission society. Shanghai and Hongkong were only short intermediary stations before our seminary found a lasting home in Manila. There the ninety students who had come with us could finish their theological studies. After their ordination to the priesthood, they would work among the many millions of Chinese who live outside of the China mainland in Southeast Asia. After the Communists' takeover of the whole mainland, the borders were closed. We could not recruit any more new seminarians from the mainland, and in 1958 we had to close the seminary.

Long before this date it was obvious that we had to find new fields of activity. While still in China I had planned the foundation of a cate-chetical institute for the improvement of mission catechetics. Conditions made the realization of this plan impossible as long as we were in China. But the situation of our dwindling seminary in Manila favored it, and even recommended a much wider radius of activity than we could have envisioned when still on the mainland. In 1953 the East Asian Pastoral Institute was founded and soon exerted a noticeable influence in the field of missionary catechesis. Until 1960 it had the awful name, Institute of Mission Apologetics.

The great opportunity for international activity arrived with my trip to Europe in 1953. It was primarily intended as an informative trip which would bring me in contact with the centers of catechetical studies in Europe. The exchange of ideas brought valuable new insights but no new orientation. The decisive event of the year was the invitation to present a paper at the International Liturgical Study Week of Lugano. I owed it to the recommendation of Father Jungmann. My topic was the missionary claim for a thorough liturgical renewal. In those years my studies dealt intensively with the momentous role of the right use of Scripture and liturgy in the process of religious education. My discourse in Latin was very well accepted by the experts of pastoral liturgy and catechesis. It immediately resulted in an invitation to teach a summer course the following summer on missionary liturgy at the University of Notre Dame.

One of the most inspiring contacts I made in 1953 was that with Rev. Josef Goldbrunner who, at that time, was editor of the *Katechetische Blätter* and pastor at Stockdorf near Munich. I shall never forget the marvelous religion classes he gave in his parish school. After I had attended them, I congratulated him and asked: "Now, Father, please tell me how do you as pastor appraise renewed catechetics? What are its fruits in Christian life?" "John," he answered, "you must already know that from your own experience in China and in the Philippines. In the lower grades everything works wonderfully. But in the upper grades it depends, in the normal case, decidedly upon the collaboration of the family. Without genuine Christian life in the family, even renewed catechesis of children will fail. It cannot work wonders." And he acted according to his answer. He took pains to provide his parish with an outstanding program of adult catechesis for the parents. In his parish I found an exemplary coordination of catechesis for children and adults. With Father Goldbrunner I share the conviction that, on the whole, even the best school catechesis works in vain with youth who live in an un-Christian environment at home. But I also share his conviction that effective care for a more adequate adult catechesis does not dispense the parish from providing a good catechetical program for children.

The trip to the United States in 1954 for the summer course at Notre Dame started a new period in my life. Each year for the next twenty years, I made extensive trips to give catechetical conferences in six continents. I circled the globe sixteen times. Soon I was being called the catechetical Sputnik. In this intensive catechetical activity, I considered my principal task was to proclaim the "A-B-Cs of Modern Catechetics." In fact, this was the title of a booklet I published in 1962 with Sadlier. I think I worked best where I could contribute to a timely catechetical awakening. My service consisted primarily in a forceful presentation of the basic principles of a catechesis which understands itself as guidance to a life of authentic faith. I always tried to present these principles in such a way that the religion teachers themselves felt challenged to a deepening of their own life of faith.

Obviously I myself learned very much from my work in many different countries with quite different pastoral conditions. Yet, in spite of all differences, I found everywhere a great need for a better understanding of the basic Christian message and of the fundamentals of Christian education. Almost everywhere I encountered the danger of catechetical activism, or lack of the indispensable reflection on the task and nature of true religious education. I became more and more convinced the main failures in Christian education do not result from lack of acquaintance with the nuances of the educational process, but from gross errors with regard to the aim, the content, and the basic process of religious education.

My international activity reached its culmination in the international study weeks on missionary liturgy and catechetics at Assisi (1956), Nijmegen (1959), Eichstätt (1960), Bangkok (1962), Katigondo, Uganda (1964), Manila (1967), and Medellin (1968). The first two were primarily on liturgy, and the following were on catechetics. But the liturgical and catechetical renewals of those years were so closely interrelated that even the liturgical study weeks had great catechetical significance. All seven study weeks were organized and directed by the East Asian Pastoral Institute of Manila, although almost always in close collaboration with a leading institution of the meeting-place or country. To act as secretary general of these important meetings was inspiring but not always pleasant. They were planned as meetings of experts, all of them individually invited with a special concern of having many bishops with us, so that our work could have a greater impact on the reality of pastoral life in the missions.

The meetings of Nijmegen and Eichstätt, especially, admittedly influenced the work of the coming Vatican Council II. In order to achieve significant results within the few days of each meeting, we gathered a select group of dynamic and mostly young people for one or two weeks before the main meeting, for its careful final preparation.

The most important of all study weeks was that of Eichstätt. It excelled in the papers delivered on this occasion, and especially the "Program of the Catechetical Apostolate" it presented. In his appraisal of this meeting in the *Katechetische Blätter*, Father Goldbrunner noted that the study week also pointed to a further development. The previous emphasis on the content of catechesis may now give way to a new thorough study of the peculiarity of catechetical method. After this, I wrote articles for the *Katechetische Blätter* and *Chicago Studies* which dealt more in detail with this momentous question: "Contemporary Catechetics: A Third Phase?" (*Chicago Studies*, 1963, pp. 257–268).

Beginning in 1965 there was suddenly a great emphasis within the Catholic community on the human conditions and the psychological process of religious education. Unfortunately the main promoters of this new trend did not distinguish themselves particularly by an interest for work done before them in the field of catechetics. They also often lacked the necessary understanding of the peculiarity of religious education as a genuine personal encounter with God in prayer and life.

With all like-minded friends, from 1959 I looked forward with great expectations to the coming Ecumenical Council. The meeting in Rome during the spring of 1961 for the preparation of the council document on sacred liturgy was one of the high points of my life. Again I owed my participation to a special intervention of Father Jungmann.

Vatican Council II was decidedly influenced by the preceding theological, liturgical, biblical, and catechetical renewal, and it accepted their best inspirations for a thorough pastoral renewal within the Catholic Church. It did not present any specific document on catechesis, but its whole tenor saw the catechetical work of the church clearly as the realization of its mission to bring man the good news of salvation, and to guide man in his response to faith. One of the most important catechetical contributions of Vatican II is its description of authentic faith: "By the obedience of faith man entrusts his whole self freely to God." The old narrow intellectualistic understanding of faith which had dominated catechisms for so long gave way to a biblical understanding of faith by which the whole man, as a free person, submits himself to God. The texts about God's intention to establish a covenant of friendship with man and about man's response to this invitation by authentic faith (*Constitution on Revelation and Scripture*, nn. 2 and 5) are the two conciliar passages I quoted most often in my countless conferences after the council.

Just as the catechism of the Council of Trent was the outgrowth of that council in the field of catechesis, the *General Catechetical Directory* of 1971 is a valuable, but unfortunately delayed, fruit of Vatican II. It presents pertinently the council's theology of religious education. It also competently incorporates the best of what the new interest in the human condition and the psychological process of religious education had to offer. The *National Catechetical Directory for the Catholics in the United States* (1979) was even more delayed. I mention this because I felt my work in the service of the church and of Catholic catechetics, like that of many others who served the same cause, suffered considerably by this delay. By the time these important ecclesial documents appeared, religious education had been unfavorably influenced by a formidable wave of secularism and an unreadiness to accept normative directions of the church. Due to this situation in the last fifteen years, religious education in home and school suffered a serious setback.

In these special circumstances, I felt called to use the remaining strength of my advanced age for paving the way for the spiritual deepening we so direly need at present. My many conferences and my books of the last years all point in this direction: *Our Message Is Christ* (1974); *Evangelization and Catechesis—Are We Really Proclaiming the Gospel?* (1976); *Living in the Spirit of Christ* (1977); *You Are My Witnesses—Spirituality of Religion Teachers* (1977); and most especially, my newest book *Pastoral Renewal in the Power of the Spirit* (1981).

In *Pastoral Renewal* the chapters which most clearly manifest my present view of contemporary catechetics are those on what I term catechesis "in the power of the Spirit." Particularly is this true of the chapter "Does Catechetics Need a Shift in Emphasis?" where I explicitly call for a fourth stage of catechetical renewal with particular emphasis on the spiritual dimension of religious education against the trend of contemporary secularism. Regarding the way to obtain this fourth state, I state at the end of that chapter: "It is important to realize that other developments in the field of religious education could be achieved by solid study of the respective areas of religious pedagogy. Yet this shift of the basic emphasis can be accomplished only by a new spiritual approach to catechetics. It is not primarily the result of studies as such but of a spiritual renewal which lets us see our catechetical work in a new perspective."

Chapter 2

A Search for Authenticity

Findley B. Edge

It happened during the mid-fifties. Vocationally, I was professor of religious education at the Southern Baptist Theological Seminary. I had been teaching for a decade and thus felt comfortable with regard to my teaching task. I had been promoted to full professor and given the Basil Manly Chair of Religious Education. As a denomination, Southern Baptists had been experiencing rapid numerical growth for more than a decade. The educational organizations of many churches were being expanded. Churches were needing help with their enlarged organizations. I was receiving far more invitations from churches to assist in this organizational expansion than I could accept. From all outward circumstances I should have been quite happy and fulfilled.

On the contrary, I was far from being happy or fulfilled. The racial crisis was seething in the South, and I had the feeling that here was a chance for Southern Baptist churches to take the lead in what seemed to me to be a deeply spiritual as well as moral issue. Southern Baptists were the largest Protestant group in the South and what we did, I felt, could have significant influence. Although some isolated voices were heard among Southern Baptists, from my perspective we were strangely silent or even, at times, reactionary. At first I was irritated, hurt, and disappointed over this response by our churches. In time this situation touched something in the depth of my inner being. The hurt I felt toward the institutional church changed to hostility. The disappointment changed to anger. As a people, we Southern Baptists made the claim that we were a religious people. But the question arose for me, "What kind of religion is it we profess?" As a people, we claimed to emphasize experiential faith, an inner commitment, and a deep personal relationship with God. Again the question arose, "Is our faith so intertwined with Southern culture that our basic commitment is more to Southern culture than it is to the living God?" With these feelings and these questions welling within me, the numerical growth we had been experiencing over the past few years became as dry bones.

These feelings and questions concerning the institutional church were so deep that I began to question whether or not I could continue in my position as professor of religious education. It seemed to me we were concerned about only the external trappings of religion. How could I continue to teach that which seemed to me to be a seriously inadequate expression of the Christian faith? Many with whom I talked, seeking to find some resolution of the conflict in my innermost being, could understand neither my questions nor my concerns in this area. They felt that our numerical growth was an obvious evidence of God's blessing upon our work. I entered a period of intense agony and struggle. Little did I know at the time that I was on the threshold of one of the most meaningful periods of my life—a period in which my philosophy of Christian education would come into more clear focus and take on a new shape.

ROOTS

No experience this profound is without its antecedents. Before undertaking to identify some of the experiences that might have contributed to the conflict I have just described, let me identify myself theologically. As one who agrees with the basic theological positions which have been traditionally held by Southern Baptists, I would be classified as conservative in theology and evangelical in approach. I follow the historical-critical approach to a study of the Bible and thus, within the Southern Baptist tradition, probably would be considered "progressive."

For as long as I can remember, I have felt that if there was a God who created the universe and if, as would be reasonable to suppose, the Creator knew what was best and wanted what was best for his creation, then the sensible thing was for one to obey God insofar as possible. If there were no God, then, I presume, one was free to live one's life as he or she desired, seeking to find or make whatever meaning one could out of this existence. Therefore it was always a puzzle to me that so many people who professed belief in God seemingly took religion (their obedience to God) so lightly. A large percentage of church members never attended the worship services of the church. Still others attended only

rarely—on special days. Others were faithful in terms of church attendance but their obedience to God in daily life seemed to be minimal.
But this was the way religion was. Everyone seemed to accept this state
of affairs as a matter of course. None seemed unduly upset about it. This
problem came into more clear focus for me during my seminary studies.

The Problem of Institutionalism

Many things of religious significance happened during my early years,
but the formation of my philosophy of Christian education began during my days as a student in seminary. Two things were particularly
significant.

The first was the influence of Dr. Gaines S. Dobbins, my professor of
religious education. During college I did not have even one course in
education, so it was Dr. Dobbins who introduced me to the field. Under
the influence of his stimulating teaching I first became aware of the
potential there was through the process of education to help people
grow. Thus, when I decided to do graduate study I chose to do it under
his direction in the area of Christian education.

The second significant influence was a question that was raised in my
thinking—a question concerning authenticity in our religious life.
Throughout my early life in the church the scribes and the Pharisees
were soundly condemned for their expression of the religious life. This
teaching was based on such passages as, "For I say unto you, that except
your righteousness shall exceed the righteousness of the scribes and
Pharisees, ye shall in no wise enter into the kingdom of heaven" (Matt.
5:20 ASV). At the seminary I was surprised to learn that the scribes and
Pharisees, rather than being the evil people I thought, were, in fact, the
religious leaders of the people. Elementary as this insight may seem, it
hit me hard. As I reflected upon this, the question came to me, "If Jesus
condemned as inadequate the religious expression of a people who
believed in God and who were committed to God and who expressed
their religious devotion as meticulously as did the Pharisees, how would
he evaluate the religious devotion and commitment of the masses who
are church members today?" On the basis of purely subjective and
superficial observation, it seemed to me that the expressions of our love
for and commitment to God were no better than theirs. As is the case
with so many issues that arise during seminary days, this question be-

came the focus of many conversations. Slowly but surely the question of the "authenticity of our faith" began to push itself to the level of consciousness in my thinking.

This question caused me to focus on a still larger issue, namely, the tendency of experiential religion always to move in the direction of becoming institutionalized. In my study of the Bible and the history of the church, I was made aware that there are various movements (varying in size and influence) that began, as reactions to some weakness or error that existed in the understanding and/or expression of religion at a given time. Those movements that might be considered to be major (generally lasting over several centuries), began with a radical rebellion on the part of a relatively small number of people against some aspect(s) of the religious scene. Those who rebelled felt they were recapturing something of the "essence" of religion as revealed by God but which had been lost by the masses who professed to be religious at that time. At the beginning of the movement the adherents had a deep, inner commitment to the ideals and values they were seeking to recapture and express. Their commitment was so deep they were willing to suffer ostracism from society and even persecution. They formed organizations designed to conserve and propagate the values to which they were committed.

When the generation who started the movement, with their deep inner, personal commitment, sought to communicate their ideals, values, and commitment to the next generation they obviously passed on the various forms that had been devised to express their "life together." However, in passing the ideals to the next generation, some of the "essence," some of the "inner dynamic," tended to be lost. If the movement survived and was successful, the forms, ideals, values, and commitment continued to be passed on from generation to generation. With the passing to each new generation, as the decades lengthened into centuries, more and more of the "essence" and "inner dynamic" was lost. Maintaining the "forms" increasingly became the major expression of the adherents' commitment. The movement became institutionalized.

The question that troubled me was, why does this happen? Assuming that which a movement seeks to recapture is in harmony with the revelation of Christ and the teaching of Holy Scripture, why is it that a movement in which one's religious expression flows from a deep inner motivation based on a commitment to God, with the passing of time, becomes institutionalized and encrusted in a cold, lifeless formalism?

Why is it that the major expression of one's religious commitment comes to be demonstrated only in the observance of certain religious forms? A corollary question is, is this sequence inevitable? Is there something psychological within our being which says that the seventh or tenth generation cannot have the same feelings of intensity or the depth of commitment as the first generation? Are there social forces that make this outcome inevitable? Is there a sort of social determinism in which, in spite of all efforts to the contrary, forces in society so modify and shape the movement that it eventually becomes institutional? Is this what has happened to all movements? Or, is it possible in society to exercise purposive control so that institutions can be used to perpetuate and propagate from generation to generation ideals and values that spring from deep inner commitment without becoming institutionalized?

The issue of the institutionalization of religion was always in the background during my graduate study, and thus it was natural that it provided the subject for my dissertation. It was not possible to explore all the questions raised above, so I focused on the area of my specialization. The title was "Religious Education and the Problem of Institutionalism." I selected what I felt were three major movements in religious history. The focus of the study was to ascertain whether or not there were principles and approaches to education that were common to all three movements when they were in their beginning stage and whether there were common educational factors that were operative when the three movements had become institutionalized. This was followed by an analysis of the principles of Christian education utilized by my own denomination to see whether these were more nearly similar to the principles and practices followed in the beginnings of the movement or were more similar to those followed when the movement had become institutionalized. I felt the insights I identified were significant but for a number of reasons decided not to share them in print. So, the dissertation was placed in the library where it could be quickly forgotten.

The Improvement of Teaching

Whatever disappointment this may have engendered was assuaged by the fact that upon my graduation I was invited to join the faculty at the Southern Baptist Theological Seminary. At the time, in addition to religious education, Dr. Dobbins was teaching church administration, psychology of religion, evangelism, worship, and journalism. When I joined the faculty he gave me the whole field of religious education. This meant that I had to be concerned about the history and philosophy of education, the practical organizational life of the church, developmental psychology, age-group ministries, recreation, and the like. However, the basic concern I had at this beginning point in my teaching ministry was to focus on seeking to improve the quality of teaching in the churches. The question of authenticity still plagued me. There was such a discrepancy between the "faith" that was taught in the churches and what was expressed in life in the world.

In those beginning years I did not set out to formulate a philosophy of education with quality teaching as a base. Rather, my primary concern was to provide some simple and practical help for untrained teachers.

The Family

Early in my seminary study I became acquainted with Horace Bushnell. Although I did not agree with all he said, I was convinced that his emphasis on the family as teacher was sound. In the late forties I attended a conference led by Dr. Ernest Ligon, who was professor of psychology at Union College, in Schnectady, N.Y., as well as founder and director of the Character Research Project. This began a personal relationship which lasted for a number of years. Again, I could not agree with Dr. Ligon's theology, and I became aware that sometimes he exaggerated his points for the sake of emphasis. Nevertheless, I became convinced that the essence of what he was doing had tremendous potential.

Theology

I took my first sabbatical at Yale University and the Divinity School in 1954–55. I went there to study under Dr. Paul Vieth, because of all the people who were writing in Christian education at the time, I identified with him more closely than with anyone else. However, when I arrived at the Divinity School, I found that Dr. Vieth, with short notice, had decided to take a sabbatical in Japan during the first semester. I was crushed! I was to take half of my work in the University Graduate School and half in the Divinity School. The only other person teaching Christian education in the Divinity School was a professor just slightly older than I, about whom I had heard nothing—Randolph Crump Miller. As it turned out, Randy Miller became one of the pivotal influences in my approach to Christian education. In terms of personal relationships, he was warm and gracious. He and his wife had my wife and me in their home on more than one occasion. He deepened my interest in the family as an agency of teaching. He taught me the "language of relationships." He introduced me to the "clue" to Christian education. All of this and more I learned and appreciated. But the pivotal learning I received from Dr. Miller was that one's philosophy of Christian education ought to grow out of one's theology. At the time I was not aware of the influence this concept was to have on my future thinking. It came to be central in the philosophy which was on the verge of emerging.

THE RACIAL CRISIS AND MY AGONY

When I returned to my teaching post in Louisville in the summer of 1955, the racial crisis was beginning to cause serious social disruption. In the midst of the moral and spiritual revolution that was taking place in society, instead of the churches becoming involved and giving leadership, they were either reactionary or uninvolved. Southern Baptist Theological Seminary had Dr. Martin Luther King, Jr. as a lecturer, and churches withheld financial support as a protest. The questions I had concerning the family as teacher were left unanswered. Even the search for a quality approach to teaching lost its excitement. It seemed to me that our problem was at another place and at a deeper level. Our statistical growth was still mounting and the programs of the church were going "full steam ahead." But I was miserable. Something was wrong with a religion that, on the one hand, was popular and growing and, on the other hand, refused to get involved with human suffering! The people in our churches, in terms of personal morality, were among the finest people to be found anywhere, yet most of them saw no relationship between their Christian faith and the racial crisis all around them. The problem of institutionalism was once again raised in my thinking, but this time it was not in terms of an academic study; it was an existential reality.

I became convinced that the problem we faced was primarily a the-

ological problem. Our problem was that we didn't know who we were—
or who we were supposed to be—as God's people in today's world. I had
always been convinced that God's people are a unique people, in some
special way different from all other people in the world. But as I reflected
upon this I became aware that I did not know the essence of that
uniqueness. I had always viewed the Christian life in terms of "being
good" and "being faithful to the church." While I believe both of these
are positive and desirable, I came to the conclusion that neither of them
nor both of them constitute the *essence* of the uniqueness of God's
people. There I was in the mid-years of my life—I believed in God; I was
a Christian; I was a clergyman; I was a professor in a theological seminary—and yet, I had to confess that I did not know the answer to the
most fundamental question in the Christian experience, namely, if
God's people are a unique people, what is the essence of that uniqueness? I set about to find the answer to that question—an answer that
would be biblical, that would make sense, and thus would be satisfying.
This search went on for about five or six years. This was my period of
agony. When I would talk with someone and try to share my search with
them, hardly anyone could understand what I was talking about. They
would say, "The church has never been in more grand shape!" I was
lonely, frustrated, and hostile. I was disillusioned with the institutional
church.

AN EXPERIENTIAL PHILOSOPHY OF CHRISTIAN
EDUCATION

The answers that grew out of this search have formed the basis for my
philosophy of Christian education. Obviously, over this period of five or
six years, the "answers" did not come in an orderly, systematic way. It
was only at the end of this period that I was able to pull all the threads
together, and I put the findings in a book, A *Quest for Vitality in
Religion*. The subtitle of the book was, "A Theological Approach to
Religious Education." In this I sought to emphasize a sound theological
base, a relationship with God that was experiential and personal (as
distinguished from cognitive and mechanical), and a commitment to
the Christian Way that was authentic (as distinguished from
superficial).

The Essence—A People on Mission

Believing that God's people are a unique people and wanting to find the essence of that uniqueness, I asked, "Why was God calling a people in the first place?" This led me back to the creation in which God looking over his created order said, "That's good!" But sin invaded human experience of such proportions it led to a brokenness in the basic nature of mankind. This brokenness was so severe the individual was incapable of achieving healing through his/her own efforts. God, in infinite love but with full recognition of man's freedom of choice, set about the task of seeking to bring man back into an authentic relation with himself where healing is to be found.

How was this to be done? We get the first clue in Genesis 12:1–3. God called Abraham and in these verses stated both his purpose and his plan. His purpose was that all nations, all people, were to know and experience his blessing. They were to have their brokenness healed and once again know the blessing of life with and in God (verse 3). The plan God will use in achieving this purpose is stated in verse 2, "I will bless you, and make your name great, so that you will be a blessing" (RSV). A very important point needs to be noted here. God's basic call to Abraham was not simply a call to bless him, though God clearly stated, "I will bless you." There was something more fundamental in God's call to Abraham. God's call was a call to a mission. God said, "Through you I will bless all nations." God's mission was the healing of the nations. God's call to Abraham was a call to be an instrument of that healing. This is why Abraham was called. This is to what Abraham was called. It was in fulfilling this mission he would receive the blessing.

This is a tremendously important point, not only for Israel but also for us today (particularly those of us who are evangelically oriented). I had always thought that God's basic call to man was a call to salvation. Thus I have spent a large portion of my life seeking to lead people to accept God's salvation. This salvation was a free gift. One could not earn it. I was taught if one accepted this salvation, then he/she was "in" for eternity. It was desirable that one should also serve God, but it was not necessary. In this view one could "accept Jesus as Savior" without "accepting him as Lord." I believe this is a tragic misunderstanding of biblical teaching. From one perspective, salvation is a "by-product." In one sense, salvation, like happiness, is not found by seeking it. Salvation, like happiness, is "found" when one is consumed in doing something else.

How does this relate to the point at hand? God's eternal purpose is to bring healing to all people, which only he can do. But his *basic* call to man is not a call to salvation but a call to mission. It is as man understands, accepts, and fulfills this mission that God's gift is given. As one "loses his life" in the mission of God in the world, one finds that God has brought healing in one's life and that the gift of salvation has been given. Thus, the essence of God's call is a call to mission.

The same call of God to Abraham was repeated to Isaac and Jacob. Then Joseph, foretelling the famine, became Prime Minister in Egypt and brought his father, Jacob, his brothers, and all their families to settle in Egypt in the land of Goshen. Several centuries passed and there arose a Pharaoh who "knew not Joseph," and the descendants of Jacob were thrown into bondage. The cry of the people was heard, and God sent Moses to lead the people out of Egypt.

Up to this point God had been working primarily through individuals—Abraham, Isaac, Jacob, Joseph, Moses. Now, God expanded his call. He called a people. This is found in Exodus 19:1–8. God told Moses the message he was to deliver to the people. He first reminded them of the demonstration of his might in their deliverance from bondage and of his tender care in watching over them. He then stated the condition for the relationship which he was about to propose. "Now, therefore, if you will obey my voice and keep my covenant, you shall be my own possession" (Ex. 19:5a RSV). This, also, is a pivotal point. God's promises are always conditional. I am aware that there are statements in the Scriptures in which God makes his promise to Israel in which this condition ("if you will") is not stated. However, we have to realize that the totality of the basis of God's relationship with Israel is not stated in every passage. Therefore the Bible must be studied and understood as a whole. God could not be consistent with his own nature without making this relationship conditional. Nor could he be consistent with his creation of persons with freedom without making this relationship conditional.

So Israel was called to be God's people. But, as with Abraham, God's basic call to Israel was not a call to receive something. It was not a call in which God was automatically going to give them something. As God's people they were to be a unique people, but what was the essence of that uniqueness? This is clearly stated. They were to be a "kingdom of priests." Like Abraham, Israel's basic call was a call to mission. They were to be a people of priests to fulfill God's mission. Faced with this call, Israel responded, "All that the Lord has spoken we will do" (Ex. 19:8b RSV).

Unfortunately, it is one thing to say one will accept and fulfill a calling; it is quite another thing actually to do it. The Old Testament is replete with Israel's struggles to be an expression of God's people. There were times when Israel "served the Lord" and was pleasing in his sight. There were times when Israel "forsook the Lord" and did that which was evil in his sight. However, the basic problem was that the people of Israel failed to *understand* clearly the nature of God's call in their lives and therefore failed to fulfill their call. The fact is they misunderstood God's call. They thought that God had called them to bless them. They thought the fact that they were God's special people meant that they were a people with special privileges instead of a people with a special calling. And so they believed God. They accepted him. They worshiped him. But they failed to fulfill the purpose for which they were called.

Throughout their history, in a variety of ways God sought to lead Israel to recognize and face the reality of their failure. However, Israel sought to convince God of their devotion and commitment to him through external forms of worship. One of the most dramatic confrontations between God and Israel in this connection is seen in Isaiah, chapter 1. The setting is a court scene. Israel is the defendant and God is the prosecuting attorney. God calls for all of heaven and earth to be the jury. Then God brings his charge against Israel. He says even animals know the master who feeds and cares for them. But, God says, those whom he called to be his children, those who have been the recipients of his love and care, do not know him (Isa. 1:2–3). God then exposes the inadequacy of external forms of worship. God says he is "fed up" with the sacrifices and the other expressions of devotion they offer (1:11–15). This does not mean that God is not worthy of worship nor that he does not desire worship from his people. It means that when one (or a people) uses worship as a means of evading the *basic call* of God (to be instruments of his mission in the world), then worship, itself, is a sin.

God, then, calls for Israel to repent. They are to seek justice. They are to relieve the oppressed. They are to care for the orphans. They are to minister to the widows (1:16–17). The broken peoples of the world, God says, are the focus of his concern and must be the focus of our concern.

To be God's people is not to be called to special privilege, rather it is to be called to special service. So God, the Father, calls Israel, the children, for a pivotal conference. "Come now, and let us reason together." God says to Israel, one more time I want to try to explain to you the purpose for which I called you when I called you to be my people. I want you to understand who I am and what I am about in the world and also try to explain to you who you are to be and what you are to do as my people in the world. It is true that Israel has tragically failed in fulfilling the purpose of her calling. But all is not lost. "Though your sins be as scarlet," they *can be* "as white as snow; though they be red like crimson," they *can be* "as wool" (1:18 RSV). (The translation "shall be" in this verse is incorrect. The second imperfect verb in a conditional sentence is subjunctive and should be translated either "can be" or "may be"). On what basis might this happen? The way is clear. "If you are willing and obedient, you shall eat the good of the land" (1:19). In essence, God said, I am about a mighty mission in the world, a mission of reconciliation, of healing the brokenness in the lives of people and society. It is to this mission of reconciliation and healing I am calling you. If you are willing to understand this and if you will be obedient in fulfilling this mission, then you will be mine and I will be yours with all this implies.

But, there is an alternative that also must be clearly faced. If you fail to fulfill this mission, whether you defiantly rebel or verbally accept it and then fail to carry it out, you need to understand the consequences, "you shall be devoured by the sword" (1:20 RSV). Then God adds, you need to take this with utmost seriousness because I am exceedingly serious in what I am saying. "The mouth of the Lord hath spoken" (1:20 RSV). Unfortunately Israel failed to understand and failed to respond to God's basic call to mission. In the fullness of time, Jesus is born. The Gospels describe the continuing confrontation between Jesus and the religious leaders of Israel, particularly as represented by the Pharisees. Their understanding of God, his purpose and call, differed radically from that which Jesus was proclaiming. The pivotal encounter is related in the Gospel of Matthew, chapter 21. Two parables are given that point up the failure of Israel in terms of their call. There was a man with two sons whom he told to work in the vineyard. The first son refused; the second son (Israel) said he would do so, but he did not do it (Matt. 21:28–32). In the second parable the owner of a vineyard let it out to some workers. At the appropriate time the owner sent servants to "receive the fruits." But instead of returning to the owner the fruits of their labor, the workers tried to take the vineyard for themselves (Matt. 21:33–41).

Then Jesus speaks God's words of judgment upon Israel. The warning given in Isaiah 1:20 finally becomes a reality. "The kingdom of God will be taken away from you and given to a nation producing the proper fruits of it" (Matt. 21:43 RSV). In essence Jesus said, for more than a thousand years you had your chance. You were called to be God's special people. But the essence of your uniqueness as God's people was that you were to give yourselves—as a people—to be the instruments of God's healing in a world of brokenness. In spite of your expressions of religious devotion, you have failed to fulfill the purpose of your calling. And so God says, I will now call a people who will hear my call, will understand my purpose, and will bring forth proper fruits. And so God calls the "New Israel." And Christians, today, make the audacious claim that we are a part of this "New Israel" of God. But the thing we must understand is, the "New Israel" is called for precisely the same purpose as was the first Israel. We are a people called to mission, and this mission is God's mission of reconciliation. We are a people called to assume a servant posture to express unconditional love to the broken people of the world—this means to all people, for all are broken in their spiritual and human situation.

What, then, is it that bothers me about those today who call themselves Christian, of whom I am one. The sin of Israel is again being repeated. The fact is, Israel was a highly moral people. The children of Israel believed in God. They were committed to God. Israel worshiped God and were careful to teach the Law to their children. They expressed their devotion to God in a variety of religious feasts, fasts, and sacrificial observances. But these were not enough. They failed to understand and fulfill the purpose of their calling. As Christians, today, we, too, are "good" people. In terms of personal morality, the people in our churches are as fine as can be found anywhere. We believe in God and have what we would call a deep commitment to him. We give our money so that religious work can be done around the world. We teach our children the Bible and seek to lead them to love God. We have our religious rituals that express our devotion to God. What more could God expect? The tragedy is, the mission of God basically continues to be unexpressed and unfulfilled. While we are expressing our religious observances, the brokenness, spiritual and human, in the lives of broken people remains largely untouched.

The Nature of God's Mission

If the uniqueness of God's people is that they are a people on mission, what is the nature of that mission? This is another question in which theology is foundational for a philosophy of Christian education. It was also the crisis question for me in this period of agony and search. In the religious tradition in which I was reared, I was always taught that God's mission in the world was to get "lost" people "saved." I was carefully warned against "the Social Gospel." This, I was taught, was a group of heretics who had so lost awareness of the spiritual purpose of God that they ministered to people simply in terms of their physical and social problems and never tried to get their "souls saved." I was taught that those churches that became involved in trying to minister to the social problems of people invariably lost their evangelistic zeal, and thus it was best for the church not to bother with social problems. Besides, the government and other agencies took care of these matters. The only institution that God ordained to care for the spiritual condition of mankind was the church and the church had all it could possibly do if it gave itself to helping individuals find Jesus as personal Savior. Finally, I was taught, the church should deal with eternal matters. Where will a person spend eternity? This was the pivotal question. It was far better for the church to give itself to the ministry of helping individuals have a saving experience with Christ, so they would spend eternity with God even if they did have to suffer some in this life. Thus I was taught. And yet here I was rebelling against the church because it was not taking the lead in the racial crisis.

Is the church an institution called into being by God whose only task is to lead individuals to experience personal spiritual regeneration? Or is man's nature such that this kind of personal regeneration is not needed, and thus the task of the church is to minister to people in terms of their human-social problems? Or is the individual's brokenness both spiritual and social so that it is imperative to seek healing in both areas in order to fulfill God's mission? God's people must understand the answer to this question with clarity if they are to be instruments of fulfilling this mission.

It is possible to give only brief conclusions here. I have dealt with this question more fully in *The Greening of the Church* (chapters 3 and 4). I believe that sin has marred the basic nature of the individual. Because of sin, man has become alienated from God, and the sin in human experi-

ence is of such nature that the individual is incapable of bringing healing in his/her own life. Salvation (healing from the brokenness of sin)
can come only through an act of God. Man's need is radical and God's
solution is radical. He gave his son. Paul says, "God was in Christ,
reconciling the world unto himself" (2 Cor. 5:19 RSV). This reconciliation is wholly gift on the part of God. The individual can do nothing to
merit it or to earn it. But God honors the freedom he gave to human
beings in creation. To receive the gift there must be a free, conscious,
intelligent response to the call and wooing of God. Therefore a part of
the early training my religious group gave me was correct. A part of the
mission that God is about is the personal spiritual regeneration of every
individual. God does not wish "that any should perish, but that all
should reach repentance" (2 Pet. 3:9b RSV). Therefore this is a ministry
which all of God's people, each in his/her own way, must be about.
Evangelism is an imperative, not an option, for God's people.

However, the mission of God in the world includes not only personal
salvation, it also includes the healing of people in terms of their human
and social brokenness. This emphasis on the physical-social needs of
people is just as integral and necessary a part of the gospel as the evangelical emphasis. In the biblical view, the individual is a unity as distinguished from Greek philosophy which views the person as a dualism,
"soul" and "body." In the past, evangelicals tended to follow Greek
philosophy rather than biblical teachings in their view of the person so
that they sought to "save the soul" while the "body" was ignored. It was
just such a dichotomy that was the catalyist for my disillusionment with
the institutional church in the mid-fifties. Fortunately, this situation is
changing and in many places those who are evangelical in their basic
theological perspective are equally vigorous in their social concern. It is
recognized that God is concerned about the total person. It is not God's
will that anyone should be cold or that anyone should be hungry;
therefore, in order to fulfill God's purpose in the world, God's people
must care for and minister to the total person.

Sometimes evangelicals who have demonstrated a social concern
have been told that such concern is simply a "gimmick" used to "hook"
persons for an evangelistic purpose. Two responses need to be given. We
confess, and make no apology for the fact that we desire to see every
individual come into a personal and saving relationship with God as
revealed in Christ, in which relationship God brings the healing that
only God can bring. This, we believe, is a fundamental part of the

purpose of God, and for God's people to fail in this ministry is to fail in fulfilling a pivotal part of God's purpose in the world.

The second response is to confess that there are those who have used social ministry as a "gimmick" simply to "hook" people, and this is exceedingly unfortunate. Those who are called to be the people of God must have a genuine love and concern for persons as persons. God's love for man is unconditional. God comes to man, loving him, ministering to him regardless of whether he ever responds or not. As the people of God we must care for man as God cares for him. This means that we will minister to man in his human needs regardless of response.

The Ministers of this Mission

There was a third theological insight that emerged during my period of agony and search. The doctrine of the priesthood of all believers was one which I had accepted for years. The meaning of this doctrine, as I understood it was, because every Christian is a priest, every Christian has the right of direct access to God without the necessity of a priest to be mediator. The new understanding that came to me was that the priesthood of all believers also means, because every Christian is a priest, every Christian is therefore a minister and he/she is accountable under God for the manner in which he/she fulfills that ministry. This was almost exactly opposite from my previous understanding.

In my youth when I felt "called into the ministry" I felt I was giving God my life so I could serve him "full-time." In my early days as a student pastor I felt that the responsibility for God's ministry rested upon my shoulders. Of course I was to try to get the laity, as many as I could, to help me in this task but I was the one who had been "called" into the "ministry" and thus the primary responsibility for "doing the ministry" was mine. I discovered, from the biblical perspective, that this understanding was a tragic misunderstanding. The doctrine of the priesthood of all believers means that the basic ministry belongs to the people of God—all the people.

The biblical basis for the ministry of the laity has been stated clearly in many books and so I will not deal with this area here. The professional minister is also a lay person and as such has the same calling as any lay person. I do not like the term, "professional minister," but all other designations are equally undesirable or worse. He/she is called by God to mission and is responsible for fulfilling that mission. On the basis of gifts given by God, the professional minister is appointed to the task of equipping the laity for their ministry. The basic call of God to "the ministry" is the calling of the laity. The professional minister is called to a special function, not to a higher calling.

What impressed my thinking so deeply was that in this biblical teaching God revealed the practical strategy for accomplishing his purpose in the world—he called a people to be the ministers of his mission. Our heresy is that we have perverted that plan. And the work of God will not be done as it ought to be done until the people—all the people—whom God has called to be his ministers understand this call, accept it, become equipped for it, and fulfill it. To follow any other approach to the life and ministry of the church is simply playing games. To continue to follow the present approach in which the professional ministers are the primary ministers is to doom the work of the church to relative failure.

The stupendous task facing the leadership of the church at the present time may be stated as follows. Given a people, most of whom, when they become a part of the life of the church (in whatever way they become a part of the church), have no understanding that they are called by God to be ministers, how does one seek to lead this people to understand that the basic call of God in their lives is to be ministers, and lead them to accept that call, to be willing to become equipped, and then to fulfill that ministry? We really do not know who we are or what we have been called to be as God's people. The church has lost much of that which it had at the beginning of the movement.

A SEARCH FOR PRACTICAL ANSWERS

Growing out of this search extending over several years, I felt I finally had a theological base that made sense, at least to me. I had found what I felt was the uniqueness of God's people. It was not enough for them simply to be a good people and a religious people.

They were a people called to mission. I also felt I had some understanding of the nature of this mission, and I felt I understood more clearly who were the basic ministers of that mission. Then my thinking began to be flooded with a number of other questions, most of them beginning with "how."

The Evangelical Academies

One of these questions was, how do we, as the People of God, bridge the gap between the church and the world? In my earlier search I found several references to "Centers of Renewal." The predominant group was Evangelical Academies, located primarily in Germany and Switzerland, with a few in France, Italy, and some other European countries. There were other Centers in Scotland and England. The word was that these places were bridging this gap. I felt that if I could study these centers I would find the answer which I sought. With the help of a grant from the Association of Theological Schools, my wife and I left for a sabbatical in 1964–65 to study these centers. We visited centers in England, Scotland, Germany, Switzerland, France, and Italy—more than twenty in all. In each place we stayed a week or more attending the conferences, talking with the leaders who ministered through these Academies, seeking to identify their purposes and goals and the approaches they used to achieve these goals. We also talked with the participants who came to the conferences. In all instances we were received with gracious hospitality. The leaders shared with us openly and honestly. I was impressed with what I saw. Though each center was unique, in their situation they were "bridging the gap between church and world." In the most serious manner they were "letting the world write the agenda" and they were seeking to minister to places of brokenness in the world. However, I came to the conclusion that what was being done in these centers was not "the answer" for the problem in the churches in the United States. I returned to the United States still looking for answers.

The Vineyard Conference Center

Much to my surprise, my book *The Quest for Vitality in Religion* received a very favorable response when it appeared in 1963. A significant number of both the professional ministers and laypersons wrote saying they, too, were disillusioned with what was happening—or failing to happen—in the life of the churches. Practically every mail brought more letters, so I decided it might be helpful to get a few of these people together. At least we could share our misery together. Using the names of the people who had written as the mailing list, I sent an invitation to attend a conference. The response was overwhelming! The conference was filled immediately and others placed on a waiting list. At the suggestion of the participants, it was decided to continue and expand these conferences. Again, the response was immediate. I became convinced that the "hurt" I had experienced was more widespread than I had thought. To lead these conferences we invited people of national reputation—Gordon Cosby, Elton Trueblood, Martin Marty, Reuel Howe, George (Bill) Webber, Keith Miller, Bruce Larson, Ralph Osborne, and others. After several years the "hunger" continued to be so great, it occurred to me that if we could have a conference center with a full-time director we might be able to touch the lives of enough people to make some changes in the life of the churches. With a grant from Lilly Endowment, Inc., the Vineyard Conference Center was started in 1972. At first we used the facilities of the Southern Baptist Theological Seminary (as had been done from the beginning in 1964). When, due to the growth of the Seminary, these facilities were no longer available, we rented a nearby building. The Conference Center grew to the point that we employed two full-time co-directors, two secretaries, and two part-time students from the Seminary. Things were going beautifully until the energy crunch hit and people stopped driving. Conferences had to be canceled. Unfortunately, our expenditures were so great and our reserves so small that the center did not survive.

The Church of the Savior in Washington, D.C.

A third experience needs to be noted. Coming back from the sabbatical in Europe in the spring of 1965, my wife and I visited the Church of the Savior in Washington, D.C. Gordon Cosby, the pastor, and I had been classmates at Southern Baptist Seminary. We had not been particularly close friends. When we graduated from the seminary, he left and I stayed for graduate study. We lost touch with each other. It was Elton Trueblood who called my attention to the fact that Gordon Cosby was the pastor of a church that was doing the kind of thing I was writing about.

Disappointed as I was that I had not found through my study of the centers in Europe the "answers" I sought, I looked forward with real anticipation to studying the limited number of places I had contacted in the United States. The Church of the Savior provided the best insights concerning a practical approach for a people on missions. Three things impressed me. I was impressed with their serious approach to study—the study of the Bible and of the nature of the Christian life. I was impressed with the serious approach they took to church membership. And I was impressed with their emphasis on the ministry of the laity and mission groups. In terms of the life and work of the church, Gordon Cosby has influenced my thinking more than any other person.

Modeling

The question "how?" continued to demand an answer. In a practical way, how do we go about the task of implementing the concepts of "a people on mission" and "the ministry of the laity." Obviously we have to start where we are. In my statements concerning the problems we face in the churches, I may have given the impression that none in the churches have an understanding of the people of God as I have described them. If so, I have given the wrong impression, for there are those who do understand the depth of God's call to mission and are fulfilling that call. For them we give thanks. There are also many who have the willingness and commitment to follow God's call, but they do not understand how to express it.

From a practical perspective, one thing that is needed in the churches today is to bring into being and make more visible a large body of people who will model the "reality" of church as it has been described here. From an educational perspective, one of the major weaknesses in the life of the church today is that we have sought to make up through *verbal teaching and exhortation* what we have failed to model in our lives.

From both the biblical and educational perspectives, this is one reason the ministry of the laity is so imperative in the life of the church today. A common misunderstanding by the laity concerning their ministry will illustrate this point. Sincere Christians want the work of God to be done effectively in the world. They also recognize that they have some responsibility for carrying out this work. However, most laypersons are engaged in some kind of work full time, either paid or unpaid. Therefore they feel they do not have the time (neither do they know how) to fulfill God's mission in any serious way. Also they hear, time and again, the plea for financial support for the work of the church. Thus the laity often reason, "Since I do not have time to serve God seriously myself and since my money is an extension of my personality, I will fulfill my ministry by giving money to the church." They feel that this helps pay the pastor's salary and he can fulfill the "ministry" locally, and it also sends missionaries, and they can fulfill the "ministry" around the world. Thus, in effect, the lay person is paying someone else to do his or her ministry. This is the attitude of the majority of the laity in most Protestant churches.

However, from both the biblical and educational perspectives, this is a tragic misunderstanding. The laity cannot fulfill their ministry by proxy. They cannot pay someone else to carry out their calling. Why? First, a brief answer from the biblical perspective. This is not to say the church does not need some money to carry out its ministry. The point I want to state most emphatically is that, in terms of ministry, *God does not need your money! He needs your physical presence in ministry!* Paul states it, "I appeal to you therefore, brethren, by the mercies of God, to present your bodies as a living sacrifice" (RSV). But this view does not rest upon a proof-text. The doctrine of Incarnation underlies this point. God sought to reveal himself in a variety of ways in the Old Testament period, but this revelation was always incomplete. When God sought to reveal himself fully to the world, he became incarnate in the person of his Son. He took upon himself the form of flesh and dwelt among us. Thus the world came to understand more clearly the love of God, the forgiveness of God, the identification of God with the poor and the outcast because they saw all of this and more in the life and ministry of Jesus—in his physical presence. The question comes, how is God going to reveal himself to the unbelieving and the broken of our world today? As the instruments God is using to reveal himself, we are using words primarily to communicate that revelation. We are saying to the broken, the poor, the alienated, and others, "God loves you." The broken of the world neither hear nor understand these words. If these people ever are to confront and understand the love of God, the forgiveness of God, and the concern of God for their wholeness, the laity will have to get in-volved personally in the lives of these people with ministries of uncondi-tional love in which the love of God is demonstrated in their physical presence. Once again, "the Word must become flesh." Incarnation is a basic and inescapable principle in God's plan of redemption and heal-ing. The laity cannot pay someone else to do this for them.

The strong emphasis urging the laity to give increasing financial support to the church, which is the pattern in most churches, may be one factor in leading the laity to have a gross misunderstanding of the biblical understanding of the ministry of the laity. It gives to them the impression they can use their money in the place of their presence in their ministry. The principle of incarnation indicates this is not possible.

The ministry of the laity is also essential from an educational perspective. In 1963 I wrote, "It is quite probable that the most powerful teaching force in the church is not the pulpit, nor the Sunday school, nor any other educational agency. It is the life lived by the church." The fact is, among all the approaches needed in the educational ministry of the church, modeling may be the most fundamental. Bandura, among secular educators, has given special emphasis to this approach. There is evidence that a person's deepest feelings, his or her deepest commitments and values, which constitute the basis of his or her functioning and actions, are not learned primarily in a formal educational setting but rather within the context of the culture in which that individual grows up, whether social or religious. One seems to learn one's functional commitments and values from the models in the midst of which one is born, grows up, and lives.

To illustrate, in the church of the first two centuries, any educational "program," in the formal sense, undoubtedly was quite limited, though worship and teaching were carried on. Yet, in these first two centuries, the early Christian movement had a profound influence upon society. The movement grew in a phenomenal manner. Granted, the early churches had many problems, yet the fact was the laity were effective witnesses. They, the laity, sought training. They had a tremendous evangelistic outreach. Many persons were won to Christ under the most difficult circumstances. The new converts were assimilated into the life of the church. They became equipped and they witnessed. How did this happen? What was the reason for the amazing transformation that took place in the lives of these new converts, and what led them to become involved in mission and ministry subsequent to their conversion? Certainly the power of the Holy Spirit was the spiritual dynamic. But we claim to have the spiritual dynamic of the Holy Spirit today, and it is not happening among our new converts. What was the educational ingredient they had that is missing in our time?

The new converts lived in the midst of a faith community that modeled what they (the new converts) were to become. It was that way from the beginning. "Now those who were scattered went about preaching the word" (Acts 8:4 RSV). In the faith community, the members modeled, lived out, expressed the life "in Christ." They expressed caring love for each other in the midst of their loneliness, or suffering, or persecution. They expressed caring love for the outsider in the midst of their hurt, or problem, or need. It is said that the world was amazed at the manner in which they loved. The "world" saw this and came to understand that if they became a part of this faith community, this was the life that was expected of them. They participated in a faith culture that modeled the life that was expected.

Recently, I read in a paper put out by the Andover Newton Laity Project that from the educational perspective, the question we are facing in the life of the churches is, HOW CAN WE CONVINCE THE LAITY THEY ARE THE BASIC MINISTERS WHEN MOST OF WHAT WE ARE DOING IN OUR CHURCHES KEEPS TELLING THEM THEY ARE NOT? We fail to model the fact that the laity are the basic ministers. What we are now modeling is that there is a small nucleus of lay persons who assist the professional staff by assuming leadership roles in the church. By our modeling we teach that "the average" member is to attend the meetings and support the church through his/her financial contributions.

We fail to model the fact that a serious knowledge of the Bible is essential to encountering the world at the points of its hurts. We fail to model the fact that it is necessary to train in order to be equipped to help people find healing for their brokenness. In most Protestant churches there are excellent educational programs. We encourage the people to attend. In these educational programs we teach people, verbally, the ideals of the Christian faith. Although there are exceptions, too often what we are *modeling* is that people should gather together and *discuss* the Christian life. That is what our people are learning, and that is what they are doing. If we are ever to move beyond words, verbalism, we must begin to model, to express in life, the ministry of the laity. The words we use in teaching the Christian life are profound and challenging. We tell each other that we are to "count the cost," and that we must be willing to "go the second mile."

But even while we are discussing these ideals we have the sinking feeling that these words have almost no relevance to the reality of our daily lives. So the problem is not in our words. Nor will a change in teaching methodology solve the problem. Our problem is far deeper. We face a serious theological question that needs to be answered and an equally serious spiritual decision that needs to be made. Theologically, the question is: In God's eternal purpose, who is the basic minister? If the answer is, the laity, then the lay person has a profound spiritual decision to make: Is he or she willing to be that kind of minister? Educationally, the question is: Will our answer to the above question be only words voiced in our meetings, or will the answer be modeled in our living?

This is not to imply that a formal approach to education is not also needed. We cannot depend on modeling alone to provide the totality of our education. Our fundamental learnings, learnings related to commitment, our deepest and most significant religious learnings, come primarily through modeling. Therefore, from the educational perspective, making real the ministry of the laity is an absolute imperative.

POSSIBLE APPROACHES TO IMPLEMENTATION

A number of questions demand attention. The first questions have to do with understanding. How do we undertake to lead the people to understand that "being good," being faithful to the church as an institution, and giving financial support to the church is not an adequate expression of the Christian life? How do we lead people to understand that they have been called by God to a mighty mission? How do we lead them to understand that they are the basic ministers of that mission and that they cannot pay someone else to fulfill that mission? How do we lead them to understand that they are to fulfill this ministry "in their bodies"? Second, understanding, difficult as it is, is not enough. What do we do to undertake to lead the people to be willing to accept God's call to mission and ministry? This deals with the problem of commitment, and it deals with the deepest levels of the lives of people. Third, what do we do to help people become equipped for this ministry? God's ministry in the world will assume a wide variety of expressions. This means there must be a wide spectrum of training opportunities provided. Fourth, how is this ministry expressed? How can lay persons seriously involve themselves in God's ministry and still make a living and have time for their families.

The Laity Expressing Their Ministry

There are a number of lay persons in our churches who do understand that they have been called by God to join in his mission and they understand that they are the basic ministers. They also have a commitment to God that leads them to be willing to get involved in this ministry if they only knew how. How does a lay person express his/her ministry?

I am sure there are many different answers that could be given to this question. In the normal routine of one's life there will be numerous opportunities for the Christian to minister to persons and in places that have need. These ministries of an incidental nature are important. However, in addition to these incidental ministries, there is a special area of brokenness to which each lay person is called by God based on the gift(s) which have been given to him or her. This place of ministry is specific and must be consciously accepted by the individual as the place in which God wants him or her to work in the world to fulfill his/her ministry. There are four major options a lay person has to express his/her ministry. In three of these the lay person is related directly with persons. In the fourth, the lay person is related to structures.

First, the lay person may find ministry primarily through one's secular vocation. Actually, in fulfilling a ministry through vocation, one may focus primarily on a ministry through structures. For example, a multinational company with headquarters in Indiana has on its staff in an executive position a former professor of ethics at Yale whose task is to help the corporation be sensitive to the social, moral, and ethical issues involved in the complex relationships the corporation has to its stockholders, its employees, the community in which it is located, the country in which it is located, and the foreign governments and people to which it is related.

However, the majority of lay persons who express their ministry primarily through their vocation will express it in direct relations with people. Certainly in one's vocation every Christian ought to be concerned about such general matters as honesty, relationships, integrity of the service rendered, the product produced, and the like. These are the kinds of things all decent people ought to do. But, to be a minister through one's vocation, one ought to be related to some specific person(s) and/or place(s) of brokenness in which one consciously gives oneself to be an instrument God can use to bring healing in the life of the person or persons involved. For example, a lawyer will certainly seek to be "Christian" in his relations with all clients and will seek to represent them to the best of his ability. However, the lawyer may feel a special leading or impression from God that his/her "ministry" is to focus on one client, a teenage boy who has been charged with a drug violation. If the lawyer is to seek to be an instrument of God to bring "healing" to this place of brokenness, he/she will not only fulfill one's responsibility as a lawyer but will also become involved with the boy and the entire family in a long-term relationship.

Over a period of time the lawyer will seek to understand the boy in the deepest ways possible and in a variety of ways seek to build a positive relationship with him. This "ministry" will lead the lawyer to be concerned about the father's vocation or lack of one. Does he make a living wage or not? Does he or does he not have work skills that are marketable? What are his attitudes about life, about his family, about himself? What about the wife? What about other brothers and sisters? How does one go about building relationships so that people are open to the possibility of change and growth in their lives?

These are some of the basic questions which the lawyer must answer. Plans are made and efforts are expended. Then, at an appropriate time and way, the lawyer is to inquire about each family member's attitude toward God. This is essential, for if one is concerned about total healing in the lives of people, one must be concerned about the spiritual brokenness in the lives of people which only God can heal, as well as the human brokenness in their life.

In making his/her commitment to this ministry, the lawyer has no idea how much time will be involved, or what the outcome will be. These are matters over which the lay person has no control. In this situation, as an expression of one's ministry in the mission of God, the lawyer is called to express unconditional love, which is God's kind of love. God only requires that one be faithful. Obviously a lawyer cannot be involved to this extent with every client. For this reason the lay person must seek God's leading to the place of brokenness where one's ministry is to be focused. But if one is serious about wanting to be a minister, an instrument of God's healing, this kind of involvement is a necessity.

As an aid in assisting the lay person in this type of ministry, it is very important for individuals who feel a sense of "call" to the same ministry to form themselves into a "mission group." That is, the lawyers in a given church (or area) who feel an impression from God that they are to use their vocation as the channel for their ministry should form a mission group. The group would consist of from four to eight people so that personal interaction is easy, and the group should meet each week. Three things are done in this meeting. First, the participants should minister to each other at the points of their hurts. Just because one has committed oneself to trying to be a minister for God in some type of serious involvement does not mean that he or she will no longer have any personal problems. Thus, when these hurts occur, one function of the group is to be a support group in expressing caring concern for one another. Second, in this weekly meeting the group is to study to become better equipped to serve in the specific ministry to which each has been called. This is the equipping the New Testament speaks about. Obviously, one's equipping and one's ministry should be directly related. Third, in this weekly meeting each individual is to make specific plans as to what he/she will undertake to do that week as the next step in building relationships to fulfill God's purpose in the lives to which the lay person has been sent.

There are several reasons why such a group is helpful. First, the group gives support to each person in the group in fulfilling his/her ministry. In isolation it is quite easy for a person to become discouraged when there are "dry spells" in one's ministry or when the response of the people to whom one is seeking to give one's self is negative or even hostile. The group gives support to one another at such times. Also, a person is more daring and more willing to get involved as a member of a group than in isolation. Second, the group holds each member accountable. If the group notes that one participant over a period of time gives evidence that he/she is not seriously involved in carrying out one's calling, it is the responsibility of the group to call this to the individual's attention and hold him or her accountable. Third, the training for this ministry can best be done with others. Fourth, the group can serve as a "sounding board" and make suggestions as each member makes his or her plans concerning what one is to do in a given practical situation to be an authentic, caring, and helpful person.

Having used a ministry through one's vocation to explain and illustrate one possible expression of ministry, the other general options for expressing ministry will be mentioned only briefly.

One may find one's ministry in any of the needy areas of society. Wherever there is brokenness there is an opportunity for ministry. But again, the ministry must be specific and personal. One may minister to those in prison, to those with drug problems, to school drop-outs—the options are limitless. A nurse, an engineer, a factory worker, and a mechanic may say I certainly want to be "Christian" in my vocation, but I feel a definite leading that God is calling me to focus my ministry in the area of teaching adult illiterates how to read. Thus, they would form a mission group.

Others will find their ministry in the organizational life of the institutional church. Some will find their special ministry in teaching small children. The ministry of others will be working with youth. Again, those who have a common ministry, for example, those who teach children, will form themselves into a mission group, for support, training, and planning.

Then there will be those who in response to God's leading will minister to and through the structures of society. Structures play a powerful role in the lives of all people. Structures may discriminate or oppress. Rather than dealing directly with the persons who suffer the consequences of certain structures, there are those who may find their ministry in improving or changing the structures. Those who have this calling should form themselves into a mission group, for they will need all the support they can get.

Gifts for Building Up the Body

There are so many areas of need and opportunities for ministry, the Christian who becomes serious about finding and fulfilling his/her ministry may be overwhelmed. There are so many places of brokenness: where in the world is one to go and what in the world is one to do? Is there no place to find guidance? The Scripture says that God has given gifts to all of his people (1 Cor. 12:7). It is reasonable to deduce that the gift(s) which God has given to a person are directly related to the ministry God wants that person to perform. Thus one guideline for helping a person to discover his/her ministry is for the person to identify his/her gift(s).

This is another area in which a biblical teaching (theology) has simply been lost from the life of the church. God has given gifts to his people. The gifts were given for the building up of the Body, for fulfilling God's mission in the world. These gifts are directly related to the specific ministries to which God has called each of the laity to engage, but the church is doing practically nothing to help the laity identify their gifts. It is amazing that, with all the activities that take place in a parish church, there is not a single one where the lay person is guided in discovering his/her gift(s).

The ineffectiveness of the church in the world is not surprising. The church is a gift-rich institution, yet it lives its life in abject poverty. Not only does the church not have activities designed to aid the laity in identifying their gifts, we in the church do not even know how to go about helping the laity identify their gift(s). This is one of the great needs within the church. Fortunately, there are a few who are taking some initial steps in this direction. Once the individual identifies his or her gift then he/she can determine the specific ministry in which that gift will be expressed.

There are varieties of gifts and therefore there are varieties of ministries in which the Body ought to be engaged. The ministries of a given congregation ought to be under the supervision of that congregation—the community. The congregation ought to approve each ministry, and the congregation in a formal service of the church ought to commission each mission group to be an expression of the Body laboring in that particular part of the vineyard.

As the various individuals and groups gather and formally or informally share together what has been happening in their particular area, worship ought to be a celebration of what God has been doing in his world.

THE NATURE OF THE SALVATION RELATIONSHIP

What kind of relationship with and commitment to God is needed so that one is willing to accept and fulfill God's call to mission? Paul says, "if anyone is in Christ, he is a new creation" (2 Cor. 5:17 RSV). The question is, what is the nature of this "in Christ" relationship? I have spent my life within an evangelical tradition. On the one hand, I believe the evangelical insistence on the necessity of a conversion experience is sound. On the other hand, I feel the traditional views that many hold with reference to the conversion experience and the salvation relationship create numerous questions which cry out for consideration. Unfortunately, such consideration will not be possible in this essay. Therefore

I will focus attention on the issue that has been the central theme of this philosophy, namely, God's call to mission—a search for authenticity. To state the issue in the form of a question, is growth and development optional for one who has an authentic "in Christ" relationship? Or, to make it even more pointed, is it possible to have an authentic "in Christ" relationship without accepting and fulfilling the mission for which we have been called by God? The answer to this question is directly related to the practical problem of personal commitment.

Evangelicals have tended to emphasize "belief" as central in the salvation relationship. This is understandable because the Bible emphasizes "belief" as central to this relationship (John 3:16; Acts 16:30–31). The problem is, what does the New Testament mean by the word "believe"? What level of understanding is involved? What level of commitment is involved? Quite often the meaning of a word is strongly influenced by the context in which it is used. For example, when Paul responded to the frightened inquiry of the Philippian jailer, "What must I do to be saved?" Paul replied, "Believe in the Lord Jesus Christ and you will be saved, you and your household" (Acts 16:30–31 RSV). The jailor was aware that Paul was in prison for the faith he professed. He had been his guard. So when Paul said "believe," the jailor was aware that Paul did not mean something shallow and superficial. He was aware that Paul was calling for him to lay his life on the line in such fashion that he, too, might suffer imprisonment for this "belief." Thus, when we seek to understand the New Testament meaning of "believe," we must ask the contextual question, to what is God calling us when he calls us to "believe"? If God's call is simply to accept his gift of salvation based on the acceptance of a certain view of how Jesus is related to God (that is, that Jesus is the Son of God) and the acceptance of a certain view of what Jesus can do for the individual (that is, that Jesus can save one from one's sin), then it would seem to me that this level of commitment could be quite limited. If God's call only means that God expects the follower to live "a good, clean, Christian life," that is, to live up to the existing cultural standards, to attend worship services, and to support the church financially, the level of commitment involved in such "belief" could be quite limited.

So, the focal question now becomes, when God calls us to be a part of his people, when he calls us into the salvation relationship, what does he call us to be and do? What is involved? We must ascertain this context before we can determine the level of understanding and commitment which is involved in the New Testament meaning of "believe." If we reply, as we generally do, that to "believe" demands a commitment of the totality of our life to God, then this seems to imply a very deep commitment. But let us see if we can be a bit more explicit. In response to the question, to what does God call us when he calls us into the salvation relationship, Matthew 7:21 says, "Not every one who says to me, 'Lord, Lord,' shall enter the kingdom of heaven, but he who does the will of my Father who is in heaven" (RSV). Thus, God calls us to do his will. But what is his will? Again, the Scripture says, "The Lord is not slow about his promise as some count slowness, but is forbearing toward you, not wishing that any should perish, but that all should reach repentance" (2 Pet. 3:9 RSV). Thus it is God's will that all shall be saved. (I am aware that these answers are oversimplifications of issues that need fuller treatment. My hope is that these simplified statements are harmonious with the conclusions that would be found in a fuller treatment.)

To answer our question, we could say that God calls us to do his will and his will is that all shall be saved. Therefore he calls us to his mission of reconciliation. "If anyone is in Christ, he is a new creation; the old has passed away, behold, the new has come. All this is from God, who through Christ reconciled us to himself and gave us the ministry of reconciliation" (2 Cor. 5:17–19a RSV).

Now we come to the question toward which the preceding has pointed. If to "believe" means that in the salvation relationship one is committed to that to which God is calling his people, and if God is calling his people to the mission of the reconciliation of the world, is the acceptance of and the fulfillment of this mission optional for the person who has experienced authentic "belief"?

Yet the reality in our churches is, we "knock ourselves out" trying to find ways to entice the members "to do God's work." When they decline with the excuse they don't know how, we plead with them to take advantage of the opportunities for training we provide. The large majority ignore our pleas. We rejoice if a few respond. Can't you imagine Coach "Bear" Bryant, after a football game, gathering the players in the locker room and in a pleading voice saying to them, "*Please* come to practice next week. Last week not enough came out to have a scrimmage. We just can't learn to play the game unless we practice, so please come out." Such a thought is ludicrous. If he says anything at all it is something like, "Practice is at the regular time on Monday. Be there!"

Thus, we get from organized sports two basic principles for the church: INHERENT IN JOINING THE TEAM IS A COMMITMENT TO PLAY THE GAME! INHERENT IN THE COMMITMENT TO PLAY THE GAME IS A COMMITMENT TO PRACTICE! This means that, for the person who is "in Christ," to accept, to become equipped for, and to fulfill God's call to mission are not optional. To have any less commitment in the salvation relationship makes the Christian faith and the church a shallow mockery.

Thus, we end where we started. Our problem is, there are so many in the church who do not know what game it is we are playing as God's people, and if they did know they seemingly have no intention of getting involved. They do not know that to which God called them when he called them to be his people. And once again the spector of institutionalism in the church rears its ugly head. As the Christian faith has been passed from one generation to the next through the centuries, the authenticity in terms of understanding, commitment, and dynamic has been lost many times. Sometimes it may have taken centuries; sometimes it happened more quickly. Also throughout the centuries there were various reform movements as different groups sought to recapture the authenticity of the early movements as they understood it. In time, these reform movements themselves became institutionalized. Today the church has many needs. We need a clearer understanding of how we learn. We need to have a better understanding of the practice of teaching. We need better forms of worship. We need to know how the family should relate to the task of Christian education. These and many more things we need. But our basic need is for a theological and spiritual reformation in which we seek to recapture more of the authenticity of the reality and the dynamic of the Christian faith that were characteristic of the early movement.

Chapter 3

How I Became A Religious Educator—Or Did I?

Randolph Crump Miller

In 1919 my father, an Episcopal minister, built a large parish house as a base for the religious education program of a growing congregation. Six years later a beautiful church was opened. In the meantime the congregation had grown rapidly because of the educational ministry. In 1947 I also built a parish house, and the church was constructed some seven years later after I had left. I remember the discussion in the congregational meeting that made the final decision to build the educational building. The younger adults, most of whom had children, were strongly in favor of beginning with an educational ministry. Some older people were afraid that they would not live long enough to see the new church structure, but they did.

The priorities of my father's ministry meant that I was early exposed to good education. I remember that we used *The Christian Nurture Series*, a closely graded approach based to some extent on the views of Horace Bushnell. We had contests that were fun. We had good people as teachers, and my brother went to Sunday School because he liked Mrs. Welbourne. Worship was still by departments, and our building was arranged for informal worship as part of the total program. Already I was being influenced by a kind of religious education that I still believe in.

There were other influences. I became at about the age of ten the crucifer, carrying the cross and assisting in the services. My father had no acolytes' guild, so I was the church's jack-of-all-trades during early adolescence. Two pews near the front of the church were usually occupied by attractive girls from private boarding schools, and this added to my interest in being the crucifer.

During my senior year in high school I was the teacher of a sixth-grade class of boys, and I met with some of them on Monday nights as

"The Lads of Sir Galahad." Later on, when a senior in college, I drove into the city on Sunday mornings to teach a class. This continuing association with a good Sunday School during these years has led me to the conclusion that religious education can be effective in some cases because it has been. At their best, good programs prepare children and young people, and sometimes their parents and other adults, for a life of Christian conviction and action.

By the time I went to college I knew that I wanted to be a minister. Although I had no major at Pomona College my courses tended to be in the departments of philosophy and religion. I was planning on the parish ministry, and my father suggested that I study for a Ph.D. My bishop agreed that this was a sound plan, and in 1931 I found myself in New Haven at the graduate departments of philosophy and religion of Yale University. During the next four years I studied under Douglas Clyde Macintosh, one of the exponents of empirical theology. When combined with the philosophy of organism, or process philosophy, it becomes a theology of depth and comprehensiveness, a view which I have expounded in most of my books. My dissertation centered on the thought of Henry Nelson Wieman, and my horizons were broadened as I studied under H. Richard Niebuhr, Luther Allan Weigle, Hugh Hartshorne, Robert Lowry Calhoun, and others.

As I worked on the final details of my dissertation I wrote to Bishop W. Bertrand Stevens of Los Angeles suggesting that I stay in the east and take a position as an assistant minister or perhaps I would accept his offer to return to the Diocese of Los Angeles. A letter from my father changed all this. He wrote about a poor theological seminary struggling for its exis-tence which might hire a fledgling theologian. This seemed to be just what I had been training for, although not aware of it, and I wrote to Dean Henry H. Shires offering my services. He replied that indeed he would like me to come and that he could afford to pay me room and board, and perhaps I could make $10 per Sunday as a supply preacher.

At Berkeley

For the next sixteen years (until 1952) I taught at the Church Divinity School of the Pacific in Berkeley, California. My major field was philos-ophy of religion, and I also taught apologetics and Christian ethics. From 1937–1940 I was also the chaplain to the Episcopalians at the

University of California, and we had a well-rounded program of seminars and discussion groups as well as worship and recreation.

In 1940 the dean asked if I would teach an additional course on lesson materials in Episcopal Sunday schools. The course at the Pacific School of Religion dealt with all sorts of lesson materials and did not deal specifically enough with those recommended for the Episcopal Church. I did not recognize it at the time, but this was the beginning of my dual interest in teaching both religious education and theology at the seminary level.

The following year the dean asked me to teach the introductory course in Christian education. I protested strongly that I did not have sufficient background and no overall concept of what such a course should contain. The dean suggested that I consult my wife and the outline of a course she had taken with Sandford Fleming at the Berkeley Baptist Divinity School. With his outline and bibliography, I worked out an introductory course that I followed in general in my *Education for Christian Living* (1956, 1963) and in my courses until 1981. At this time I became involved in many teacher training programs in local congregations. In 1943 the Cloister Press published my *A Guide for Church School Teachers*, which contained most of what I knew about the subject.

Symptomatic of how my work was expanding, in 1943 the Church Divinity School of the Pacific celebrated its fiftieth anniversary with a jubilee volume edited by Dean Shires and me, *Christianity and the Contemporary Scene*. I wrote two essays, one on what was happening in American theology and the second on the situation in Christian education. Already the germ was developing on the relation of theology and educational theory. I wrote: "Until the connection between the Christian tradition and the philosophy of modern education is made clear, there can be no satisfactory solution to the problem. In brief, the problem is this: Someone has to make a Christian out of John Dewey! By this I mean we must show how the fundamental insights of progressive education can be made consistent with the Christian way of life and belief" (p. 197).

Already I was looking for the organic connection between a live theology, relevant content, interpersonal methods, and worship. I was concerned about age groups and the growing edge of persons as a basis for the application of content and method. The social applications of this process were noted by Adelaide Case, who saw the radical implications of Christianity for political, social, and economic reform. The Christian imperative brings tradition and faith to bear on social problems. This positive note was threatened by the unsolved problem of untrained teachers, the difficulties with teacher recruitment and training, and the lack of adequate courses for prospective ministers in the theological seminaries.

Beginning in 1940 I was vicar of a store-front church. We had about fifty children and young people in a small store, with a kindergarten space behind the altar. We had classes by age groups, although some were small. By limiting the size of classes they could meet together with no great confusion, much like buzz groups a few years later. On clear days some classes met in a teacher's station wagon. We called this "the divide and conquer technique." We had a brief worship service at 9:15, followed by classes. At 11, there was a regular service of Morning Prayer.

The congregation remained in the store for seven years until 1947, when the new parish house was completed. At this point, we instituted a parents' class, which I taught. Our 9:15 service became a family service, which we identified as "modified but not mutilated Morning Prayer," in which we would "break a rubric to save a child but never break a child to save a rubric." Later on we had a slogan in the spirit of the Lord: "The crying of a baby is a more joyful noise to the Lord than the snoring of a saint!" Such statements expressed the spirit and atmosphere of our worship, but they always seem to dismay liturgical scholars.

About this time I began to correspond with Mary Jenness, a fine writer of curriculum material, who asked for my evaluation of her manuscript on *Climbers of the Steep Ascent* for 9th graders. She was suffering from multiple sclerosis, from which my mother had died, so we quickly found much in common. I was invited by Maurice Clarke of Cloister Press to write their 10th grade course on *The Challenge of the Church*, and Mary Jenness, to whom I dedicated the first edition, made many suggestions for creative approaches and innovative methods. Our correspondence during several years helped me to understand the significance of curriculum materials and the ways in which students may be involved in learning.

By now we had built the parish house and we had a fully developed program of Christian education in process. We used the Cloister Series, to which Mary Jenness and I had contributed. This was an excellent series which sold well for several years. We established a Sunday School in a nursery school building, and this became the nucleus of another congregation. Our staff included two seminary students and one woman from St. Margaret's House, but the teaching responsibility was strictly on the shoulders of the lay people. One advantage of this pastorate was that when seminary students were skeptical about what was said in class I could invite them to St. Alban's, where they could see for themselves.

The Seabury Series

In 1947 a committee on a new curriculum for the Episcopal Church was formed, and I was invited, probably because of the need for someone from the Pacific Coast. The first few meetings were not fruitful, as there was no staff and the committee was not sure of its task. But it quickly became a think-tank for educational theory. At first there was no secretary for education, and we were also looking for an editor-in-chief. It is hard to imagine how lacking in educational ability the church as a whole was. But the personnel of the new committee represented the best that the church could offer: Adelaide Case, of the Episcopal Theological School; Dora Chaplin, of General Theological Seminary; John Heuss, who became the director of the department; Reuel Howe, of Virginia Theological Seminary, whose theory of interpersonal relations was influential; Charles Kean, from Kirkwood, Missouri; Marion Kelleran, of Virginia Theological Seminary; Gardiner Monks, who chaired the committee through the whole process; Vesper Ottmer Ward, who was editor-in-chief and whose design was finally followed; Theodore Wedel, who turned the College of Preachers over to the church for the education of the clergy in the theory and practice of Christian education; and Bishop Lewis Bliss Whittemore, who became the watchdog of the editorial staff. The committee brought in James Smart, of the Presbyterians, Frances Eastman, of the Congregationalists, and Charles Penniman, who managed to stimulate the entire editorial staff and finally became so controversial that Ward and his staff resigned. David Hunter became the new director of the department and William Sydnor became the editor with a new staff.

From 1947 to 1952 the committee met four times a year, usually at Seabury House in Greenwich, Connecticut. Each meeting was an opportunity to develop new ideas, refine old ones, and share our insights. The struggles in the editorial board were difficult ones. The vision of the curriculum as developed by V. O. Ward was maintained even after he was fired by Bishop Whittemore, and most of what Ward outlined at meetings at the College of Preachers appeared in the Seabury Series. During this time, Reuel Howe developed a series of lectures at the College of Preachers that emerged in 1954 as *Man's Need and God's Action*.

The interpersonal theory at the center of Howe's thought, so close to the thinking of Martin Buber, became a permanent part of my educational theory. However, I was already at work on a statement of educational theory, and in 1948 I read a paper to the editorial board on theology and education, which became the first chapter of my *The Clue to Christian Education*. This point of view had been developing for a long time, at least back to the time I began teaching in the field. I had stated the problem in 1943, and I waited for someone to respond in terms of the differences between H. Shelton Smith's *Faith and Nurture* and Harrison Elliott's *Can Religious Education Be Christian?* I had regularly assigned to my classes a paper comparing these two books from the time they were published, and I believed that the answer would be the clue to educational theory. I found the answer in theology.

The Clue

"The clue to Christian education," I wrote, "is the rediscovery of a relevant theology which will bridge the gap between content and method, providing the background and perspective of Christian truth by which the best methods and content will be used as tools to bring the learners into the right relationship with the living God who is revealed in Jesus Christ, using the guidance of parents and the fellowship of life in the church as the environment in which Christian nurture will take place" (p. 15). I then spelled out what I meant by a *relevant theology*, for one's theology is crucial. But this is not teaching theology, for I qualified my statement by saying that theology was in the background and faith and grace were in the foreground. This assumes that God is involved in the processes of our lives, that faith is a relationship of trust, and that grace has to do with a gracious personal relationship. This final assumption that God is involved in the process of education (we plant and water and God provides the increase) caused consternation among some theologians and led to exciting responses in issues of *Religious Education* in 1965–66.

After I had written the first chapter of *The Clue* and used it as a paper for the editorial board, I did nothing more for six months. I returned from the committee meeting and found that my wife, Muriel, was ill with polio. She died on May 13, 1948, at the age of 35. Besides the immediate problems (What does a man do with four daughters aged 2, 4, 6, and 8?), there were some matters of faith. What kind of theology assists one in trusting God's love? What does one think of God when one's spouse dies? Here theology, faith, and education come together. The answer may be that of Job, or of Job's friends, or the question may be put in a different way. I had found an answer that suited me when I tried to understand my mother's multiple sclerosis. William James provides a picture of a pluralistic universe in which God is at work as love. Because God is love, there are things that God cannot do, and whatever force comes from God is one among many. God is persuasive rather than coercive. God does not undo what has been done. God does not make square triangles. God acts in persuasive love and does not take away human freedom and responsibility. God did not take away my mother's multiple sclerosis and did not stop the polio process that led to Muriel's death. What God does for those who remain open is to offer the grace of God's healing power and persuasive love. "God is a very present help in trouble," but God does not take our troubles away. God may make them bearable, but not pleasant. So I sought to come to terms with Muriel's death as I preached to my congregation about God's love (see my *Living with Anxiety*, pp. 157–162; *Live Until You Die*, pp. 141–147). But it was six months before I could return to writing the manuscript for *The Clue*. I continued to teach and preach and minister to the congregation. The children's grandmother helped in many ways, and there were always friends to provide genuine interpersonal relations.

I think of *The Clue* as a rather middle-of-the-road or conservative book. I was seeking to answer the question posed by the Shelton Smith-Harrison Elliott dialogue, and my book brought my interests in theology and religious education together. I succeeded in describing a theory of Christian education practice that was both theologically acceptable and educationally helpful to many people. I included a portrait of a deity who makes all things new. There is in the world emerging novelty, and our response to such creativity makes God available to us.

Both the Seabury ideas and the theory behind *The Clue* were at work at St. Alban's. The only Seabury material available in 1950 was the adult "Church's Teaching" volume on the Bible, which we used in the adult class, but we began to enlist two teachers for each class. We had a fifty-minute class period for all ages. We had a genuine family service. We had regular teacher training sessions. And we correlated the parents' material with what their children were learning.

Because of lecturing in connection with the development of the Seabury Series, in 1949 I met a young widow in Richmond, Virginia. We both responded to a momentary encounter, and in June 1950 Elizabeth Williams Fowlkes and I were married. Shortly after we were settled with our six children in Berkeley, there came a phone call from Dean Liston Pope offering me a position at Yale in Christian education. I had fancied myself as a theologian who gave religious education a high priority, and now I was being asked to be a religious educator with some theological roots. This was really a change in vocation, as I saw it, and it was not an easy decision to make. At the same time, it was to some degree a continuation of a path I had already chosen. I had published a book in popular theology, *Religion Makes Sense*, in 1950, just before *The Clue to Christian Education* appeared. I finally decided that we would go to Yale, and in 1952 we moved from Berkeley to New Haven with the six children.

Yale Again

My colleague at Yale was Paul Herman Vieth, one of the wisest and best balanced of the religious educators. He had continued the Yale tradition after the retirement of Luther Allan Weigle. Hugh Hartshorne was also active. We had a graduate program that was tied in with the department of education in the graduate school. I adapted the introductory course I had built in 1941 out of the outline of Sandford Fleming and proceeded to develop some seminars on the relation of theology and education. Vieth and I worked together on joint seminars, and I learned from his experience in the field. I continued as a consultant to the Seabury Series.

Even before I left California I was working on the drama of redemption model as an approach to teaching the Bible. It had been developed by the leadership training team of the Episcopal Church. I began working on the five acts of the drama: Creation, Covenant, Christ, Church, Consummation, and added the response of Commitment and Criticism. I supported this approach with studies in the field of biblical theology, such as Ernest Wright's *God Who Acts* and finally Bernhard Anderson's *Unfolding Drama of the Bible*. I quickly saw the teaching values of this interpretation and began offering a seminar on it. This emerged into a series of lectures, and then became my *Biblical Theology and Christian Education* in 1956. In the meantime I was asked to produce a textbook for college and seminar courses. This took me back to the Sandford Fleming outline, and I spent a year providing the balance of chapters, plus the bibliography needed for a textbook, *Education for Christian Living* (1956).

The Seabury Series had received a mixed reception in the churches. Most of the reviews by professionals were approving, and a team headed by Ronald Goldman evaluated it positively in terms of how it fit the learning curves of all the age groups. In those congregations where it was taken seriously, it worked well. I was the director of religious education in a local church in New Haven, and the teachers fought for the privilege of teaching the Seabury courses which dribbled from the press three courses per year. But only about a third of Episcopal parishes even tried the Seabury Series, and it was a financial failure before it got started, although about two-thirds of the clergy had some special training at the College of Preachers. I still strongly believe that the Seabury Series is both educationally and theologically sound, and it is probably the best curriculum material produced by any group. But the best is not always likely to sell. It did not demand any special expertise, but it did require a conviction of the significance of Christianity, a deep sense of devotion, and a willingness to spend a great deal of time in preparation.

I had begun to take an active part in the Religious Education Association as soon as we moved east, and I was chairman of the board in 1957–59, thanks to my old friend who was the general secretary, Herman E. Wornom. In 1958, after the death of Leonard Stidley of Oberlin, I became the editor of *Religious Education* and continued for the next twenty years. In this position I came into contact with the religious educators among Catholics and Jews as well as Protestants. There was a constant stream of submitted articles. We had many special symposia and convention issues, often due to the suggestions of Herman Wornom. As book review editor I received most of the books worth reviewing and sent them to reviewers. This broadened the basis of my ministry. There were six issues a year, so the job was a constant one but never burdensome. Three times Paul Vieth became acting editor when I was away on leave, and John H. Westerhoff III succeeded me as editor

Godin and Georges Delcuve, at Lumen Vitae in Brussels; and Rabbi Marc Kahlenberg, in Brussels, as we traveled across Europe. Later on, four of these men wrote articles for *Religious Education*.

A major project of that sabbatical was the writing of *Christian Nurture and the Church*. The time at Bossey and the visits along the way provided the needed stimulus, although I had been working on the basic ideas in lectures since 1954. We settled in for about nine weeks at St. Deiniol's Library, Hawarden, Wales. This library is a memorial to Gladstone, and it provides room and board and 40,000 books. It is an ideal place for uninterrupted work. The emphasis of the book was on education to be the church in the world. In every act of the church as a people or family, it can become a group who are followers of "the Way" in their daily ministries. Education is not limited to the schooling model but is concerned with the quality of life in the congregation as it worships, experiences fellowship, shows pastoral concern, seeks to recreate society, offers Christianity to the world, and expresses itself in ecumenical relations.

At Oxford I heard Ian T. Ramsey speak on empiricism and religious language, and we had several conversations on these topics which influenced considerably a portion of my chapter on communication. I also met Basil Yeaxlee, whose book on *Religion and the Growing Mind* had influenced the editors of the Seabury Series and had become a staple in my own teaching. I preached for R. S. Lee, Vicar of St. Mary's, and read the manuscript of his *Your Growing Child and Religion*, which was a Freudian approach to religious development. I visited several educational colleges and discovered the care that the British give to the training of teachers to teach religion in the schools. I also had the opportunity to read some of the dissertation of Kenneth Hyde, of Birmingham, who examined the results of such religious teaching when it is not connected with the students' religious upbringing. Much of what I learned has been incorporated in my thinking and writing since then.

The World Council of Christian Education in making plans for the 1962 Institute in Belfast asked me to write the study guide, which I accomplished while at St. Deiniol's. *The Educational Mission of the Church* was based on Bible study and followed the basic thesis of my *Christian Nurture and the Church*. The guide was translated into several languages and became the basis for study prior to the institute. At the institute, I led the Bible study each day. Participation in such an international gathering increases one's awareness of both the similarities and differences among people of other nationalities, races, cultures, and religious traditions. The World Council of Christian Education included all major Christian groups except the Roman Catholics, who sent observers and participated fully. I found a readiness on the part of many people to understand what I was trying to communicate. For me, exposure to this great variety of experts in Christian education was a challenging and stimulating experience. Russell Chandran, of Bangalore, India; José Miguez Bonino, of Argentina; Processo Udarbe, of the Philippines; and J. W. D. Smith, of Glasgow, Scotland, were among those who made an impression on the institute. At this assembly the first steps were taken toward the merger of the World Council of Christian Education and the World Council of Churches, consummated in Peru in 1971.

I had given an address in Naramata, British Columbia, on "The Age Group Characteristics of Parents Between the Ages of 35 and 50." This became the opening chapter of a book on *Youth Considers Parents as People* (1965), written for the Youth Forum Series and backed by the research of Merton Strommen. It brought together my studies of adolescence and parenthood. It was written shortly after our six children had ceased to be adolescents, and they provided some of the illustrations. It is one book all six read.

I had become excited about Ian Ramsey's studies in religious language while at Oxford in 1959, so I spent a summer reading in the field, and in 1965 I developed a course for a summer session at the United Theological College in Vancouver, British Columbia. This led to a seminar at Yale. I am not sure that I came fully to terms with Wittgenstein, but I appreciated many of his criticisms and began to examine the whole field of linguistic philosophy. The empirical bent of Ramsey's position was particularly attractive to me, because it was broader than the verification theory of the stricter empiricists. Further study took me as far back as Horace Bushnell's 1849 essay on "The Nature of Language, as Related to Thought and Spirit." The full impact of this kind of thinking led to *The Language Gap and God*, the first draft of which was written in Beirut and given as lectures at the Near East School of Theology in 1967.

The World Council of Christian Education

The World Council of Christian Education sponsored our sabbatical in 1966–67. I taught for one term at Serampore Theological College in

India, and our trip was arranged so that we met religious educators in each country that we visited. It was a deeply enriching experience as we were exposed to a variety of cultures. In most situations our common interest in the educational work of the church led to seeming agreements across cultural and denominational boundaries. We learned of many problems in India as the churches cooperated in trying to solve the problem of teaching religion in the colleges without the process becoming evangelism, much the same situation as in the state-supported colleges and universities in the United States. The dominance of the Hindu religion even in the Christian colleges led to some tension, and there seemed no easy resolution. We were impressed by the achievements of the Church of South India as the only ecumenical venture that successfully brought together the various traditions of Protestantism including the Anglican, and we observed the similar process that led later to the formation of the Church of North India.

We were asked to be consultants to the Oriental Orthodox Churches' committee on Christian education curriculum meeting at Antelias, Lebanon. There were twenty-five people present, with representatives from the Coptic Orthodox Church of Egypt, the Syrian Orthodox Church of Syria, the Syrian Orthodox Church of South India, the Armenian Orthodox Church of Lebanon, and the Ethiopian Orthodox Church. They were Nestorian in their theology and had ancient roots in tradition and liturgy, and they were concerned to develop curriculum materials to be used in five languages besides English. Their endeavors were sponsored by the World Council of Christian Education, and consultants were provided. The committee members were open to discussion of educational methods and age-group characteristics. I found difficulty in their outright rejection of the interpersonal emphasis and the I–thou relationship, which had been a key factor in the theory behind the Seabury Series. Paul Verghese of South India (now Bishop Gregorias), who was the chairman, explained that in the Arab world and the Eastern cultures, the relationships were always corporate rather than individual, and that the sense of the tribe or the extended family was paramount in one's identity. One carries out the commands or the traditions of the family even when they are opposed to one's own judgment.

Later on I met with the committee and its changing membership in Cairo and in Beirut. We worked on age-group characteristics, probable topics for study, and finally lesson outlines. In one meeting in which two bishops disagreed, the Metropolitan Athanasios of Beni-Souef in

Egypt would ask what I thought rather than argue with the other bishop. Athanasios knew that I agreed with him, and as a foreigner and non-Orthodox consultant I could say what he wanted without offense to Bishop (later Pope) Shenudah. It was a form of scapegoating which helped the meeting run smoothly, and it was done later also by Paul Verghese, the chairman. We finally shaped the material so that the lesson writers could take over on their own and produce the lessons in five languages.

The World Council of Christian Education played a significant part in my development as a religious educator. Beginning with the writing of the study guide for the 1962 assembly in Belfast, I was able to meet with educators in many countries. The WCCE sponsored both the 1966--67 and 1970 sabbaticals and involved me in the curriculum development of the Oriental Orthodox Churches. Both Nelson Chappel and Ralph Mould, who were the general secretaries during this period, did much to make these travels possible. I ended my sabbatical in 1967 by attending the WCCE assembly in Nairobi.

In 1970, after meetings in Fiji, New Zealand, New Guinea, and Australia over a period of several months, I was the leader of a summer program in Singapore, sponsored by the Theological Education Fund, for those teaching religious education in the seminaries of Asia. Prior to this program we visited seminaries in Indonesia, Thailand, Burma, and Hong Kong.

Out of the Singapore study institute came important responses, including the Indonesian and Filipino reflections in a committee report published in *The South East Asia Journal of Theology* (Autumn 1970, p. 46): "Christian education assumes a dynamic aliveness which involves the whole of a person and the totality of one's concerns with the Gospel story. Christian education puts the faith of the church in a dialogical relationship with the world even as it seeks to incarnate God's grace there. This understanding of Christian education will surely revolutionize our life and work as Christians in Asia. . . . Christian education does not so much attempt to fill individual Christians with a body of knowledge as it does to enable them to have a perspective that arises out of one's being saved and made righteous by God in Christ."

My survey of the thirty-one papers presented to the institute, which was published as "Some Asian Contributions to Christian Education" in *Religious Education* (March–April 1971) and in *South East Journal of Theology* (Autumn 1970), was read to the entire group at the conclusion of the institute. It led to two conclusions: 1) There is a "need to make Christianity intelligible in the languages and thought forms of Asia, and this cannot be done by Westerners." 2) "There is a common humanity under God, by whatever name (or no name) God may be called. In spite of language, conceptual, and cultural differences, what stands out is our common problem of seeking to be human, to enter into relationship, to see the divine as 'the inbetween' as human beings relate to each other. . . . This message came originally from the East to the West, and it lies deep in the unconscious mind of us all. This is not the whole story, for the East also points to the mysticism that makes us aware of the hidden mystery that stands behind all that we can know of reality. In a dialogue of equals, perhaps we can recapture the essence of what it means to be both religious and a Christian in today's world. But to achieve this, both East and West need to develop radically new models of Christian education." This goal is a far cry from the more common "English educated westernized snobbish elite who because of their estrangement from the larger community in which they lived created problems for themselves and their nations."

Papers by some of the thirty-one constituents stressed the theological base, the social-action implications, and the need for understanding the context of Christian education in Asia. Donald Kanagaratnam, of Sri Lanka; W. P. Napitupulu, a lay person in the Indonesian government; Levi V. Oracion, of Silliman University in the Philippines, and José Gamboa, Jr., of Manila, contributed articles to the March–April 1971 issue of *Religious Education.*

The meetings leading to the merger of the World Council of Christian Education and the World Council of Churches marked the end of my ecumenical ministry in other countries. For almost ten years I had participated in conferences and made two trips around the world meeting with significant religious educators in each nation. Now a change was in the air, and I had participated in the moves toward the inclusion of the World Council of Christian Education in the World Council of Churches. The merger was a splendid accomplishment, enabling the World Council of Churches with its network and resources to carry out the educational mission of the churches. It was also a loss, for the tie with volunteer educational associations and the professionals in the field was lost. Some of the specific projects sponsored by the WCCE were abandoned.

We gathered in Peru for the final assembly in July 1971, coming from various *encuentros* where we learned about the conditions in particular countries as we proceeded to Lima. I joined the group in Mexico City for an exciting week of considering religious education in Mexico. As we came together in Huampani near Lima, I discovered that I knew educators from almost all the countries, either having been there or having met them at previous assemblies. The committees had done their work well, and the vote for the merger was 149 to 7, with two abstentions. Whether the results were satisfactory is hard to tell, for both groups had lost some of their financial support and therefore the new division was unable to mount as many programs as the religious educators hoped for. But at least Christian education was where it belonged within the World Council of Churches.

Similar influences in the United States paralleled those of my travels. Beginning about 1952, when I began to think of myself as a religious educator, I began to attend meetings of professors, either those set up by the Association of Theological Schools or by the National Council of Churches. This last group became the Association of Professors and Researchers in Religious Education (APRRE), and it was in this group that I found a common interest and developed important friendships. The papers presented at the annual meetings were significant, and as editor of *Religious Education* I often asked to publish them. The genuine exchange of views in this group was sometimes invigorating, as were the informal conversations as we caught up on the new thinking of our friends.

Combined with this experience was the continuing connection with two parishes as director of Christian education. I could put my theories into practice and evaluate the results. So I came to specific conclusions about the need for the careful selection of teachers, the need for continuing teacher training, the careful grading of age groups, the keeping of classes at a number suitable for genuine interpersonal interchange, sufficient time for teaching to be effective, and a program of worship as part of the total picture. I preferred two leaders for a class, and I liked the idea of a process observer to evaluate what actually was going on. I was also convinced that the element of romance and an appeal to the affective domain were essential along with a theological honesty, a need for precision, and a capacity to distinguish between a variety of language games.

Graduate Students

The greatest satisfaction in my teaching at Yale was the graduate program. Paul Vieth, and before him Luther Weigle, had developed an effective approach through the department of education. The students who received their Ph.D.'s were the leaders in the field. At one time, Luther Weigle counted sixty college presidents among them. They also dominated the educational boards in the churches, and were the leaders in the National Council of Churches and in the religious education division of the World Council of Churches. The program was restricted after Yale abolished its department of education, and from then on the degree was given through the department of religion in the Divinity School, which fitted in with the rising theological emphasis that was emerging in the 1950s. From 1916, when Weigle came, until 1968, when the program was destroyed, it was a fine academic and professional degree. But the internal politics of Yale took the Christian education degree out of the new graduate department when it was transferred to the graduate school.

The canceling of the Ph.D. degree was my biggest disappointment while at Yale. The students were highly competent, and they became fast friends. We were closely together in discussions, tutorials, and rewriting dissertation materials. Some of them were teaching assistants. The last doctoral degree was awared to Charles Melchert in 1968. The elimination of graduate students from the seminary courses limited the number of subjects to be offered and lowered the level of scholarship. Paul Vieth retired in 1964, and we were helped by visiting faculty, including Campbell Wyckoff and Kendig Cully, for a few years. Iris Cully taught part time for the next eight years. Since then, Letty Russell has taught a few courses, but otherwise it has been a one-person department.

Process Thinking

My interest in theology had always been high, but now there were more opportunities to follow the recent developments in process theology. From the beginning of my writing, I had been concerned with empirical method and process thinking, and I now began to offer a seminar that took account of the thinking I had done years before in my dissertation. Some students actually dug the dissertation out of the library and read it. I began to read some of the newer books in the field. In the summer of 1973 at the Kanuga Conference in North Carolina, I gave four major addresses for lay people on process theology. The response was favorable, especially as compared with that of a group of Episcopal clergy in Orlando, where it was reported that "some listened and others mocked."

During a sabbatical leave in 1973, I began putting together the manuscript that became *The American Spirit in Theology*. This book reflected a lifetime of theological speculation on writings I had been acquainted with since college days. Beginning with William James and his use of radical empiricism, pragmatism, and pluralism, which I took to be the three elements of the American spirit, I had a focus for looking again at the people I had studied as a basis for my doctoral dissertation: John Dewey, Gerald Birney Smith, Shailer Mathews, Edward Scribner Ames, Douglas Clyde Macintosh, and Henry Nelson Wieman. From my original acquaintance with them in the 1930s, they came to life again as the basis for understanding Alfred North Whitehead and Charles Hartshorne. With this background, chapters on Schubert Ogden, Daniel Day Williams, and Bernard Eugene Meland brought the story full circle. This was probably the most satisfying of my books, although not as central to my career as *The Clue to Christian Education*. What *The American Spirit* did do was bring into sharper focus my theological interests that served as background for my *This We Can Believe*.

These studies led to a reconsideration of how one can relate process theology to religious education. The origin of this project was an invitation to write an article on process theology and black theology. The key question was whether process theology provided a basis for dealing with the issues being raised by all the liberation theologies, black, feminist, minority, Third World, as well as ecology. My first venture was written for *Black Theology II*, edited by Calvin E. Bruce and William R. Jones (1978). The chapter was rewritten and expanded for *The Anglican Theological Review* (July 1975), and it became the basis for a new seminar on process thought and religious education, which I offered at the School of Theology at Claremont, where the Center for Process Studies is located. We were in Claremont on sabbatical for the spring term of 1976, which gave me the opportunity for discussion with faculty and graduate students interested in process theology. Potentially, the position developed in this course was covert from the first formulation of the relation of theology and education in 1943, when I wrote that one problem "is to come to terms with the philosophy of 'organism' and Dewey's operationalism, of making Christian theism adjust itself to the findings of science and metaphysics" (*Christianity and the Contemporary Scene*, p. 14). In the same chapter, I wrote that "just as Thomas Aquinas christianized Aristotle, so modern theologians must come to terms with Whitehead. This perhaps is the great metaphysical task of modern theology" (p. 11). This position, held consistently since the days of my dissertation and explicitly since 1943, became the primary focus of my thinking with the writing of *The American Spirit in Theology* (1974). The course, begun at Claremont, I repeated at Yale each year and offered twice at New York University in summer school and at the Presbyterian School of Christian Education in Richmond. It is a promising field for continuing exploration. As process thinking is modified by those holding to a form of Christian theism, as for example in the thinking of John B. Cobb, Jr. and David Ray Griffin, it will become more suitable for the experiments of religious educators.

Horace Bushnell

The invitation to give the Martin Lectures at Perkins School of Theology led to a special study of Horace Bushnell, who had had a significant influence on my thought since I began to teach religious education in 1940. I had read his *Christian Nurture* at this time, and his theories quickly became a part of my thinking. When I concentrated later on theories of religious language, I found his treatment of that subject to be relevant. Also, I found that he was an insightful theological thinker, and I saw a consistent theological pattern running through his rather untidy system of thought. This pastor–educator–theologian, with his intuitions of something deeper than the purely rational, had attracted me at an early age, and I still find Bushnell to be one of the great spirits of the nineteenth century. I had written a portion of a chapter on Bushnell for my *The Language Gap and God* (1970).

For the purposes of Christian education, what made Bushnell significant was his concept of the family as an organism, which is related to the church, also conceived as an organism. These organic relations were tied in with the language of relationships, so that how we treat each other communicates more than the words we use, although we always need words to tell our loving. Bushnell understood that such relationships were crucial prior to the emergence of language in the child, and that only such relationships could make words come alive. By the time a child is three, taught Bushnell, the parents will have done half of all they can do for their child's moral and religious development. Bushnell also provided support for my view of the importance of children in a worship service that involves the family in a meaningful way, including the preaching. "We do not preach well to adults," he wrote, "because we do not preach, or learn how to preach, to children" (*God's Thoughts Fit Bread for Children*, p. 36).

Bushnell's emphasis on the significance of the home and the organic nature of the family carried over into the experiments with approaching the family-as-a-whole, which was essential to the Seabury Series. The basic research was due to the work of Ernest Ligon, who worked out a system in which families worshiped together, came together for discussion of their lessons, and evaluated their changes in behavior. Ligon used this approach for a rather sterile type of character-trait development, but within an organic view it became a basis for relationships expressed by love, as in the thought of Reuel Howe. In Howe's thought it is the basis for an understanding of infant baptism and of the responsibility of parents as effective ministers. This has led to a changed perspective on the way a parish handles its baptismal services and its ministry to infants, so that they are incorporated into the organic life of the community.

The kind of continuity emanating from my study of Bushnell is also evident in my theological development. My first book, *What We Can Believe* (1941), was based on my studies under Douglas Clyde Macintosh and on my interpretation of the thought of Henry Nelson Wieman in my dissertation. I claimed then that theology is based on experience as interpreted and tested in life. This empirical base could be supplemented by what William James called "overbeliefs" in a pluralistic world view. I sought to make the best use I could of biblical scholarship and scientific evidence, without losing the stress on commitment that is the essence of trust and faith. Looking back on this book from a perspective of forty years, I do not find it far out of line, except for possible improvements from a more overtly process point of view. This is evident in my *This We Can Believe* (1976). Starting with the same assumptions about theological method and with a little more theological and metaphysical insight, I found that I could make use of much of the earlier book, but that it could be enriched and made more useful by greater use of the philosophy of organism. Following the same outline as in 1941, I was clearer about such concepts as the incarnation, the resurrection, the problem of evil, the meaning of responsibility, and eschatology.

In 1978 Iris and Kendig Cully, who have been close friends for many years, edited a *Festschrift* written by former students and colleagues.

The title of the book was appropriate: *Process and Relationship*. The authors dealt with some of the emphases and stresses of my position, but quite rightly followed their own interests in fourteen too-brief chapters. It was primarily an act of friendship on their part, and I was greatly honored. These women and men, highly competent and imaginative, were doing what I would want them to do. They were developing new ideas and testing them in front of their colleagues. Perhaps they were moving beyond or against positions I have taken, which is what one would expect. Boardman Kathan concluded with a personal biographical sketch. In it, he ties in an interpretation of my position with events in my life, and does so with accuracy and appreciation. Note should also be taken of Sara Little's interpretation of my position in the *Festschrift* for Herman Wornom, *Pioneers of Religious Education in the 20th Century*, in the special edition of *Religious Education* (September–October 1978) in which she evaluates my position in the light of her expert knowledge of the whole corpus of my writings.

Delayed Retirement

In late September of 1978 the State of Connecticut changed its laws to eliminate mandatory retirement. I was just 68, had retired as editor of *Religious Education*, and assumed that I would be through at Yale in June 1979. But the temptation to continue was attractive, and Colin Williams, the dean, said that I was free to do so. Later the age of 70 was made mandatory for university people, so I had what I call two "bonus years" before I retired as of June 1981.

I had been exploring various aspects of theology, ethics, and education in articles in journals, and I put a selection of these together for a new book, *The Theory of Christian Education Practice* (1980). H. Richard Niebuhr had used the phrase, "the theory of practice," for an understanding of the relation of the more academic studies in the seminary and the application of Christian insights to daily living. It seemed to me that this phrase described much of what I had been doing in Christian education through the years in relating theology and method, and I took over his phrase for my attempt to relate process theology and religious education in a restatement of educational theory and practice. The first two chapters of this book describe what I see to be the relation of process theology to Christian education. In summary form, I have tried to establish the dynamic quality of organism as a primary model, using the human body as an illustration. I have identified "God with the creative order of the world, a process which transforms human beings, brings values from a potential to an actual state, and works to overcome evil with good. God is that process by which we are made new, strengthened, directed, comforted, forgiven, saved, and by which we are lured into feelings of wonder, awe, and reverence" (p. 15). This implied much about God's relation to human freedom, to the powers of evil, and to the creativity at the center of all. It points to God as working through persuasive love and not through coercion. The future is open, and thus is the basis for hope. As Whitehead wrote, "the power of God is the worship he inspires."

At the center of the theory and practice of Christian education, there is a vision, and our response to that vision is the experience of worship. We worship a deity of persuasive love, who never coerces or overrules us. Children and adults alike discover their worth in the sight of God as they respond to a commanding vision. This is the empirical anchor of our faith. Worship does not have predictable results, for in worship we may face emerging novelty, unexpected challenges, and the freedom to act as transformed persons. We need to reform our worship to take account of the multirelational connections of the complex organism which is reality.

The dual concerns of theology and Christian education have shared in my priority in ministry and teaching. Christian education was a top priority when I was a child, and I see no reason to change now. There is hope for the future as we clarify our theory of education practice, provided that the community of the faithful exhibits that quality of life that makes faith contagious. We share a life together, and we bring others into it through personal relations, so that we learn to worship together and act together as disciples of Jesus Christ.

Chapter 4

From Practice To Theory—And Back Again

D. Campbell Wyckoff

One of my favorite exercises is the "Who Are You?" game, but the most fascinating thing about it has been that I have never come up with a completely satisfying answer to the question. Genealogically, I am a Wyckoff (go back ten generations to 1637 and the ancestor who took the name—Wijkof—arrived on these shores), a Campbell (two different clans), a Dripps (a Scotch-Irish family that would be Fergusons had they not clashed with the authorities generations ago), a Millar (Irish Moravian), and Brokaw (French Huguenot, originally "Broucard"), a Mac-Donald (Canadian Scot), and a McKenzie (western New York, the family stemming from the Highlands)—just to go back three generations. In citizenship, I am an American; in religious faith, a Presbyterian. Family-wise, I am a son, a husband, a father, and a grandfather (also a cousin and nephew, but not an uncle). Functionally, I am a layman, a missionary, a professor of Christian education, and more generally a learner-teacher. I am also a neighbor, a colleague, and a friend. I am a university graduate (all three degrees are from New York University), a Democrat, and a pacifist.

The list could be extended. But it (even with other things that could be added) is more than a list, for I have incorporated its manifold elements into a self-identity. That self-identity, in turn, is one of the major elements that I project into my function as Christian educator. I cannot imagine my not being a Christian educator, and all the other things that I am are caught up in one way or another, into that functional identity.

That has its great advantages. It brings a rich variety of experiences, memories, and anticipations to doing Christian education and thinking about it, and it provides a perfectly normal, natural, and personal focus for a holistic approach to Christian education theory and practice. As a result, nothing in experience is alien to Christian education, and there is no insuperable problem about getting theory and practice in focus and keeping them there.

There are disadvantages as well. I was once quite an authority on Christian marriage—then I got married. My expertise on the Christian family ceased when I started trying to raise two children. It is painfully embarrassing to remember conversations and lectures in which I shared my views on these (and, unfortunately, many other like) matters, those views to be shattered later by the realism of experience. In fact, memory and experience seem to operate on expertise systematically to diminish it as time goes on.

Christian Education As Enterprise

My primary conviction about Christian education is that it is an *enterprise* in which I, along with others, am engaged. This means that it is not primarily a set of ideas, but a task to be accomplished. That task is as concrete as the Sunday School and the theological seminary in which I teach, and as broad as the combination of work at the various age levels, intergenerational work, and work in the various institutions that undertake the task—the church, the family, the school, colleges and universities, seminaries, and their various related functions and agencies.

Furthermore, it is an interpersonal enterprise, in that it takes place when persons meet and interact with one another and with the triune God. It happens between me and another person, or several other persons, in the presence of and by the grace of God. Some of these meetings of persons are planned and formal; some are unplanned and informal. Thinking back over how I learned the Christian faith and the Christian life, it is likely that, powerful as were the planned and formal occasions of Christian education, the unplanned and informal occasions were probably just as, if not more, telling.

To stress that Christian education is an enterprise is to be down-to-earth about it, but does not minimize the importance of rigorous thought about it and on its behalf. The planned and formal aspects of the enterprise cannot become more effective if they are not subjected to principled analysis and critique, and even the unplanned and informal occasions benefit from the kind of character, habituation, stability, and principled flexibility that are the product of deep reflection on these very experiences.

This line of argument has led me to the title that I have given to this article—"From Practice to Theory—and Back Again." We start with our involvement in Christian education as an enterprise. We reflect on our experience in it, that reflection leading to considered theory about it. Considered theory is then brought back to the enterprise to inform it, enrich it, and correct it. But if in any way we withdraw from engagement in the enterprise itself into some ivory tower of theory, it is not long before we become obsolete as Christian educators, however brilliant and fascinating our thinking may be.

Ages, Stages, and Periods

"Ages and Stages" do not appeal to me very much as a way of understanding personal growth and guiding Christian development, especially when they are used diagnostically and prescriptively. To describe a person as having a "mental age" corresponding to a "chronological age" is less important, in my opinion, than to come to know the integrity of that persons's self-identity. This conviction stems from an observation of my own self-perception over the life span. When I was a child, I knew myself more as a self than as what they were describing as a child. When I was an adolescent, the same thing applied—I knew myself more as a self than as what they were describing as an adolescent. When, in college, I was taught the "characteristics of adolescence," I guessed that they might possibly prove useful in describing other people and in planning and doing youth work, but I could not really take them seriously as terribly important ways of thinking about myself.

Perhaps this basic attitude toward "ages and stages" came to a head in a family incident in which my father became enraged with me over something that I had done, and backing me up to the wall with his forefinger, declared vehemently, "I know that adolescents are supposed to act like that, but *no son of mine* is going to act like that!" It had never occurred to me that being an adolescent was anything important, but I knew that being his son *was* important. (Freudians, have your picnic, courtesy of the superego! That has never been convincing to me either.)

To go back to the self that I knew as a child, as a youth, and that I now know as an adult: My experience is that it is the same self—grown,

expanded, enriched, altered in some respects, and subject to decline—
but essentially the same. When I think of myself as a child, it is my self
in those years that I remember, and likewise with my thinking of myself
as a youth and as an adult. I am more the same person than I am
exemplar of different "ages and stages."

I bring this up because I am going to recount certain "periods" in my
development as a Christian educator, and simply do not want you to be
misled into taking the idea of "periods" too seriously. I have not been
one person at a particular period in life, and another person at a later
time. Rather, I have been the same person growing and responding,
with a rather stable sense of self.

You will understand, in light of this, that even finding labels for my
"periods in life" has been difficult. At one point I almost called them
"first educational period," "second educational period," and "third
educational period," and then decided, even though these were accurate labels, that they were not sufficiently descriptive to do for my
purposes. So I have decided to call them my "formative period," "missionary and first professional educational period," and "second professional educational period," with the understanding that they have more
in common than differentiates them.

Formative Period

The "formative period" includes everything up through the college
years—an amalgam of family, community, church, and school.

My father, Dewitte Wyckoff, was a native of the Finger Lakes. Early
orphaned, he made his way through schools in the region, and graduated with the "Order of the Coif" from the Cornell University Law
School in 1910 (having entered from high school, as was then possible).
After working briefly for a law firm in Brooklyn, he joined the staff of the
American Law Book Company, and found his lifelong vocation of
"legal research."

My mother, Christabel Campbell, was born and reared in the western
New York Scottish enclave of Caledonia, spent what must have been
two very happy years at the Geneseo Normal School, and went to teach
on Long Island. Eventually her teaching career led her to Brooklyn,
where she and my father met while each of them was teaching a Sunday
School class at Gregg Chapel, a mission of the Lafayette Avenue Presbyterian Church.

Cleland B. McAfee was pastor of the Lafayette Avenue Church at that time. When he left to teach at McCormick Theological Seminary in Chicago, they determined to follow, and after a brief period of teaching back at Cornell, did so. The Law Book Company thought enough of my father's work to keep him on its staff and to mail his work out to him in Chicago.

Besides Dr. McAfee, the person who seems to have had greatest influence at that time was another faculty member, George Robinson, who deeply impressed my parents by his outspoken opposition to this country's entrance into World War I. As a child, I often heard the story of Dr. Robinson standing before a class on the day after that war was declared, saying, "My lips are sealed!" Years later, I happened to meet him while we were traveling west in the same railway car. He recalled the incident, and chuckled over it, implying that they didn't stay that way very long!

When they came back to New York after two years in Chicago, it was to finish with another two years at Union Theological Seminary. By that time I was on the scene, complicating things. Being married and having children was not the norm for seminary students in those days.

My father felt that his two greatest teachers at Union were George Albert Coe in religious education and Harry F. Ward in Christian ethics. For a period he served as Dr. Ward's teaching assistant, and remained devoted to him as mentor and friend until his death. The outcomes of the Union years were, for both my parents, dedication to involvement in parish life, concern for religious education, a passion for Christian and social action, and a liberal theology.

Another quite different outcome of the Union years was disappointment at not being ordained and becoming a minister. Presbyteries were not ordaining Union graduates in 1921! My father took a position in the legal department of the American Bankers Association, and remained in that position until his death in 1957. (We are a family of laity!)

My father and mother lived what they believed, and they shared that belief and life with me fully. When they taught evening courses for workers on strike in Passaic, they took me with them. (We went by trolley car. The family automobile was a much later and very traumatic innovation.) They were indefatigable workers in the church's Christian education program, and I was there. (I still count as personal friends some of the young people whom they taught.) Regularly, they organized study groups in our home around the annual study books on home and foreign themes, published by the Missionary Education Movement (now the Friendship Press). Pioneering in leadership education, they taught in and helped to organize the "High School Leadership Curriculum" at the New Jersey School of Methods, held each summer at Blairstown. (It was there that I came to know people like Harold Donnelly, who was later the first Professor of Christian Education at Princeton Seminary.) They were the first ones who systematically worked to bring the black Sunday schools of Bergen County into the membership of the Bergen County Council of Religious Education, and I went along as they visited those schools.

In 1929 the Federal Council of Churches asked my father to take on a six-month investigation of the so-called "Centralia Case," in the State of Washington. This was a shooting and lynching affair involving the American Legion and the I.W.W. (Legionnaires had been killed and I.W.W. members lynched in the process, just after World War I.) He took a leave of absence from the Bankers Association and undertook the assignment. Characteristically, we went as a family. When the plans were being made, an aunt of mine remonstrated with my parents, "You surely aren't taking the children out of school for six months!" My father's reply was, "I don't believe in letting schooling interfere with education!"

During the junior-high years an incident took place that has remained central and important. In a class at a youth conference at Blairstown during the summer, we were talking among ourselves about some aspect of religious belief (I do not remember exactly what it was), when the teacher, who had been quiet, said, "From what you are saying, I don't believe that you have had a personal experience in the presence of God." Then she led us into his personal presence. Later she talked to us about Brother Lawrence and the "practice of the presence of God." I have to confess that I have never been able to do much with Brother Lawrence himself, but since that day I have not lost the sense of meeting a personal God and living in his presence. The 1930s (my college days) were probably as secular and agnostic as any period in this century; yet, as I listened to professors sneering from the podium at the idea of a personal God, I found myself asking, "How is it that I know something that they do not know?"

This experience has had its dry times and its fruitful times. It has deepened and changed. But I think it is something like this that the Westminster Confession of Faith means by "the assurance of salvation," which may be "divers ways shaken, diminished, and intermitted," while we are "never utterly destitute of that seed of God, and life of faith; that love of Christ and brethren; that sincerity of heart and conscience of duty; out of which, by the operation of the Spirit, this assurance may in due time be revived, and by the which, in the meantime, (we) are supported from utter despair."

Schooling did become important toward the end of the high-school years through the influence of two teachers. The mathematics teacher of my junior and senior years, Doris Smith, uncovered for us some of the philosophical and historical roots of the subject in a way that has tantalized me ever since. My senior English teacher, Selma Wasson, gave me a love of poetry, a conviction that writing was important, and a sense that I might be able to do it.

During the high-school days, leadership of what would now be called "ecumenical" youth work served a significant purpose in my experience. The county youth council was strong, and I was in the thick of its planning and program. For a year I served as its president. No one had to convince me of the possibility and importance of interdenominational Christian education work. I had seen that in my parents' work. But the experience of my personal leadership in it gave me a realistic inner view of its tensions, problems, and opportunities, its advantages and limitations. It resulted in a personal commitment to ecumenism.

At the same time, parish life became more personally meaningful. The churches of my childhood were the First Presbyterian Church of Rutherford and the Reformed Church of Hasbrouck Heights. In Rutherford, the experience was one of gracious and authoritative pastoral leadership, and nurture in a loving Christian community. In Hasbrouck Heights the experience was of a congregation alive, growing, experimenting, innovating.

The church of my high-school and college years was the First Presbyterian Church of Englewood. If there is such a thing as religious quality, the Englewood Church had it. Its worship was an experience of the beauty of holiness. In education, mission, and Christian social responsibility it exerted local, national, and international leadership.

During college years, I had to find my own places for student teaching in religious education. At one time I served as a student teacher in music in the parish school of Corpus Christi Church, near Teachers College. Father George Ford became a friend and mentor. Later when I read *The Seven Storey Mountain*, I discovered that it was about this same time that Father Ford had been the one who brought Thomas Merton back to

Christianity. But I never met Thomas Merton. Before his conversion he had been involved with radical campus groups, while I was giving leadership in the Student Christian Movement. My other piece of more or less self-assigned student teaching was at the Morningside Presbyterian Church, a congregation struggling to stay alive. The Morningside building later became the Church of the Master, and throve under the ministries of James Robinson and Eugene Callender. But at the time I was there, it was dying.

When it came to college, I was in no mood for the ordinary, and I found exactly what I wanted across the river in Columbia University's Teachers College—an experimental school called New College. One of the things that drew me there was that Paul M. Limbert was on the faculty. I had come to know him at Blairstown and also at camps and conferences conducted by the International Council of Religious Education in New Hampshire. Under his leadership I could develop my interest in religious education in an atmosphere of free educational innovation.

New College's educational plan involved the systematic expansion and integration of experience and learning. The expansion of experience and learning was done through a series of basic courses in the arts, sciences, humanities, and education. In all of these courses there was an alternation between mastery of theory and research, on the one hand, and going out into the community and world, on the other hand. The resources of New York and its environs were constantly being explored and used (one of the permanent results, in my case, being a loving attachment to the place). When the necessary experience was not at hand, you went out to get it. Two kinds of experience were identified as the chief ones not at hand: life in a rural setting and experience abroad. New College students were required to spend a period at the New College Community (at the foot of Mount Pisgah, in Western North Carolina) and in a study–travel experience in Europe. The "clouds of war" in the late 1930s prevented my going to Europe at that time, but the experience at the Community was important.

The idea of the Community was not just to expose city boys and girls to life in a rural setting, but to have them experience at first hand how life is supported and maintained in such a setting. If we wanted electricity, we built a waterwheel and generated our own power. When it failed, we fixed it. All our food was raised on our own farm by the students. Milk meant looking after a dairy herd. Beef meant raising the herd, slaughtering, and preparing. Vegetables and fruit came from the gardens that we planted and cultivated and the orchards that we tended, or from the canning and preserves that we had done ourselves. In this setting, the professors of geology, biology, and botany, got in their systematic instruction. When the electricity failed, we found the instruction in physics highly pertinent.

At the same time, if we wanted social life and entertainment, we had to create them for ourselves or go out and find them in the neighborhood. Creating them for ourselves was no great problem, except to get them organized, keep them going, and take care of the spats and sulks that developed along the way. (The psychology people figured prominently in helping us deal with these matters.) Going out and finding them in the neighborhood was another matter. We were miles from the nearest towns, with no transportation except the Community truck. The immediate neighbors were mountain people, at first almost inaccessible to us for lack of roads. Then we discovered their square dances and revivals, their arts and crafts (which they did not even think of as such), and their way of life, which we took in avidly because of their knowing how to cope with the difficulties that were baffling us in trying to "live from scratch" in the Community. (The sociology people did some skillful instruction in this connection.) Eventually we found that we could make contact with the towns and cultural centers at some distance from us, but we found that we were more selective and discriminating about what we wanted from them than we would have been before getting to know our immediate neighbors. We did get dressed up and ride the back of the truck to church; we did join with the chorus and orchestra at Lake Junaluska in a performance of the "Elijah"; and we did take our singers and chamber orchestra to give a Sunday afternoon concert in the Central Methodist Church of Asheville.

Paul Limbert did more than anyone else to expand my experience while at New College. In addition to everything else, he was particularly influential in stirring both personal and scholarly interests in philosophy and religious experience. His course in the history of philosophy provided the base for later explorations and developments of more specific interests. His work with us in the psychology of religion introduced me not only to the theory and research of Starbuck, Coe, James, and their followers, but to the traditions of mysticism and prayer as well. A keen interest in what James Bissett Pratt called "mild mysticism" was generated in the process.

He also proved to be a wise and well-informed guide to the theological currents that were beginning to flow at that time. He set me to reading Henry Nelson Wieman, whose thought showed me what the dynamics of the general processes of religious experience and growth were. He also set me to reading Karl Barth and his American followers. That gave me a whole new idea of the richness and importance of the Christian tradition, classic Protestantism, the Bible, and the relationship of the church, faith, and culture. He helped me to become personally acquainted with Reinhold Niebuhr, then a vigorous and ubiquitous campus figure on Morningside Heights.

All this could not help but set a direction for my theology. I had grown up in a liberal atmosphere, shot through with the imperatives of the social gospel. Now my theological thinking began to become more conservative and biblical without losing its educational focus or its concern for social responsibility.

My professional interest in curriculum stems from another New College teacher who contributed to the expansion of my experience—Florence Stratemeyer. She was just then laying the groundwork herself for what was to become the curriculum theory and analysis to be found in *Developing a Curriculum for Modern Living* (1947). She helped us to see the crucial importance of education's being conducted according to a systematic plan, and showed how the curriculum might be designed so as to achieve selective comprehensiveness, balance, and integration, organized according to a principle that did no violence to either the logical or psychological nature of the educational process.

While insisting on the systematic expansion of our experience in formal and informal ways, New College also stressed the integration of that experience. There were "central seminars" that dealt with philosophical and educational issues, designed to help us draw together what we were learning and experiencing. Every member of the faculty engaged with us in these seminars at one time or another.

A personalized advisory system kept us individually in touch with the faculty members who could be of most help to us in putting things together. No grades were given in the courses, but we were given probingly critical written analyses evaluating our work in each course. (Graduate admissions offices subsequently found these difficult to assess, but I think they were finally translated into conventional grades for their benefit.)

The culminating experiences designed for integration were a year-long internship and a thesis. We parted company before the thesis, but the internship did take place (prematurely, they thought) and, in my judgment, served its purpose admirably. I had spent the summer of 1936 at Asheville Farm School, a boarding high school for mountain boys run by the Presbyterian Board of National Missions, working at various tasks ranging from manual labor to cultural enrichment for the boys, and including considerable responsibility for Christian education. My advisers and supervisors were H. S. Randolph, the superintendent of the school, and A. L. Roberts, the teacher of religion and Bible. This summer had been factored in as part of New College's emphasis on the expansion of experience. (Asheville Farm School has since evolved into Warren Wilson College, a four-year liberal arts school that still maintains its character as intercultural, interracial, international, and combining work and study.) I returned for the full year of internship under A. L. Roberts' supervision in the school year of 1937–38. My appointment from the Board of National Missions was the Presbyterian Church's first appointment of an intern. The internship plan, as it developed, was based on the New College pattern.

As I have indicated, the internship, from my point of view, served its purpose admirably. It pulled together what I had learned, experienced, and was becoming. It gave me a realistic picture of my abilities and limitations, at least for the time being. More than that, it clarified the two major elements in my professional direction—mission and education.

First Professional Education Period

The internship was the watershed between the formative years and the "missionary and first professional education period." The sense of professional direction that it gave was grounded rather firmly by now in rich educational experience and in theology that gave meaning to personal faith, the church, and mission as a combination of education, evangelism, and social action.

During my internship year, however, Paul Limbert was absent on sabbatical, and the New College authorities and I reached an impasse on the direction that my future work with them was to take. In the meantime I had become increasingly impressed with Samuel L. Hamilton and the work that he was doing in the Department of Religious Education in New York University's School of Education. I made arrangements, then, to transfer to the New York University to finish my bachelor's work under his leadership. So in the early summer of 1938 I transfered from the Heights to the Village.

The association with New York University was to last a long time, from 1938 until 1954. My academic degrees—B.S., M.A., and Ph.D.—are all from there. When I joined the faculty, it was as a lecturer, and I proceeded through the ranks to full professor and chairman of the Department of Religious Education. The experience was one of maturing as a student, as a person doing research, as a teacher, and as an administrator.

Most of the years there as a student were a combination of working and studying at the same time. After the B.S. was conferred in 1939, I went as a summer worker under the Presbyterian Board of National Missions to Alpine, Tennessee, where the church maintained a program that combined a high school (day and boarding), a full church program (including a number of outstations), a community program that extended beyond Alpine to the whole presbytery of Cumberland Mountain, and a model program in agriculture and sylvaculture. Instead of returning to New York after the summer's work, I stayed on (for two years) as a teacher in the high school, Alpine Institute, and as a community worker. My teaching responsibilities were in Bible, music, and modern history. The tasks as community worker were to conduct Sunday schools at several of the outstations, vacation schools throughout the county in the summer, give leadership to the presbytery youth conferences, organize and conduct what would now be called continuing education events for the clergy and laity of the presbytery, and to itinerate throughout the presbytery with workshops in Christian education and music. My colleagues were a resourceful, creative, congenial, and hard-working lot, with whom it was pleasant and stimulating to work. It was a very satisfactory period of "settling in" as a Christian educator in a mission setting.

During the summer of 1940 I began my graduate work at New York University, and the fruitful interplay of work and study began to become evident. I had the year's experience at Alpine to work through in the context of summer courses that I was taking, and the process, I discovered, was one of gaining real insight and achieving real integration.

My enthusiasm for and belief in this educational dialectic of work and study grew tremendously, and I began to make my future plans to take full advantage of that dialectic.

In 1941 I was invited to become director of the Youth Division of the Greater New York Federation of Churches. The federation was a coalition of the Protestant churches in Manhattan, The Bronx, and Staten Island, working actively in church planning, evangelism, Christian education (children's work, youth work, and family life, including other units for servicing leadership education, vacations schools, and the kind of weekday religious education that was called "released time"), social welfare, and social action. I was the novice on the staff, but I approached it, on the basis of my previous work, with some confidence and thought of it as a transfer of my commitment to Christian education and mission from an extremely rural setting to an extremely urban one.

One expectation that seemed to have a complete priority in that job was that I organize and direct a city-wide, weekend youth conference, whose chief criterion was that it was to be attended by 1,000 young people. I took it as a challenge and did it, managing to put together in that context a rich variety of educational experiences around the theme, "The Challenge of International Christianity." One of the things that I enjoyed most about it was that we housed the conference in the churches of the neighborhood around Stuyvesant Square, with the big meetings in St. George's, and smaller group meetings in the Friends Meeting House, Labor Temple, and a number of the ethnic churches in the area. It meant some traipsing around for everyone, but it was a real experience, in miniature, of "international Christianity." We concluded with Sunday rallies in each of the boroughs of the city (the one in Manhattan was at the Salvation Army Temple), to which we beamed a radio broadcast whose main speaker was Edward Hambro, then in exile from Norway and teaching at Princeton University. As the first large organizational job that I had ever tackled, it gave me many hours of real anxiety, but in the end it left me feeling confident that I could handle this sort of thing, even though it was something I would not choose to make a life work! At least, the turn-out was satisfactory, and the federation executives were happy! (Years later, when Charles West joined the Princeton Seminary faculty in Christian ethics, we enjoyed reminiscing about his having been one of the group leaders for the conference.)

Being in New York allowed me to continue and finish the degree of Master of Arts in 1942, and I immediately applied for admission to the

Ph.D. program and was accepted into it. It was in 1942, also, that I was invited to become a member of the headquarters staff of the Presbyterian Board of National Missions, in the Unit of Rural Church and Indian Work. All this enhanced the value of the work–study combination, which was proving to be increasingly productive.

The association with the Unit of Rural Church and Indian Work was to continue until I was invited to teach at New York University in 1947. Those five years carried a number of enriching duties. For one thing, I traveled the whole continental United States in carrying on the administrative and supervisory work given to me by the Unit. I learned how to deal with personnel problems and to manage a large (large at least for those times) budget. Working so intimately with both the Appalachian and the American Indian cultures led me to convictions about cultural specificity in religious education whose implications I have explored now for almost four decades. The specific responsibilities were administration of the board's work among the American Indians (work with over thirty tribes in twenty-three states), assistance in the administration of the work in Appalachia organizing and providing executive leadership for the Presbyterian Rural Fellowship, looking after what the board used to call "contact work" with a number of synods (a matter of helping the national missions people in various sections of the country—in my case, places like Kentucky, Utah, and Idaho—with budgeting, programs, and personnel for the local mission projects), and carrying on the kind of rural church surveys that were basic to planning and strategy in the areas for which we were responsible (I had been trained for this kind of demographic survey work by Edmund deS. Brunner at Teachers College, and in the area of community organization at New York University).

At that time, H. S. Randolph, who had been my superintendent at the Asheville Farm School, had succeeded Warren H. Wilson as secretary of the Unit of Rural Church Work (to which the Indian work had been added). One of the great lures of the position was to be able to work with him again, and from him I gained great insight into this kind of leadership and the administrative processes involved. Dr. Randolph would hand over an area of responsibility—really hand it over. His delegation of responsibility carried with it complete confidence in you and your ability to carry it. The sense of his directives was: "Take this job and do it. Use your best judgment, and make the decisions that have to be made. When you make a decision about something that is particularly sensitive or important, tell me what you have done, so that I will be able to defend it when the people who hold me accountable ask about it." Directives like that constitute an administrative approach that I believe in and have tried to practice ever since.

Another lure in the position was the promise of close association again with A. L. Roberts, who had been the supervisor of my internship at Asheville Farm School. As a matter of fact, the position I was invited to take was one that he had just vacated when promoted to a higher responsibility with the board. Al Roberts, in his Farm School days, had determined that the personnel policies and practices of the board needed drastic overhaul, and it was not many years before he became the board's personnel secretary and was able to put his ideas into practice. The result was a unified program of selection, training, orientation, placement, in-service training, promotion, transfer, and reimbursement of the field personel. I watched all this develop, knew what his aims and methods were, and as a result got a liberal education in the field of personnel management.

I have highlighted the matter of alternation of work and study between my work at New York University and my work at Alpine, with the Greater New York Federation, and with the Board of National Missions. There were other important aspects of the academic work accomplished during those ten years.

New York University taught me how to organize the academic field of religious education. First, the curriculum juxtaposed studies in religion with studies in religious education. Thus, the "sciences of religion" became basic to the theory and practice of religious education. Courses covering the psychology of religion, comparative religion, religion in world culture, and biblical studies were considered to be not only appropriate but necessary in the university curriculum. They in turn, fed into the studies of religious education theory and religious education practice.

Second, the curriculum rested solidly on a base of liberal, cultural, and scientific studies (what we would now call "liberal education"), and on the "sciences of education," specifically, educational psychology (including developmental studies), educational sociology, history of education, and philosophy of education (which, in turn, juxtaposed with itself the history of philosophy). The basic studies and the sciences of education also fed directly into the studies of religious education theory and religious education practice.

Third, the religious education curriculum itself focused in studies in depth of religious education theory, working out to specific studies in method (a variety of courses), curriculum, and administration (courses in organization and management, evaluation, and supervision). There was a special emphasis on counseling. An integral program of student teaching was devised for each person, and carefully supervised on the field and by university personnel.

Fourth, a constant motif was theological discussion. This was the time when the "new theology" (neo-orthodoxy, Barthianism, the dialectic theology—it had many labels) was being discussed on every hand. It is hard to recreate the atmosphere of excitement and ferment of those days when Barth, Brunner, and Tillich were first becoming known. The chief exponent of the new theology in our field was E. G. Homrighausen, who was one of the earliest translators of Barth, whose *Christianity in America*, published in the mid-1930s, was a theological hair-raiser in its repudiation of religion as a contradiction of the Christian faith, and who succeeded Hal Donnelly in the Christian education chair here at Princeton. (Incidentally, I have known and worked with all my predecessors in Christian education here—Donnelly, Homrighausen, and, before Donnelly, James Armentrout, who lectured in Christian education here on a part-time basis before the chair here was established.)

Perhaps the most remarkable thing about studies in religious education at New York University was this rich context in which the studies were conducted. As a result of the training there, it would be hard for me to think of any sharp dichotomy between liberal and professional studies. It would be equally hard to separate religious education from studies in education, the sciences of religion and theology. It would be unthinkable to separate foundations, theory, and practice.

One of Professor Hamilton's remarkable educational habits was to teach you to swim by pushing you off the diving board. He saw religious education as a complex of practical enterprises, informed by the relevant disciplines and oriented to theology and education, but also requiring commitments, skills, and habits that could be acquired best by doing what needed to be done and reflecting systematically on the experience thus gained.

One day when I went to see him on some routine matter, he told me that he had a request for a faculty person for a leadership education course to be offered in the Community Leadership School in Mount

Vernon, and that he had decided that I was the one to do it (this was when I had not yet received my bachelor's degree, and was perhaps twenty years old). The minister who headed the school would be in later in the day to see me. When the unsuspecting clergyman arrived, he could not believe that I was the candidate, and asked whether I was really serious in thinking that I could do it. My position was that if Professor Hamilton thought I could, I could! I got the appointment and fulfilled it acceptably by doing the job and learning to do it at the same time. That was exactly what Professor Hamilton had in mind. When I checked in with him and reported that I had discovered a formula for getting it done (plan it—do it—assess it—plan the next step), I found that that was exactly what he had had in mind that I discover.

Professor Hamilton was a remarkable teacher. Insight flashed in the give-and-take in his classes. An incidental reference could send you into a huge reading program that had to be finished before the next session. His leadership in the university, the church, and the community was a model for us of what a religious educator ought to be. We were over-whelmed by his scholarship, and sought to emulate it. At the same time he was a loyal friend, but without an ounce of sentimentality in that friendship. When he was dying in a hospital in Newark, as I was visiting him just before he entered a coma, the last thing he said to me was a criticism of a decision that I had made, and a declaration that that was not what he would have done!

Herman Harrell Horne, who taught philosophy and history of educa-tion, was another superb classroom teacher, but of another sort. I have often thought since that being in his classroom was as close to being with Socrates as possible. Every session sparkled with the challenge of his dialectic. He was a staunch German idealist, but I used to say that he never made a disciple. That was not quite true, for the fact is that J. Donald Butler, later a colleague at Princeton, faithfully developed Horne's position and method in his *Four Philosophies and Their Practice in Education and Religion* (first published in 1951). When I read Butler's book, I was transported back into Horne's classroom! Louise Antz followed Dr. Horne, and became a good personal friend as well as a faithful and inspiring academic adviser and teacher.

Representing another important strand in the New York University tapestry was Hughes Mearns, whose work in creative education has not been surpassed. He had developed his approach in his work with the young people in the Lincoln School (Teacher College's experimental and innovative elementary and high school), and brought that approach and all the detailed experience of it to his teaching at the university. In his classes we were absorbed into the beauty of the arts, and became convinced that not only could we appreciate the creative work of others, but could be creative ourselves and communicate that creativity to our students. Mearns was another person who got us out into the excitement of the cultural riches of New York City.

My master's thesis was on John Dewey, under the sponsorship of Professors Hamilton and Horne. The work on Dewey was a confirmation of what I had discovered in Wieman about the generic processes of religion in human life. It clarified the key roles of values and commitment for me, and helped me to relate them, on the one hand, to my Christian values and commitments, and, on the other hand, to educational dynamics. I could not accept Dewey's strictures against what we called "the supernatural" in those days, nor could I make Wieman's substitution of the "superhuman" for the "supernatural," but I could appreciate and accept gratefully the clarification of the processes involved in the human side of Christian education. I came to realize that my arrival at rather conservative religious views could only be explained as the result of the use of "liberal" educational growth processes. Later on, Ward Madden had the last word on the Dewey-inspired approach to religious education in his *Religious Values in Education* (1951). Madden was a doctoral student and instructor in philosophy of education who worked with George Axtelle and Theodore Brameld when I was first teaching at New York University. Since the philosophers of education, historians of education, and religious educators all had their desks in the same room, there were frequent discussions of his project. In the book he acknowledges the painstaking critique Professor Hamilton did of the entire manuscript.

My Ph.D. dissertation centered on Jonathan Edwards. I had wanted to do a critical history of the saga of the Stockbridge Indians (and still have two large notebooks of raw material for that project), but was dissuaded from this by wise faculty heads. There was one piece of that saga, however, that provided my focus—the period when Jonathan Edwards, having been voted out of his church in Northhampton, undertook to preach to and teach the Indians who had been gathered in the model village of Stockbridge. This expanded in another direction, and became a theological and educational investigation of Edwards's theories of knowledge and responsibility, in which I found clues to the solution of Christian education's most pressing theoretical problems. The study began with a critical analysis of the conflicts in theology, philosophy, and education found in the work of George Albert Coe, William Clayton Bower, Harrison S. Elliot, H. Shelton Smith, and E. G. Homrighausen. These conflicts, found to be centered on the issues of knowledge and responsibility, were finally examined in light of Edwards's positions, which took the conflicts to a deeper level of analysis at which it became possible to resolve them. One of the things that sustained me through the arduous work (supervised by Professors Hamilton, Antz, and John Payne) was the way in which the research brought together my interests in theology, education, and mission.

An important aspect of the missionary experience of these years was the ecumenical aspect of the work. In rural work, the Protestant and Catholic people vested with responsibility for fostering rural church work and rural life had for decades been working and planning together, even keeping in close touch with persons in government service who could help. Working in that area, I was immediately thrown into an atmosphere of cooperative thought and action. The city work was definitively ecumenical, and not only that, but intercultural, interracial, and international. In that context I was a representative for ecumenical interests as well as a participant. Indian work was much like rural work in its ecumenical orientation, except that there was much more direct personal contact with the nonprofessionals, mostly Indians themselves, in the interfaith meetings and groups. In the Indian work there was an additional side in which we worked rather constantly with the various groups seeking to serve Indian interests, agencies both public and private. The person in whom much of this centered was Mark A. Dawber, who with Edith Lowry headed the Home Missions Council. Dr. Dawber seemed to me to be the kind of scholar, leader, and colleague upon whom I would like to have modeled myself in that aspect of my life.

Supplementing and supporting this ecumenical experience was the very character of the situation at New York University. The student body in religious education included Protestant, Catholic, and Jewish students. The theological spectrum among Protestants ran from Unitarian to Seventh Day Adventist. Classes were always interracial and international. This broadening element in my experience was becoming permanent and normative.

The various developing characteristics of my professional life seemed to converge at the point where I was asked to present a position paper to a gathering of the Division of Christian Education of the National Council of Churches. The subject was "Education and Mission," which gave me the opportunity in an ecumenical setting to say what had become deep convictions—that Christian education is rooted in action in mission, and comes to mature fruit through critical reflection on that action.

In 1947 Professor Hamilton invited me to join the faculty of the Department of Religious Education, contingent on my finishing the dissertation. (Having since guided doctoral work for decades, I think I now see part of his strategy!) It would be a wrench to leave the people and fields of work I had come so to value in my work in national missions. Yet teaching in religious education at New York University would scarcely be a matter of leaving the areas in which mission and education, theory and practice, and action and reflection meet. The offer was a real challenge, and I accepted it.

Second Professional Education Period

Teaching at New York University in the fall of 1947 I entered what I have labeled my "second professional educational period." The heavy teaching schedule (six two-hour courses each semester) ranged over both sides of the curriculum, and it required some ingenuity to keep ahead of students. Most of the students were mature working people who brought their own wisdom, experience, and demand for excellence to the classroom. The character of the student body required that courses be given in the late afternoons and evenings, and on Saturdays, and the days were spent in office work, advisement, study, and other duties.

Early on, Professor Hamilton assigned me a course in sociology of religion. I remonstrated, never having taken the course, but to no avail. His "plunge in and learn in the process" policy held. He told me to take Joachim Wach's *Sociology of Religion* (1944), and lead the class through it systematically. It was my introduction to a discipline that I have used centrally in my work, and my first contact with phenomenology as an orientation for scientific research and thought. I discovered that Wach's footnotes were an education in themselves, and that sociology of religion could serve as a discipline that pulls things together, both in religion and education. Perhaps it was this orientation through Wach that prepared me much later to appreciate and use the work of Peter Berger.

The practical focus of Professor Hamilton's work was leadership education, an interest that stemmed from the time of his executive leadership of the New Jersey Council of Religious Education (and its School of Methods). The "laboratory school" for volunteer religious educators had proven its worth, combining practical experience in the classroom under supervision with instruction in the principles involved. He wanted, however, something on a high academic level that would really succeed in producing a professional level of class-room competence. A year or two before my faculty appointment he put together a summer-school program that did what he had in mind. It was an eight-week affair, beginning with a crash course in theory (two weeks), followed by a one-week demonstration-observation school in which age-level specialists taught actual classes in the mornings, while students observed. The afternoons were given to critical review of what had taken place, with the students planning for their own teaching responsibilities. For four weeks following the students taught in university and church-sponsored vacation church schools throughout the New York metropolitian area, under the supervision of the age-level specialists, who visited each school once a week. In the afternoons everyone returned to the university for critical analysis and further planning. During the eighth week there were all-day sessions in which critical review was intensified and the whole experience focused. In later years we located the program in the Riverside Church. I took over its administration when Professor Hamilton retired. I do not believe that this combination and sequence of experiences could be improved on in the professional training of religious educators.

I began to wonder if there might be some interest in the publication of a version of my dissertation, and sent it to Paul Payne, who turned it over to Paul Meachem, editor for religious books at the Westminster Press. Dr. Meachem did me the honor of coming to New York to see me—with bad news and good news. The bad news was that they were not interested in the dissertation. The good news was that they were looking for something on the principles of Christian education, and would be interested in having me submit such a manuscript. The outcome was *The Task of Christian Education*, written at New York University, but published after I had gone to Princeton.

Dr. Meachem's editorial work was just what I needed. He suggested that I submit an outline of the book. That was all right. Then the first chapter. That was all right. Then the first half of the book. At this point there was a pause. He came to see me, and gave me his judgment that it would not do! My style made it difficult to identify my reader. The answer, after I had thought it through, seemed to be to write to a real audience. I took my chapter outlines and delivered them as talks to teachers groups I was asked to address. (I bought one of those new "tape recorders"—a heavy, bulky contraption that I hauled around with me from place to place.) The tapes were transcribed, and from the transcripts I wrote my chapters. Just to be sure, I picked out a lay leader in my own parish, and wrote the book for her (but never told her so). The result was, according to Dr. Meachem, "exceedingly readable" (a judgment that one reviewer emphatically did not share).

In the spring quarter, 1952, I was asked, on the spur of the moment, because of an emergency that had arisen there, to teach a course one day a week at Princeton. In 1952–53 it became two courses, and in 1953–54, three. The first invitation to occupy the chair of Christian education there was for the fall of 1953, but I had to decline because of duties at New York University that could not be completed by that time. The offer was renewed for the fall of 1954, and I was able to accept.

In one way the change was an easy one to make, in that the Christian education program at Princeton had been patterned after that at New York University, Herman Harrell Horne having been one of its advisers. In another way it was a difficult change. I was used to working in an educational orientation in which theology was the essential added ingredient. Now I would be working in a theological orientation in which education was the addition. The Princeton students were much less mature, on the whole (later, Princeton developed a somewhat older and more mature student clientele in Christian education). The breadth of theological viewpoint could not match what I had been used to. A little later, when Paul Lehman left to go to Harvard, we talked about the real differences in teaching in university and seminary settings.

Princeton Years

The years at Princeton continued my "second educational period." In my inaugural address, "Toward an Informed and Valid Practice of

Christian Education," I developed the direction that I wanted my work to take. In the first book I wrote at Princeton, *The Gospel and Christian Education*, that direction became a program that put theory in dialogue with practice, and that set the three aspects of practice as method, curriculum, and administration.

Why theory in particular? Theory seems to me to be the most appropriate way to deal with Christian education in a seminary setting. A theology of Christian education would have to be done in theological categories, and when it is done that way certain rigidities and imbalances are likely to develop. Furthermore, a theology of Christian education, because of its direct doctrinal connection, becomes somewhat untouchable. The same considerations generally apply, in my mind, to a philosophy of Christian education.

A theory, on the other hand, is purely functional. Its categories derive from the issues and problems of practice to which it seeks to address itself. The sources to which it goes in the search for answers to its questions are, in principle, unlimited. It consists of a comprehensive set of hypotheses that are as carefully drawn, as intelligently informed, and as directly applicable to practice as possible. It is not at all sacrosanct and may thus be subjected to rigorous criticism, experimental testing, and judicious revision. At the same time, it may be normatively theological and may address itself to every appropriate educational question.

Because the questions that Christian education has to answer boil down to method (fundamental educational relationships), curriculum (the educational plan), and administration (effective ways of implementing the plan), these three may be considered theoretical categories. While they are especially handy, there is an even more defensible (though perhaps not so immediately useful) set of categories in the sixfold breakdown that I have developed and used during my Princeton days: the objective of Christian education (its basic purpose, *why*), its scope (*what* is to be taught and learned), its context (*where* Christian teaching and learning take place), its process (*how*), the participants (the parties to the Christian education transaction, *who*), and its timing (the exceedingly complex question of *when* Christian education takes place).

The two sets of categories intertwine. Method corresponds, of course, to process. Curriculum involves all six (which is one of the reasons that I find curriculum to be the most challenging and interesting aspect of Christian education). Administration takes its cue from the category of context, yet uses all six criterial as well as functional ways.

Paul Payne took occasion in his review of *The Task of Christian Education* to chastise me for my chapter, "Methods Are Tools." What I was trying to say was that they were not ends in themselves, but had to be functional to Christian education's objective and curriculum plan. But he was right, and from his criticism I came to realize that fundamental method is always prior to curriculum. The educational relationships sustained between God and his people, and by his people as teachers and learners, have to be known and understood before a Christian education plan that is defensible is formulated. How does God teach? How do people learn? What is the role of the human teacher under God? How do persons at various points in their experience learn effectively, and what roles do God and human teachers play in that process? Later on, Nels Ferré helped to clarify and answer such questions in his chapters on "God as Educator" and "Learning from God," in *Christian Faith and Higher Education* (1954). My attempt to get method in right perspective was *In One Spirit: Senior Highs and Missions* (1958).

Dealing with curriculum concerns has been a major occupation of the last three decades, starting from the early attempts to construct curriculum for rural churches and American Indian groups. The pragmatics led to theoretical questions, and the answering of those questions made dealing with the pragmatics both possible and fruitful.

The real curriculum challenge came when A. L. Roberts (then head of the Department of Educational Development of the National Council of Churches) asked me to help with the committee that was to revise the council's objectives for senior highs. The other consultants at that point were Nels Ferré and Lawrence K. Frank. An exciting and productive research began that led from *The Objective Of Christian Education for Senior High Young People* (1958), through my *Theory and Design of Christian Education Curriculum* (1961), to *The Church's Educational Ministry: A Curriculum Plan* (1965). In my book, the findings of the National Council's Curriculum Study were reported and placed in a theoretical and practical context. Among the concepts that were clarified were: the objective itself as awareness of revelation and the Gospel and response in faith and love; the scope as the whole field of relationships—divine human, natural, and historical—in light of the Gospel; curriculum areas as existential vantage points on the scope of Christian education; the context as the community of faith living its life and doing its work; and the process as active and reflective involvement in the life and work of the community of faith, utilizing the model known as the "learning tasks."

Associations that grew with Don Newby, Rowena Ferguson, Ray Henthorne, Rachel Henderlite, Peter Gordon White, and others were profoundly influential. They were people who knew Christian education thoroughly, both in theory and practice. Their dialogue was "iron sharpening iron." I came to count them as my closest friends.

I was not satisfied even yet that we had the questions right, nor that we really had all the clues that we needed to the answers. Working further, I prepared a paper that I considered to be the first comprehensive outline of the matter, in connection with the consultation held by the World Council of Christian Education in Switzerland in 1964. The paper was published later as "Understanding Your Church Curriculum," in the *Princeton Seminary Bulletin* in 1970. The six categories were outlined and used to present a curriculum theory that I thought to be internationally, interculturally, and even ecumenically valid and useful.

The immediate reaction was anything but encouraging. It was greeted with suspicion, hostility, and neglect. Later I discovered that its poor reception was due to the fact that it seemed to threaten those who represented the old Sunday School interests and the remnants of the British Empire in what we were coming to think of as the Third World. A few took interest in it, leading, for instance, to my being able to work closely with "New Life in Christ," the curriculum for preliterate people in Latin America.

Much later have come similar opportunities to work with Joyce Bailey and her colleagues on "Fashion Me a People," the curriculum project of the Caribbean Conference of Churches, and with Harold Davis and John Spangler (of Joint Educational Development) on the Appalachian Church Education Project. There have also been opportunities to test out the curriculum theory through the writing of courses and units for the United Methodist Publishing House, the Christian Board of Publication, and for my own church.

Questions of administration took practical turns. The administrative work with the Greater New York Federation of Churches and the Presbyterian rural and Indian work was in the background. At New York University I worked at various levels, including that of chairman of the Department of Religious Education, doing year-round program and faculty planning, promotion, and recruitment, the maintaining of financial stability, intraschool relations, and church relations. At Princeton I handled the School of Christian Education in the more than two decades between Dr. Butler's leaving and Freda Gardner's appointment as the school's director, directed the seminary's doctoral studies for seven years, and the summer school for the past eleven years. Having been ordained as a ruling elder (a lay status in the Presbyterian Church) in the late 1940s, I have served in many capacities in the congregation, and at presbytery, synod, and national agency levels.

My resultant understanding of administration is that it carries four functions, which are guided by particular principles: planning (which is purposeful in terms of Christian education's objective), organization (which is rigorously functional), management (which is to be democratic), and supervision (which is to be cooperative). Supervision, in turn, has a threefold function: the determination of criteria, evaluation, and systematic improvement according to the evaluative findings. My chief writing in this area was *How to Evaluate Your Christian Education Program* (1962).

Leadership is an administrative concern, and involves (among other things) the professional Christian educator. Recognizing that many professionals are ordained ministers, there are still thousands of unordained professional Christian educators whose lay ministry requires training, recognition, and support. I suppose that the most effective thing that has been done for the professional is the strengthening of the training programs in seminaries and graduate schools. Even with these strong programs of training, however, it has proven difficult to move effectively toward an organized, recognized, and stable profession. There is promise in the denominational organizations of Christian educators, now attempting advocacy on behalf of the profession, and there is promise in the attempts to write the standards for certification, supervision, and protection into church law. I have worked on this matter in my own denomination, through the National Council of Churches, through the Association of Theological Schools, through Joint Educational Development, and in wider ecumenical circles. Yet it seems like a place where the ratio of productivity to effort is pretty poor.

Undergirding theory is research. I have learned the value and potential of research in religious education through four means. The first was the supervision of doctoral work at New York University and at Princeton. In addition to supervising doctoral candidates in my own field, I served at New York University as the chairman of the "outlines committee," the body that screened dissertation proposals for the School of Education. Second, for more than a decade I chaired the research committee of the National Council of Churches. Third, I have participated in the projects in religious education research sponsored by the

Religious Education Association. Fourth, in attempting to strengthen the doctoral work in Christian education at Princeton we have co-opted members of the staff of the Educational Testing Service, our neighbors in Princeton, in a program in social and educational research, measurement, and evaluation.

A final concern in the "second educational period" has been the development of the discipline of religious and Christian education. This was the focus of attention the year that I served as chairman of the Professors Section of the National Council of Churches (predecessor to the Association of Professors and Researchers in Religious Education). The "learned community" in our field has, however, been small and extremely varied in its background and interests. Dialogue has tended to be desultory and spotty. The important books are few, and my attempt to expand the knowledge of international scholarship in the field has not been very successful. There remains a great deal of ambiguity about the theological-behavioral-educational "location" of the field.

Concluding Remarks

There are no aspects of the field of Christian education, as I have discussed them in this account, in which my interest does not continue. There are three special matters, however, on which I am currently trying to focus special attention.

The first is the aesthetic aspect of Christian education. Many years ago I was convinced by Jonathan Edwards that religion is a matter of the affections. That (perhaps strangely) reinforced for me Dewey's notions about education and commitment. The hurdles are formidable—the dangers of amateurism in an area that requires years of disciplined training combined with talent, the complex dynamics of the aesthetic processes themselves, and the mysteries of their relationships to cognition and will. This is an area that is slow going, that requires patient experiential growth, but that I believe may yield itself to fruitful understandings and rich resources both in individual Christian growth and in the church's educational work.

The second is the cultural dimension. Christian education is culture-specific because learning is culture-specific. Yet is is ecumenical in that the Gospel is universal. Long-range investigations in the curriculum development, and more recently William Foreman's work with the

U.S. Army Chaplain Board, have convinced me of the validity of this cultural specificity in curriculum, on the one hand, and the validity of multiethnic and multicultural religious education as a response to pluralism, on the other. These are, I believe, two separate questions, and I propose to try to deal with them as such.

The third is the importance of attention to the local in Christian education. Christian education is not going to work unless it happens at the congregational and local community level. Yet there is little guidance for local planning and conduct of the enterprise that is practically useful and theoretically sound at the same time. I think we are in a position to provide this help. Workshop courses that I have taught at the Presbyterian School of Christian Education in Richmond and at the New Brunswick Theological Seminary have shown me that it is feasible to provide necessary guidance. But it remains to be worked out in detail.

Chapter 5

A Journey into Self-Understanding

John H. Westerhoff III

Confessions

My decision to write this biographical essay turned into an unexpected ordeal. After the feeling of pride at being asked had subsided and I began to contemplate my impulsive positive response, I had to confront the realization that someone believed that I have made a contribution to the theory and practice of religious education worthy of my inclusion. My anxiety increased when I faced the fact that my identity is not as a scholar or practitioner in the discipline or field of religious education, but as a parish priest engaged in the formation of clergy with a deep and abiding concern for the catechetical dimensions of practical theology. More startling was the awareness that my life as a priest and practical theologian is at most half completed—God willing.

The task of writing this essay, therefore, was more difficult and more time consuming than any I have ever accepted. I was asked to write the story behind my professional journey as it relates to the development of my present theory and practice. Even contemplating that task is painful, for I suffer from a general dissatisfaction with my life and work to date. I simply do not believe that I have been an adequate priest, husband, parent, teacher, scholar, author, or lecturer; I do not believe that I have yet developed a theory or practice worth reflecting upon. I never keep copies of my lectures or writings. As a matter of fact I have been unable to locate a complete record of my publications. My basic orientation is to the future. I lecture and write because I must; I am driven to create and always dissatisfied with the creation. Just as painters move from internal conflict, to sketches, to paintings, and back into conflict, so I move from one lecture, essay, or book to another. Each is a creative attempt to resolve an internal struggle; none are intended to resolve it for more than a moment. I do not value past efforts, only the continuing need to try again. Perhaps that explains why it is so difficult for me to look back and face the confusions and errors of my voluminous attempts to make some sense of an experience, to share a moment of partial illumination or to attempt a reconstruction of reality.

Once, therefore, I agreed to write this essay I entered a period of depression. I was frightened at the thought of either facing my creations or revealing the interior side of my life and work. While all my work is in reality autobiography, I resist reflecting aloud in public on the life experiences out of which it has emerged. It is not easy for me to be honest, let alone objective, about my personal life. There is much I choose to forget, and some I have suspicion I unknowingly distort. The accomplishments to which others point do not mean much to me; indeed it troubles me to think I may have significantly influenced someone. My life at best has been a collection of surprises and graces. The opportunities in my life have sought me, my limited accomplishments I owe to others, and the attention I have received is neither deserved nor desired.

A friend wrote the Duke faculty before I was awarded tenure, "While it is doubtful that in the future anything John Westerhoff has written will ever be remembered or quoted, I am confident that the history of this period will not be written without some mentioning of him." If anything, that honest and gracious comment is too grand. I am not, nor will I ever be a scholar. In fact, I never expect to make a scholarly contribution to the discipline of religious education. I am not, nor will I ever be a practitioner or administrator of note; I never expect to make a significant organizational or institutional contribution to the field of religious education. My intention is not to be humble, only honest, when I confess that I do not believe that I will ever make an impact on either the world of religious education theory or practice; at best I may influence, stimulate, or encourage others to do so, and if I do that I will be satisfied and indeed proud.

Perhaps that explains why some of my most cherished compliments have come from students who later make a contribution to religious education. One once said, "All you ever did was put into words what I have always known but could not adequately express." Another commented, "I believe you are wrong in almost all your theoretical constructs, but you have continually stimulated me to be creative, to think for myself, and to risk my own convictions." And yet another wrote, "I have found little you taught practically useful, but I want to thank you for helping me to believe in and feel good about myself and my life as a religious educator."

With this necessary confession in mind I labored to write this essay because I became convinced that doing so might help you to understand my work, but perhaps more important, to free you from my errors. I pray the risk will be justified and that in the future my continuing feeble efforts to communicate ever-changing thoughts and feelings will stimulate you, to discern enlightenment for yourself. However, before I can continue I need to make one last confession. The editor of this present volume asked us contributors to write, "not our life story as a person, but our life story as it represents the development and working out of our theoretical stance on religious education." I wish I could easily separate the two; my life and my work are synonymous. I do not have a theory developed over time to which I can attach influences, events, persons, ideas, books, and the like. All I can do is reveal those biographical moments which I believe provide a basis for better understanding my work; I trust that is enough.

An Inherited Temperament

Before I can turn to the environments and experiences that I believe have affected my work, I need to attempt a description of the "me" who has over the past forty-eight years interacted with them. After two years of Jungian analysis I have gained some helpful insights into my inherited temperament. Permit me to share them.

I am fundamentally introvertive. I prefer private space, solitude, and silence to social contact. Most often I experience loneliness when surrounded by people and become exhausted rapidly at social gatherings. While I enjoy people and appreciate opportunities to emotionally interact with one or two at a time, it drains my energy.

While my inner life is unusually rich, I am reserved and tend not to share except with those I trust. Because of my vulnerability, I can be hurt rather easily. I tend to be very private. I care deeply for people, am sensitive to others' needs and have a strong need to communicate in a personal way. Still, I am painfully shy and need encouragement to socialize. Pursuing solitary activities, working quietly alone, reading, meditating, participating in activities which involve only a few people are necessary for survival.

Of course, I compensate by assuming the role of a public person who, when on a stage, appears outgoing, sociable, and gregarious; more important, I reveal myself fully and interact deeply when with a single individual. Still, if I do not have private space I am emotionally, physically, and intellectually devastated.

Further, I am an intuitive-feeling person as contrasted with a sensate-thinking one. More innovative than practical, I am a dreamer, most at home in the world of mystery and imagination. I enjoy solving problems, but I'm uncomfortable in dealing with details or following through on a new idea. The future is of more interest to me than either the past or the present. Indeed, the present is of little interest. The life of fantasy is appealing and the world of visions and dreams quite real. Typically I am happiest when speculating about possibilities; I experience dissatisfaction and restlessness when life is not changing. Most content when skipping from one activity to another, I am like a farmer who plants a field and then goes off before the crop begins to break ground. Instead of staying around to see my vision come to fruition, I am off looking for new fields to plow.

My greatest joy is making up stories and dramatically recounting them with vivid emotional imagery. Sometimes I have been accused of lying when in fact I was only exercising my imagination to improve on reality. I am more at home with nonverbal tacit ways of knowing and subjective relational experiences than with explicit ways of knowing and objective reflection. I am more comfortable with ambiguity, chaos, imagination, mystery, and surprise than with certainty, order, analysis, logic, and control. The world of artistic endeavors and of symbols, myth, and ritual, are more life-giving to me than the world of scientific endeavors and of signs, concepts, and reflective actions.

While my verbal skills are well developed, I am happier with fiction and poetry than with nonfiction and prose. I write well, but I am a poor editor. I typically gloss over details and seek only a general impression of what I read. I am most interested in framing a gestalt and an impressionistic grasp of reality. Precision confuses me; cause and effect relationships trouble me.

I have been blessed, or perhaps better cursed, with charisma, a haunting empathy for people's feelings, creative artistic talents, and an idealistic nature. A pacifist by temperament, competition does not appeal to me and I am hypersensitive to hostility and conflict. Painfully shy, I am easily devastated by criticism. I fear rejection and need a great deal of positive affirmation.

Abstractions disinterest me. When asked what books or ideas have influenced me I am at a loss to say. But people and relationships are different. My greatest difficulty, however, is naming those persons who have influenced me, for every person with whom I have ever spent a private hour has deeply affected my life and thought. I am uncomfortable with impersonal, objective, rational judgments. While surely not an antiintellectual, I am more comfortable with personal, subjective, intuitive judgments.

My personality is best understood as a self in search of itself. My life has been a quest to be who I inwardly and actually am. "How can I become the person I really am?" has been my perennial question. I hunger for self-actualization. A life of significance or making a difference in the world is not enough for me, I am continually seeking to become a perfect whole while having an identity which is perfectly unique.

Surely it is a complex personality; even I find it extremely difficult to know me. I experience all of life as a great drama, each encounter and relationship pregnant with significance. My struggle is for meaning and fulfillment. Flitting from one experience or person to another, I am always trying to touch the life of another, significantly and deeply, to improve the conditions under which people live, to creatively communicate visions and to stimulate people to think, feel, and act in new ways.

Often I have wished that I was different. Being of my temperament has caused me and others whom I love great pain. I am extremely difficult to live with. My somewhat rare introvertive, intuitive-feeling nature, my Appollonian temperament, my mystical inner life, my artistic character, my charismatic gifts, and my complex personality have through the years confused and troubled me. There have been days that I set out to change. Not long ago I contemplated developing a theory and writing a scholarly book. I know I will not. Once I considered turning my energy toward making an institutional contribution of some lasting significance. But in my heart I know I could never be a dean, bishop, or rector of a large parish. While I cannot be sure where God will lead me, I do have some insight into the temperament through which I am called to live. I therefore suspect that I will continue to be a generalist, a priest-practical theologian flitting from interest to interest, problem to problem, concern to concern using my creative imagination and charisma to inspire and stimulate others to make the theoretical and practical contributions I might wish I could make and then find my satisfaction and joy in saying that those who do are my friends.

This is the personality traits with which I was born. I am beginning to see how they have influenced my life through these forty-nine years. I am learning to accept them and perhaps to understand them. I only pray that this incomplete and surface description of my inner self will help you to understand how my life and work have been affected by the life experiences and human relationships I hold dear.

The Mystery of Beginnings

Where to begin? Perhaps a few comments as to roots will help. My father's parents emigrated from the Netherlands to a Dutch ethnic community in New Jersey. My grandfather, a prison guard, my grandmother, a homemaker, maintained their Dutch heritage, but while both had been born into the Dutch Reformed tradition they maintained only a surface relationship with the church. As a result, my father had little or no religious nurture. My mother's father, a seaman, was a committed, practicing Roman Catholic but he drowned off the coast of Argentina just before her birth. Her mother, a Protestant by birth, and an agnostic by conviction, brought her up to respect religion in general but without a particular religious tradition.

I was born at the Jewish hospital in which my mother had trained as a nurse. My parents, without a religious tradition of their own, brought me to be privately baptized in the church at which they had been married—the First Presbyterian Church of Patterson, New Jersey. The day was October 28, 1933, the festival day of St. Simon and St. Jude. I count that day among the most significant in my life. That event was kept alive in my unconscious mind through many years and on occasion, mostly in dreams and once in a vision, surfaced to haunt me. While I suspect that my baptism was at best an act of magic by both my parents and the church, I experienced my baptism as the day God chose me for ministry, gave me a new identity and vocation as a redeemed person, adopted me into my true family—the church, called me by my new name "John Henry Christian," and branded me for life with the sign of the cross so that I might someday know who I really am and to whom I really belong.

On October 28, 1933 I was made a Christian, St. Jude became my patron saint, and from that day to this the church in a strange and mysterious way has been my mystical family. It hurts me when outsiders are critical of the church or when the church doesn't live up to its calling. I have my own love–hate relationship with the institutional church; I have my own critical judgments to make, but they seem different for I'm family. All this may appear strange, but my life and work can only be understood in the light of my mystical baptismal experience.

When I was three my mother, out of duty, I suspect, began to accompany me to Sunday School at the church of my baptism. The large group of children frightened me. I cried a lot and longed for solitude. I always felt more at home when, on Christmas and Easter, my parents and I would attend the liturgy which, while terribly lacking from both a liturgical and child's point of view, still provided me with silence and holy space for contemplation. It was not that I understood or participated in the liturgy, but the environment provided me with a context for a number of profound religious experiences which I am only now able to name, explain, or understand. Nevertheless, since my parents' convictions were weak and the church was some distance from where we lived, we soon stopped attending altogether. During those years I recall an inner drive to worship and the inability to explain that need to my parents.

Then one day, I believe I was seven or eight, a neighbor offered to take me to her church. My mother agreed and I eagerly went off to attend a revival meeting within a small sect community. I cannot recall its name, but I always remember at the close of the sermon having a vision of Jesus, who looked like a woman, beckoning me with open arms. I ran up the aisle crying and fell to the floor. I felt her arms holding me and saying, "I have found you . . . I have found you." I don't remember much more except that the minister began to take a sincere interest in me, and I joined my neighbor regularly for worship.

One day the minister came to visit my mother. He told her that I was a "holy man," that God had called me to be a minister of the Gospel and that she should encourage me to hold revival meetings in our garage for the children in the neighborhood. My mother was so upset by this visit that she refused to let me attend that church ever again. Shortly later we moved.

By the time I was twelve I was ready to make my own decisions on how I would spend Sunday morning. One day I wandered into a Dutch Reformed Church in Glen Rock, New Jersey. Soon I was befriended by the pastor, Dr. Vernon Oggell. He too told me that I was destined to be a minister. He encouraged me to assist him in the Sunday services and he gave me my own Sunday School class to teach. They used David C. Cook curriculum and I loved filling in the blanks with the right answers from the Bible. I had a passion to convert everyone to *the* truth. My parents were troubled, but people at church kept telling me I brought God to them.

In college my fraternity nicknamed me "Preach," a strange title, since by now I had entered a period of intellectual relativism and had a new passion to illumine others as much as I had once had a passion to convert them. Few, including the religion faculty and chaplain, could understand me, for while I said I was a Christian and loved the church, I never attended services and spent hours arguing against Christian doctrine and biblical fundamentalism.

My present understanding of the spiritual journey and the development of faith is simply my continuing attempt to make sense of these early experiences. My convictions concerning the necessity of a faith community and the essential nature of the liturgy for religious nurture is founded on my recollection of early needs partially met. Indeed my awareness of the evangelizing nature of the Sunday School and my positive attitude toward conservative evangelical faith can be traced to my own history.

On The Boundary

My next stop was the Harvard Divinity School. Here my education and my life really begins, or at least that is how I like to remember it. While there were moments of tremendous religious significance in my early years, until I entered Harvard my life, with the exception of meeting my wife while in college, was fundamentally unhappy. Without her support and encouragement, without her belief in me and her willingness to stick with me I might not have made it. For years I tried to repress my childhood and the negative feelings I had toward my family. For years I wouldn't admit where I had attended college for while on the surface they were good years they were years dominated by spiritual lostness and a painful struggle for self-identity.

My admission to Harvard was somewhat of a fluke. I had no church or religious community yet I felt called to the ministry. My B− average didn't qualify me for graduate school, but Harvard had just begun an attempted comeback and was eagerly looking for students. It was providence that brought me to Harvard; no other explanation is satisfactory.

My Harvard experience has two parts: The first comprises faculty relationships; the other a relationship with the Rev. Dr. Herbert R. Smith, pastor of the First Congregational Church (United Church of Christ) of Needham, Massachusetts.

I entered Harvard at the height of my intellectual search for truth. I was questioning whether or not it was possible to speak meaningfully of God. I went with a secular scientific world view. I accepted the assumption that the natural world functioned according to its own inherent logic and that social and personal life results from comprehensible, predictable cause and effect relationships. Having been introduced to religious pluralism and the truth claims of Jews, Muslims, Hindus, and Buddhists, I tended toward philosphical relativism and doctrinal skepticism. Still, I nursed a longing for the sacred and haunting memory of days when the holy was alive within me.

It was my relationships with five faculty members that transformed my life; they were: Father Georges Florovsky, whose life embodied the Russian Orthodox tradition; Krister Stendahl, whose Lutheran sacramental tradition captured my imagination; James Luther Adams, who lived an incarnational moral life that integrated the intuitive and the intellectual; Amos Wilder, whose life as a poet touched my spirit as much as his New Testament wisdom; and Paul Tillich, whose dialectical thought and eclectic concerns helped me make sense of reality. There are a host of experiences and relationships with these men I would like to share, but one I must. One night a small group of us were recounting the struggles of our souls in the presence of Paul Tillich. Instead of an intellectual response he turned on Bach's B Minor Mass. I will always remember that the only answer this great theologian had for his students' doubt was the church singing its faith, singing credo: "I give my love, my loyalty, my heart to. . . ." Ever since those days I have been convinced that the arts and liturgy, better than the sciences and theology, express and illumine the spiritual dimensions of life. They helped me to understand that to affirm the intuition was not to deny the intellect; indeed, they taught me to move from experience to imagination to reason to action. They reinforced my own personal conviction, concerning the foundational nature of the intuitive, affective, responsive mode of consciousness and the prior nature of subjective experience to objective reflection.

Further, from them I learned the paradoxical, inclusivistic nature of truth. Heresies are truths run wild; that is, which deny the complex, dichotomous nature of truth. Two seemingly contradicting truths can both be true depending upon what question is asked. Attempts to reconcile paradoxes and dichotomies has never appealed to me. Indeed, whenever I have felt that one aspect of truth was being overemphasized, I have been quick to become the advocate of the neglected. Since then, asking new questions and the continuing quest to reveal the complex nature of truth is at the heart of my quest for understanding.

Each of these men (there were no women in the faculty) also taught me something important about teaching and learning as it relates to the holy. By educational standards they were all inadequate. To the best of my knowledge they never formulated an educational objective, developed a lesson plan, or evaluated what they had done. Nevertheless, they helped me to realize that significant learning is dependent upon three things. First, that there is no learning unless someone is passionately searching. Second, that all anyone else can do is offer their life in all its brokenness and incompleteness as a resource for other learning. And third, that any truth which is discovered breaks in from a source that transcends both the seeker and the sharer.

Needless to say, these insights can be found throughout my work. From the beginning I have focused on relationships rather than educational systems or structures, and I have defended the arts as foundational to the spiritual life and the affect as primary to all necessary but secondary cognitive efforts.

The other side of my days at Harvard involved the church where for three years I engaged in what was then called field work. Within this community of faith I experienced the fundamental insights concerning nurture about which I have written. Here I learned what induction into a community of faith implies. Here I also learned that I was called by both God and a community to ordination. And here I learned what it meant to be a "pastor and teacher."

Most of what I learned about liturgical leadership and preaching, about the care and cure of souls and counseling, and about teaching and religious education, I learned by observing, participating with and reflection upon the ministry of Rev. Dr. Herbert Smith. I had taken a course in the history of worship with Father Florovsky which focused on the Orthodox liturgy and the Roman Mass; I had taken a course on religion and mental health with Hans Hoffman which focused on theology and psychological theory; and I had taken a course on the history of religious education with Robert Ulich, from the school of education, which had focused on the role of religion in the history of education. But everything I learned about the ministries of the church I learned by participating in the life of the First Congregational Church of Needham. Herb Smith understood his role to be "pastor and teacher." He never let an opportunity go by, whether it was in a formal or informal setting, to intentionally engage people in learning. He focused his efforts on adults, for he felt they were the key to the church's educational ministry. Christian worship and nurture were priorities for him. While he always offered a formal course, he did most of his teaching in the contexts of meetings, parish visitation, church gatherings, and preparations for baptisms and weddings. He understood himself as the church's teacher and he taught me by first encouraging me to share in this ministry and then by reflecting with me on our experiences. Ever since I have assumed that the clergy were called to be teachers and that education involved every aspect of parish life.

At the age of twenty-two, on November 1, All Saints Day, I was confirmed, acknowledged publicly my call to the ordained ministry, and was taken under care by the United Church of Christ. In 1958 I was ordained at the First Congregational Church of Needham. In preparing this essay I discovered the paper I delivered at my ordination council.

By then I was at a new point in my journey. No longer the relativist, I defined theology as "moving back and forth between two poles—eternal truth as revealed by God and the temporal situations in which it must be received and interpreted." Faith, I suggested, always belongs to the church before it belongs to any of us individually. This faith, I contended, is caught by participation in the life of living, worshiping, learning, acting faith community rather than by being taught in a classroom.

"As clergy," I wrote, "we are called by God and the community to bring God to people and people to God by conserving the holy tradition of the church and by prophetically criticizing it, both of which we do as pastor and teacher," and I prayed that "my life in the Holy Spirit might unite Word and sacrament to the glory of God."

Upon that theological stance the United Church of Christ ordained me and the Congregational Church of Presque Isle Maine called me as their "pastor and teacher."

Life in the Parish

At the time when I entered the parish the United Church of Christ had published a new church school curriculum. Enthusiasm ran high. At last, I believed we had a resource for quality education in the church. I recall my own excitement in introducing this new resource, securing faithful adults as teachers, and providing teacher education and support. We redesigned and redecorated our educational plant and secured the latest in audio-visual equipment. I was confident that we could develop an exemplary schooling-instructional program.

Then I came face to face with two unexpected realizations. First, I became aware that the informal hidden curriculum of life in the congregation was more significant and influential than our formal educational program. Second, I became aware that on those special occasions when all ages gathered together for a church event or liturgy, learning seemed to be more involving and vital. I also discovered, somewhat to my surprise, that education takes place in a particular historical, social, cultural context and that no curriculum resource, educational model, or structure is adequate to the particular life of a parish. I also learned with some pain that the pressing needs of people do not always correspond to either a schooling setting or the content of an instructional design. Before I could resolve these new awarenesses, I was called to return to Needham and join my old friend and mentor Herb Smith. By now the church had grown to over 2,000 communicants, at least half of whom were children. While there was pressure that the church call a minister of education, Smith insisted on co-pastors sharing the total ministry of the church. Together we were to engage in a shared educational ministry. Neither our ministries nor the church's program were to be divided into specialized areas. My own positive experience in this situation influenced my negative convictions concerning the specialized ministry of education.

With our large number of children, youth, and adults and a limited plant and resources, we were forced to develop alternatives to the traditional Christian education program. While maintaining a well-administered church school, we continually looked for new contexts and methods. We intentionally built learning experiences into our numerous choirs, youth fellowships, church organizations, and meetings. We began an evening intergenerational experience, combining education, worship, and fellowship. We organized small family clusters and provided educational resources for families who were away on weekends. We developed extended programs for parents before and after a baptism, a two-year integrated confirmation program, a lengthened marriage preparation program, a program for our commutors in the business community, and many others. Soon we discovered that these programs had greater interest and were evaluated as being of greater significance than our traditional church school.

However, before we could build these experiments into an overall strategy and design for Christian education as an integral part of the church's total program, I was called to be pastor of the First Congregational Church on the campus of Williams College in Williamstown, Massachusettes. Bringing with me our learnings in Needham, I became increasingly committed to adult education as the most important aspect of parish life. Unless we could transform the lives of adults and reform our community life, our other educational efforts were limited. While we continued to do our best to maintain a viable church school, we put our emphasis on imaginative programs for adults. Our physicians met in the hospital, the university faculty met in the faculty club, our business men and women met in the Williams Inn, and our parents met in homes. In those settings we explored the relationships between our faith and lives. The process was simple: We shared how we were living and the problem we were confronting as we explored our Christian tradition; we reflected on the dissonances which emerged; and we sought to arrive at a conviction as we also discussed the changes necessary in our individual and corporate lives which these convictions entailed.

During this same period we also experimented with numerous ways to improve the quality of our church school. But, instruction in a schooling setting just did not appear to be satisfactory. We knew that, yet we had difficulty believing it. Worse, we could not imagine an alternative. I began to be convinced that liturgy and the sacraments within the context of life in a faithful community was the answer. But that was as far as I could go at the time.

Nevertheless, my eight years of experiences as a pastor provided me with an understanding of Christian nurture as a ministry of the Word, a lifelong pastoral activity in which a faith community shares its faith verbally and nonverbally so that together they might grow in faith and aid that faith to become living, conscious, and active in their individual and corporate lives. Still, I had no name for this process of what appeared to be more religious socialization than instruction and little sense of how it could become an intentional aspect of parish life.

Expanding Awareness

My years with the United Church Board of Homeland Ministries, which followed my years in the parish, influenced me in other ways and provided a context for reflection on past experiences: The BHM had a long history of attracting creative mavericks, encouraging them to act imaginatively on behalf of the church's mission, and supporting them when their ministry was unpopular. In 1966, while happily engaged in the parish, I was enticed to join the BHM's Division of Christian education to develop and edit a new magazine on education in church and society. I can recall admitting that I knew little about education (I had more questions than answers) and nothing about journalism. Their response was even more memorable: "That is why we need you. You don't know what cannot be done."

A year later we gave birth to *Colloquy*, and as its editor I began to formally work out my understanding of Christian education. In preparing to write this biographical essay I went back and reread each issue of *Colloquy*; as a result, I surfaced some interesting insights into my work. For example, I discovered that I chose as the theme for the first issue "Environment and Education." In my first editorial I questioned the wisdom of focusing the church's educational ministry as instruction in a schooling context. I advocated attention both to every aspect of life in a worshiping congregation and to every aspect of the society in which persons are socialized. That theme has remained constant in my thought. It began with my experiences in the parish and three years later it became the focus of my first book *Values for Tomorrow's Children*.

Though many questioned my choice of the title *Colloquy*, I wanted to create a relational magazine founded upon conversations between people—my own way of learning. The interview, therefore, became a regular feature, reflecting my own constant travels throughout the United States and around the world to meet and talk with a host of varied imaginative people who framed many of my own convictions. The list is long, but it includes Malcomb Boyd, Stephen Rose, Harvey Cox, Cardinal Bea, Brother Christopher of Taize, Ivan Illich, Paulo Friere, Ben Chavis, John Holt, Sid Simon, Gabe Moran, Noam Chomsky, Sister Corita, and many others. As I look back over the names of the people I sought to inverview I realized they all shared certain characteristics: They were all critics of the status quo, all creative visionaries, all persons of some deep and abiding faith.

The second issue of *Colloquy*, February 1967, was on the theme of the "Local Church as an Educating Community." I discovered that I focused on liturgy in its dual expression of ritual symbolic actions and personal–social action in the world. This theme has been with me ever since and later found expression in *Tomorrow's Church* and in *Inner Growth/Outer Change*.

In 1968 *Colloquy* began to focus on the issues of war and peace, justice and civil rights, or as I put it in the January 1968 editorial (whose theme was Politics and Religious Education): "We must prepare persons and communities for responsible action in society on behalf of shalom." The next years took me to Latin America and Africa with the World Council of Churches. My concern for the Third World, the voices of the poor, the oppressed, the hungry grew. So did my awareness of the world education crisis, the ecumenical character of the church, and liberation theology.

By 1972 it became increasingly clear to me that we could not separate education, worship, evangelism, social action, or other aspects of the church's ministry. The nature of culture and socialization theory began to creep into the issues of *Colloquy*. I began to make friends with a group of anthropologists, especially Gwen Kennedy Neville, with whom I later wrote *Generation to Generation* and *Learning Through Liturgy*. These folk, and others I met at the Education and Anthropology meetings of the American Anthropology Society, opened up for me a whole new world of insight into enculturation.

By the last years of my editorship a subtle change was occurring in my mind. Still committed to the prophetic transforming social actions side of ministry and the necessary radical reform of church life, I began to be concerned about the Christian tradition and the more conserving, nurturing side of life in a community of faith. The themes of spirituality and liturgy emerged again as they have once more in my latest books, *Liturgy and Learning Through the Life Cycle* and *The Spiritual Pilgrimage: Learning East and West*.

And then it was 1974. Church life was changing. Management by objective began to replace our older more creative lifestyle. Many felt that the BHM had ignored the needs of the churches and magazines like *Colloquy* were irrelevant to the educational needs of the churches. A more responsive bureacracy was desired and indeed needed.

As subscriptions radically dropped off, program money was being used to pay the deficits of *Colloquy*. Perhaps *Colloquy* was ahead of its time; surely its understanding of the Gospel and education were not popular. And something was changing inside me.

New Opportunities

A sabbatical during my last years at the BHM took me to Boston. While living and administrating a BHM program in religious education at Andover Newton I spent the majority of my time as Lentz Lecturer in religion and education at Harvard Divinity School.

It was good to be back again. During my four years as a minister in the Needham Congregational Church I had helped to design and develop one of the early seminary programs in field education. Now I had come to the conviction that until we could reform theological education, Christian education as I understood it and as *Colloquy* wrote about it would be difficult if not impossible to achieve. I, therefore, looked forward to this opportunity to find out what it was like to prepare clergy for the church. Mostly, I made friends who have continued to influence me. One was Jim Fowler who was beginning his work on faith development; his influence is obvious in my early work. Another was Christianne Brusselmans whose work on the adult catechumenate is just now finding its full influence in my work. Then there was William R. Rogers who got me interested in Carl Jung and Wilfred Cantwell Smith whose work opened for me a whole new way to understand faith and interestingly introduced me to Anglican theology.

During this time I began to talk with my old friend, confidant, and editorial consultant, Robert Wood Lynn, at Union Theological Seminary in New York. The more we talked, the more sure I was that I belonged in a theological school preparing men and women for ordination. He convinced me that if I wanted to do that I needed a doctorate. It all seemed impossible until I talked with Phil Phenix at Columbia University Teachers College. He convinced me it could be done and helped me organize a program. In fifteen months, while continuing as editor of *Colloquy*, I finished my degree. Once again it was the people with whom I related at Columbia and Union who influenced my work.

First, there was Bob Lynn through whom I learned the importance of an historicist perspective. He helped me to realize that the more comprehensive our knowledge of our inheritance, the less likely we are to imagine that we have to begin our quest for understanding from scratch, the less likely we are to take one aspect of our tradition over-seriously, and the less likely we are to romanticize the present. As a result I increasingly turned away from my North American Liberal Protestant tradition and began to explore both the patristic and medieval periods of the church's history and the Roman Catholic catechetical tradition. Phil Phenix not only gave me the support and encouragement necessary, but helped me to imagine a new understanding of both religion and education and the relationships between them especially as they related to ways of knowing. Dwayne Huebner helped me to develop a creative, critical approach to all accepted wisdom. He is perhaps the most imaginative teacher I have ever known. His example of combining the radical exploration of roots with an imaginative construction of alternative visions continues to influence me.

Then, there was Lambros Comitas, the anthropologist who provided me with an anthropoligical perspective on both religion and education and C. Ellis Nelson, whose theological foundations and insights into religious socialization provided me with the theory upon which I have built my own work. During this same period I met Berard Marthaler, who from a Roman Catholic perspective enlarged my understanding of religious socialization and helped me to understand the history and nature of catechesis. All this now can be found developed in my latest book *A Faithful Church: Issues in the History of Catechesis*.

And then a tragic car accident. My neck was broken. It is a miracle that I am alive. Time in the hospital provided me with time to think. What was I doing with my life? Where was I going? What did God have in mind for me? And perhaps most important, where was I to find a religious community to nurture and sustain me. While working for the

BHM I had lost contact with a local congregation. My own tradition did not seem to meet fully my spiritual needs. I needed a community of faith in order to live out my vocation but did not have one. This tormented me and then it happened: an invitation to join the faculty at the Duke Divinity School. It was like an answer to prayer. I accepted with enthusiasm and then finished my recuperation, said my sad farewells to my friends at BHM and went in search of both roots and new beginnings.

Roots for the Journey

My eight years at Duke have been among the most productive in my life. Duke is an environment that facilitates my growth and development. The past seven years have made possible my teaching in ever new and larger areas related to practical theology. Duke has encouraged me to integrate catechetical, moral, ascetical, liturgical, and pastoral theology and to develop an alternative to our current professional model of ministry with its specializations in religious education, pastoral care and counseling, worship and preaching, policy and administration. I have had the opportunity to travel, lecture, and write. Wherever I have traveled, I have made new friends and been influenced. Among the list of people who have touched my life and affected my work are clergy and lay people from almost every Christian community around the world. New friends and colleagues in the Association of Professors and Researchers in Religious Education, especially my Roman Catholic sisters and brothers, and the members of the Religious Education Association, especially my new Jewish friends, all continue to affect my life and work. My responsibilities as the editor of *Religious Education* expand my contacts and enlarge my visions.

Duke University has provided me with all the stimulation and creative possibilities I need. But for five years I still searched to find a homeland for my soul, a community of faith to nurture and sustain my spirit. Little by little I was increasingly attracted to the Episcopal Church. I had been interested in that community for many years, but I had some difficulty with the theology of the 1928 Prayer Book, and in principle I could not accept their stand on the ordination of women. Then a new Prayer Book, the acceptance of women for ordination, and the experience of a call. I had been leading Episcopal Christian Education conferences at Kanuga in North Carolina for a number of years, but three summers ago I found myself having hands laid on me by three hundred Episcopal lay folks and clergy. It was to me a call to ministry in the Episcopal Church. I contacted my old friend and colleague in Christian education, now the Bishop of Missouri, William Jones. He sent me on retreat and in prayer my decision was made. On December 4, 1977 I was confirmed in the Episcopal Church and on September 23, 1978 I was priested. I look at that event as among the most important in my life. I feel like I've come home. The Episcopal Church's understanding of the sacramental life and priesthood, its desire to be fully Catholic and Protestant, its attempts to combine a concern for formation and transformation I share. Within this evangelical catholic tradition I find it is easy to develop an understanding of catechesis that is both old and new. I have been accepted into a new family and, perhaps more important, introduced to a new set of friends; among the most influential has been Urban T. Holmes. In almost everything I now say and do can be seen his influence.

And so the present. I am a priest at the Chapel of the Cross. I need this community and this place to live out my priesthood and spiritual pilgrimage. My spiritual director, a Roman Catholic nun, and my therapist, a Protestant lay person, are helping me to grow. My regular retreats give me the solitude and silence I need. My friends throughout the world enhance and enliven both my life and my faith. I continue to live out my personality in the various places and among the various persons I meet. I continue to move from concern to concern, interest to interest, problem to problem. My work continues to provide me with a context for imaginatively dealing with my own internal struggles. Like a good Anglican, I begin and end with the doctrine of creation, always emphasizing an incarnational theology in which Christ is the transformer of culture. Like others in the Anglican community, I live with *via media*, a yes and no for every possible position and the struggle to integrate life while affirming its dichotomies. With them I hold as my authority the teaching of the church (Scripture and tradition), reason and experiences of the Holy Spirit, but most of all I understand life sacramentally. As I have sometimes put it, I am an Anglican, fully Catholic, fully Protestant, but more Catholic these days than Protestant, and more Lutheran than Calvinist. Perhaps it is my own need to regain a sense of tradition and establish a meaningful continuity with the past, my own sense of loss at not being socialized into a faith community, and my positive experience as a Protestant in search of Catholic substance that has encouraged me.

To focus my work on a community of faith as the context for catechesis or intentional religious socialization that integrates the liturgical, spiritual, moral, and pastoral aspects of intentional communal life in a tradition bearing community, I suspect I will continue to work on this problem while seeking balance between "Catholic substance" and "Protestant principle." I also suspect I will always be uncomfortable with objective theories, rational analysis as the basis of truth, practical realistic programs, and organizational structures. I suppose I will always be speculating on possible futures through imaginative efforts to provide a highly personal order to the gestalts of parish life and the struggle of persons in community to live into their baptisms.

Conclusion

What this painful effort has taught me is that my life has been one attempt after another at self-understanding. Through the years I have used my work as the context for living out my struggle to become who I am. I can now admit how much my life and work is a result of relations with those people who in small and large ways have touched my life. My work, if so far as it has any value, is a tribute to their influence.

I close with a realization of how difficult this task was and how inadequately I have done it. And so perhaps you will permit me to share the Hasidic story that best explains my life and work to date. It is a story about Rabbi Zaddoc, known for his wisdom, but in reality for many years Rabbi Zaddoc has been lost in the wilderness. One day a group of pilgrims are going through the forest and also get lost. In their confusion and trouble, they meet Rabbi Zaddoc. With joyful anticipation they cry out "Rabbi Zaddoc, can you help us find the way out." And he responds, "That I cannot do, but I can share with you the hundred trails that lead further into the forest. However, if I do that, perhaps we can find the way out."

Chapter 6

How I Became What I Am as a Christian Religious Educator

Howard Grimes

It is often a humbling experience to read what one wrote twenty or thirty years ago. In preparation for writing this essay, I have read such material to see how my mind has changed during my teaching career in religious education. Although I am glad that some of what I wrote was never published, I actually find that I have not changed as much as I thought I had. Perhaps this is due to the fact that I was eclectic when I began my career, and still am. I have assimilated many points of view, not always, I suspect, as fully as I ought. One of the major differences now is that there are so many more resources than were available when I began my professional career as a religious educator in 1949. When—or if—I rewrite an overview of Christian education which I completed in 1961 and used for several years with my classes, I will make many changes, but my *basic* stance has not changed radically.

Perhaps I should say at the outset that I am not an original thinker. Such persons are rare; they are often exciting; and they often make a major contribution to their field. But there are not many Galileo's and Einstein's, nor many John Dewey's and George Albert Coe's. I am not being falsely modest when I say that I am a collector of ideas; it is, rather, a fact. Sometimes I find that reliable ideas must be held in juxtaposition with one another even when my aim is to synthesize them.

There are dangers in being a collector of ideas. I have sometimes embraced too enthusiastically something I later viewed with more reserve. Perhaps my students have suffered because of this tendency. By the time I have written something, however, I have usually come to a more balanced view.

A by-product of being eclectic is that one is usually perceived as at best unexciting. The person with a "message" to proclaim is the one who

most often stimulates others to think and act. Generalists may be productive in the long run; those with a specialized point of view are more
likely to stimulate immediate change. John Westerhoff was not the first
to understand the context of Christian teaching as the whole congregation, but he said it so dramatically that people listened. James Michael
Lee was not the first to recognize that the social sciences are crucial for
the religious educator, but his writing and speaking caused people to
listen. The "charismatic" nature of their personalities also has helped in
the dissemination of their ideas.

I should also say that I am basically a theorist, with a strong practical
bent. Again I make no apologies for this interest, for I believe that
theory-building is the most practical exercise possible if one puts his or
her ideas into practice. The problem, I realize, as Harold W. Burgess,
Didier-Jacques Pivateau, and J. T. Dillon have recently pointed out, is
that the best theories in religious education are often ignored and,
instead, practicing church educators operate out of unexamined theories which may be quite inadequate. To paraphrase my spiritual ancestor, Charles Wesley, we need not only to unite the two so long divided,
knowledge and vital piety; we need also to join theory and practice in the
life of the church. I gladly acknowledge the value of my colleague
Richard Murray for his constant reminder of the importance of the
practice of education in the church. By his complementary concern, he
has freed me for more time in theory-building, and at the same time, has
constantly reminded me of the necessity of going beyond theory. In
turn, I believe I have encouraged him to become a better theorist.

All of this prologue is by way of offering a rationale for the manner in
which my thought-world concerning the church's teaching ministry has
evolved. "I am a part of all that I have met"—or more accurately, "All
that I have met is a part of me"—from my earlier and later experience as
a person, from the classroom and lecture hall, from my reading, and in
other ways in which people's ideas and experiences have made an impact on me.

Some Key Influences

It is appropriate for me to begin this account of my intellectual odyssey
by noting that my life has always centered in the church. I find that I
cannot separate my personal life from the professional. Horace Bushnell

has been, and ought to be, questioned; but there *is* a sense in which I never knew myself as other than a Christian—sometimes an unfaithful one, at times perhaps even an apostate, but always one who knew himself in relationship with God. Even in times when I doubted the very reality of God, there was a residual faith that would not let me go.

My life has been so church-centered that I have had recently to adjust to the fact that more and more students in schools of theology are there because of a dramatic conversion experience in their adult life. Sometimes this has been after a long period of inactivity as a Christian, sometimes with no such early experience of Christian believing and belonging. Perhaps one of the reasons I turned to the field of religious education professionally was the fact that a steady upbringing in home, childhood church, university campus ministry, and finally in theological school made me aware of the value of continuous nurture and instruction in faith.

The faith that nurtured me in my childhood and youth was Methodist, which, if we must use labels, I suppose I would call "liberal-conservative." By this I mean that it was a non-Calvinistic interpretation of essential faith and practice with a strong overlay of nineteenth-century liberalism especially as found in Adolf Harnack's emphasis on the coming Kingdom of God, the infinite worth of the person, and the commandment of love. That is, the belief *structure* was essential Christianity; the *special emphases* had been taken from a strongly ethical understanding of the Christian religion. The emphasis on "experience" was Wesleyan as that understanding had developed through the Sunday School movement.

I can remember some doubts which I had about traditional Christianity from this early period, but I became a serious doubter only in my last year of university education. I never stopped being active in the church, however, and one year after graduation from the University of Texas I entered the school of theology of Southern Methodist University.

Not much shocked me in the "liberal" interpretation I found common during theological study. Indeed, the three years were actually years of rebuilding. Several people were of special help to me in what was then a small, fairly parochial, denominational school. One person in particular became my teacher, mentor, and friend. Paul Root's field was sociology of religion; his graduate work had been done at Duke University under the social philosopher Charles Ellwood. He combined in a remarkable way the piety he had learned at home and at Asbury College, a genuinely live intellectual emphasis, and a Christian humanism that embraced many sources of truth and insight. He was later elected dean of Duke Divinity School but died of a heart attack before assuming that position.

It was in an additional year of study at Union Theological Seminary in New York that I first came into contact with the "new theology"—this was in 1940–41. I have never been certain whether it was Sigmund Freud or Reinhold Niebuhr who was more influential in shaping my thinking concerning human nature. Suffice it to say that the most significant change that occurred in my thinking during that year of study with such giants as Niebuhr, Paul Tillich, James Moffatt, and Harry Ward concerned how I thought about the human. Niebuhr's lectures for nine months were based on the yet unpublished book, *The Nature and Destiny of Man*. The person, he was fond of saying, stands at the juncture of nature and spirit; hence he or she is forever both striving for the good and falling prey to the instinctive urges of nature—and in danger of being proud of his or her goodness. T. S. Eliot's *Murder in the Cathedral* also had a profound influence on me, as, later, Arthur Miller's plays did. It seemed both ironic and accurate to me than—and still does—that the good Thomas à Becket falls victim to the most insidious sin of all, pride in his own martyrdom!

What is the significance of this change for my career in religious education? Although this all happened some years before I had even thought of doing graduate work in that field, it provided one of the crucial ideas in the formation of my understanding of Christian teaching. It caused my rejection later in the basic assumption by many religious educators that human nature is neutral. It made me aware, to paraphrase another of Niebuhr's statements, that there is enough good in persons to make Christian nurture possible and enough evil to make it necessary. In my early professional career, when I was openly rebellious against the twentieth-century liberalism still embraced by most Christian educators, a colleague once told me I had no right to be in the field of Christian education with the view of human nature I held. (I might add that a few years later he told me he had come to agree with me.)

Local church experience led me to the discipline of religious education for graduate work. During two terms as associate pastor at First Methodist Church, Houston, Texas, interspersed by three and one-half years in the army chaplaincy during World War II, I became involved in and interested in furthering the cause of local church education. In the local church, I worked closely with the director of religious education, Johnnie Marie Brooks (who later became my wife), and with the pastor, Paul W. Quillian. These two persons, more than any other, changed the direction of my interest toward working with individuals and small groups.

My years in graduate school were the final years of Harrison S. Elliott at Union Theological Seminary. Elliott was an unreconstructed liberal in religious education, but allowed me to disagree. He was a superb director of graduate work, and though my ideas were, and still are, quite different from his, I recognized his greatness then, and still affirm it. In *Can Religious Education Be Christian?* Elliott's incisive mind, in replying to Shelton Smith's *Faith and Nurture*, produced what I still believe is one of the important books in the field of religious education. Smith's *ideas* influenced me more, as did those of a slightly later book, Paul Vieth's *The Church and Christian Education*. Elliott's book helped set the agenda for my thinking, however.

Unfortunately my work at Teachers College, Columbia, was less than exciting. Teachers College in the late 1940s was, I suppose, between the times—either that or I took the wrong courses. John L. Childs, John Dewey's chief interpreter, was a superb teacher, however, and helped me understand both the strengths and weaknesses of the education he espoused. I find the issue raised now by those who oppose "secular humanism" in public schools an understandable one. Dewey *did* find the source of values strictly within the human enterprise. The solution these opponents of public education propose is obviously an impossible one in schools which represent a plethora of understandings and interpretations, but I do understand their concern, as I think many public educators do not, because Childs did such a good job of interpreting Dewey.

Thus far I have presented a brief chronological overview of some of the shaping forces of my life and thought prior to beginning my teaching of Christian religious education. To continue such an account would be neither productive nor, I suspect, of interest to others. So I have chosen in what follows a more natural approach for me, the "issue-centered" way of thinking, which I suppose I learned from Harrison Elliott both from his book and a seminar he regularly offered on issues in religious education. I have continued this approach with many changes in what issue was in the forefront of my thinking—all except human nature, which has remained a constant. A correlative approach in which I was encouraged by an early colleague Charles Johnson, who had been educated under Lewis Sherrill, is the "foundations" way of organizing the various aspects of teaching theory. My method here, as it has been in my teaching, is to divide my remarks into basic foundational areas for Christian religious education—that is, sources and origins—with issues related to the foundations.

Theological Concerns

It should be obvious by now that theology was my major concern—almost my only concern, I fear—during the early years of my professional work as a religious educator. Further, the theology which shaped my thinking after my first experience at Union and throughout my later graduate study was that which is rather loosely called "neo-orthodoxy," the theology of Barth, Brunner, Reinhold Niebuhr (and, to some extent, his brother Richard), and others. Let me hasten to add that I *never* considered myself a Barthian. There were aspects of this neo-Reformation theology that were contrary to my Wesleyan heritage, since the former was considerably influenced by John Calvin. Not only was I an enthusiast about this "new" kind of thinking, however; I was determined that other people would be too.

I suppose that Methodist education had been more fully influenced by nineteenth-century liberalism than most of the major communions, and therefore I began to make a nuisance of myself, I fear, as I called this to the attention of various Methodist meetings which I attended. I am not naturally a person who enjoys conflict, and I wonder now at the brashness with which I took on the Methodist (now United Methodist) Church! I have said that I tend to be eclectic; at this point in my life I was so intent on theological change that I acted somewhat against my nature.

Up to my second year of teaching, there was not much to assign in theory courses that reflected the new theological thought. It was therefore with much enthusiasm that I embraced Randolph Crump Miller's *The Clue to Christian Education* in 1951, and a few years later James Smart's *The Teaching Ministry of the Church*, and Lewis Sherrill's *The Gift of Power*. (Parenthetically, I wonder why Sherrill's book has not been reprinted. It presented a balanced view of Christian education that could speak to us today.)

Some time later I received a new colleague, Charles H. Johnson, who had worked closely with Sherrill and helped in the development of the material that went into *The Gift of Power*. Joe, as he was called for reasons I never learned, was a kindred spirit and meant much to me during the years he taught at Perkins School of Theology.

Certain key issues emerged during this early period, and many have remained of great concern to me through the years. I have already noted the crucial place that a view of human nature occupied in my thinking. Barth never convinced me of what appears to be his somewhat fatalistic view of the person—cut off from the Lord of the universe until God's initiative, almost without human response, makes reconciliation possible. There was too much of Wesley in me to buy this view. Wesley's doctrine of prevenient grace—God's grace operating in everyone's life with God waiting, like the father in the parable of the Prodigal Son, for a response.

I came to realize, however, that the Methodist movement had taken Wesley *too* seriously in one respect—his emphasis on the moral life. Under the stimulus of Reformation theology, I came to see that much popular theology advocated a view of "salvation through good works"—mostly, I might add, personal morality. Although John Wesley never intended that this should be the case, it had occurred, and the Sunday School, I think, had contributed more than its share to this development. I do not remember many things I learned in Sunday School, but I do remember an illustration used by a beloved Sunday School teacher who considered himself more conservative than the Methodist church in general was. He told us one Sunday that when we were judged, God would put all our bad deeds on one side of the scales, our good deeds on the other, and our fate would be determined by which outweighed the other!

I am not at all sure that Christian education in general, nor I in particular, have fully assimilated what it means for nurture and instruction to take seriously the doctrine of salvation by grace through faith. Perhaps the grace-works issue must always be one in which there is a tension between two extremes. For me, at least, this is still the case.

A theology of the church also became an area of great interest to me. For reasons which I do not fully remember, I had written my dissertation on the place and training of the laity in the Methodist tradition. What began as an academic exercise became a matter of great interest, and the impact of the research and writing was considerable. A few years later I began a rewriting of my dissertation, but it became, instead, a book on the church and its life and general ministry, *The Church Redemptive* (1958). Here too I was out of step with much early twentieth-century religious education, which at times became almost a movement alongside rather than an integral part of the church's ministry. As I explored on a deeper theological level a theology of the laity, there was no place to turn except to a theology of the church, and F. W. Dillistone's *The Structure of The Divine Society* was a seminal influence in this process. This line of thought has continued, leading in more recent years to an in-depth consideration with some of my colleagues of the meaning of practical theology.

The nature of revelation and the relationship of revelation and Scripture became still another significant issue for me in these early days of teaching. In the attempt of theologians to hold to "biblical criticism" but at the same time take the Bible seriously, some understanding of revelation other than the propositional became crucial. William Temple, John Baillie, and others helped me formulate a doctrine of revelation emphasizing God's *self*-revelation, especially in the Word made flesh. There was nothing new about this, for it is essentially what the Bible itself understands by revelation. It became, and is still, an important aspect of my theology which has direct impact on Christian teaching.

Indeed, there is a major difference implied for teaching in the two opposing views: If revelation is propositional, then the purpose of religious teaching is to impart the propositional formulations of the biblical faith. If, on the other hand, it is personal, then the incarnation of the biblical message becomes the core of Christian teaching through relationships. If it is *basically* personal but is *expressed in propositional* forms (the text of the Bible), then both instruction in the content of *the* faith and nurture *in* faith communities are legitimate aspects of religious education.

There is one issue—among many others—that has not been considered in much detail by theologians in general nor by many religious educators: how one becomes a Christian. It has been an intriguing question to me for many years; it is being thrust to the fore of our thinking in our time by the "born again" Christians who insist upon one particular way of answering the question. John Baillie's little book, *Baptism and Conversion*, does not treat the way of nurture (or education) at all. Most works on Christian initiation assume baptism (and perhaps confirmation) as the normative means. Roman Catholic writers are increasingly using the word "conversion," and John Westerhoff has recently joined in the emphasis. Charles Foster and Robert Browning have discussed the issue in a set of casette tapes, and have included much of the material in a booklet *Foundations for Teaching and Learning in The United Methodist Church*, published anonymously by that denomination's Board of Discipleship. The most complete listing of differing understandings I have seen is by Daniel B. Stevick in his chapter of *Made, Not Born*, from the Murphy Center for Liturgical Research.

My usual response to questions like this is a pluralistic one, in that I am unwilling to select any one way as normative. I have come to appreciate more fully the conversion experience as the way many people enter a life of discipleship, but I can see no New Testament, theological, or psychological reason for assuming that every person must have a dramatic converting experience. Developmental theory, as I shall point out later, has provided me with a deeper understanding that most people, in fact, do not enter and continue a life of discipleship with only one experience. In any case, this issue seems to me to be one that needs more attention than religious educators have usually given it in the past, and developmental theory provides genuine help for the process.

It should be obvious that my neo-orthodoxy was tempered by a number of forces and persons. I have already noted one factor—my Wesleyan, non-Calvinistic heritage. The experiential emphasis of the Wesleyan stream of thought prevented my embracing a rigid transmissive view of education. Contemporary theologians were also influential, Paul Tillich in particular. His "method of correlation" in theology became a permanent aspect of my understanding of the bi-polar nature of education with a dual emphasis on Bible and experience. Others to whom I point with appreciation include John Baillie, Martin Buber, Richard Niebuhr, the existentialists, and many others.

Eventually the so-called "secular theologians" entered into my thinking and effected a major shift to a more inclusive understanding of the activity of God in human life and history. For reasons I have never understood, I was asked to do a basic book for the National Council of Churches' weekday series, on the Christian understanding of history.

The preparation for and the writing of *The Christian Views History* stretched my thinking in an incredible way and helped me see as I had not previously seen the breadth of God's activity in the world. I had never fully embraced the separation of history and "holy history," but I came to see even more clearly that to confine God's activity to holy history was to limit God in a way that the prophets in particular refused to do. I became even more conscious of the view that "election" is a call to responsibility, not privilege. I did not lose my appreciation for God's initiative in Israel and later the church—if anything that position was enhanced—but I came to realize that the peculiar advantage of the Jew and the Christian is that they, if they are perceptive, can identify God's activity in all of God's creation.

A still more recent theological influence has been process theology. The presence of my colleague Schubert Ogden had made me aware of the movement, and Randy Miller's increasing embracing of it has encouraged me to take that view more seriously. In a sense I think I have done process thinking all my life; biblical theology, now somewhat in disrepute, appears to me to be quite in line with process thought. I recognize now that the schemes worked out by biblical theologians in a past generation were too "neat"—they were to some extent imposed on the biblical record. But the idea that God relates to humanity in changing ways seems both biblical and very much in keeping with current developmental theory that persons in different stages of development perceive God in different ways. God's love, as Daniel Day Williams so significantly said, does not change, and *if* God's love does not change, then God not only suffers with a suffering humanity; God also changes in the effort to comfort and to confront humanity. I shall always remember the line from Mark Connally's *Green Pastures*, as De Lawd, played by the great black actor Richard Harrison, looks out over the parapet of heaven and hears the cries from earth, "Crucify him! Crucify him!" "Must God suffer, too?" he asks the angel Gabriel. This is obviously an unconscionable simplification of process theology, but it provided a beginning from which I have increasingly recognized the truth in that perspective.

I have found this understanding especially fruitful in dealing with the problem of evil and suffering, a reality that became quite personal in our son's illness and death from cancer. As I have become increasingly appreciative of the role God plays in bringing order out of our chaotic lives and the world, I have also recovered the meaning behind the Kingdom of God emphasis of the synoptic gospels. Kingdom of God as present, as coming, and as yet to be realized in some distant future—a view which I explicated in a paper I wrote for Reinhold Niebuhr in 1941—has become increasingly real. While I had tended to ignore the Kingdom for many years, the influence of a new colleague, David Watson, has recently helped me recover this central biblical metaphor.

This new appreciation has also been enhanced as I have studied the apocalyptic movement of the intertestamentary period, including the emergence of the idea of Satan as the adversary and tempter and the resulting emphasis on the *ultimate* triumph of God over evil. In a real sense the Good News is that Jesus has already inaugurated the Kingdom, into which we can enter and to some extent participate. The struggle with evil continues—God is *in process* of bringing order out of chaos. What seems even more breathtaking to me is the conception of Paul regarding the redemption of *all* creation: "The creation itself will be set free from its bondage to decay and obtain the glorious liberty of the children of God" (Rom. 8:21). I do not pretend that I have integrated this Good News into my theory and practice of Christian teaching; I am convinced that in our day of great worldwide travail, this "theology of hope" is an urgent message which we need to assimilate in both theoretical and practical ways.

It may be that I have done injustice to process thought by my way of internalizing it. In any case, I find that that to which it has led me has been both personally helpful and intellectually stimulating.

As I have noted earlier, my entire theological odyssey is as fully personal as it is professional. What began as an academic enterprise in fact—an attempt to *explain* the reality of God, the human, and their relationship—has ended as a personal faith. What I once perceived as an intellectual exercise has become a means of reappropriating truth as mystery, pointing to a deeper reality which cannot be fully grasped, which must, in fact, finally grasp me. As Paul Tillich observes in a footnote in *The Protestant Era*, we are no more saved by right belief than by good deeds. Our destiny is in the hands of God, and I have a deeper sense of shalom because I can now trust God without knowing the dimensions of heaven or the date and place of Armageddon. As I move beyond this personal response I hope more fully to integrate these new insights into my educational theory.

Psychosocial Issues

As I have not been able to separate the personal from the professional with regard to theological concerns, neither will I be able to do so for those matters which I label "psychosocial." I use this term somewhat loosely to refer to the person in community. I also separate "human nature," a term I use theologically, from "the person," which I attempt to understand from a social science perspective.

My academic interest in the psychosocial dates from my discovery of the psychology of religion when I was writing an S.T.M. thesis on the sociology of conversion. G. Stanley Hall, William Starbuck, William James, James B. Pratt, and others whetted my appetite to know more about the human psyche. Somewhat later, Gardner Murphy, Gordon Allport, Goodwin Watson, John Dewey, Harry Stack Sullivan, and a host of others gave me "clues" that never quite satisfied. The influence of Freud was less direct, and I never found his sexual interpretation of the person adequate. W. I. Thomas's delineation of the four basic personal needs (security, response, recognition, and adventure) and Gordon Allport's reduction of these to two (tribalism, or the need to belong, and individuation, or the need to be separate) provided a basic structure for my thinking for many years. Later, Abraham Maslow's hierarchy of needs seemed illuminating but not quite adequate, and the depth psychologists entered more fully into my thinking. The Gesell studies of children and young adolescents I found interesting but in such detail that I was overwhelmed by them. I was intrigued by all that I could read about the person, and when I developed my first, still unpublished, "survey" of Christian education, I began with the person.

These sources never fully satisfied me, however, partly because of what they failed to say. Erik Erikson began to fill the gaps by his description of the ages of the person, and I, like many others, found his emphasis on the identity needs of adolescents especially helpful. I was never fully satisfied, however, that his findings were not more culturally conditioned than he believed. Randy Miller introduced me to the British psychologist Basil Yeaklee, and eventually I began to try to read the works of the Swiss "genetic epistemologist" Jean Piaget.

I was first introduced to Lawrence Kohlberg's work at a meeting of the Religious Education Association. I discovered the work of James Fowler a short time later, and he, in turn, made me aware of the work of Robert L. Selman. Developmental theory filled many gaps of which I had been only half-conscious previously, and provided an explanation of persons for which I had been searching.

A short time later my colleague Leroy Howe held his first seminar on Jean Piaget, and I took part as an auditor. I, in turn, told him of the work of James Fowler, and he and I have since been co-leaders in seminars in which students have both learned the theory and done the interviewing associated with Fowler's faith development. Although I recognize that Fowler's work is "in progress," as he does, and that cultural factors may be more prevalent in it than he recognizes, I believe that his approach, growing out of the work of Erikson, Piaget, Kohlberg, and Selman, offers the most fruitful way of thinking about the growth of faith that has yet been advanced. Two doctor of ministry students, Ben Marshall of Richardson, Texas, and Barry Kiger, of Dallas, have added to my keen interest by the work which they have done in their parishes using Fowler's theory and interview form.

Fowler has also enhanced my recent theological development by the emphasis on faith as a way of construing life rather than as organized religious thought. This approach was not new, for I had read and generally agreed with Tillich's *Dynamics of Faith*. I knew something of the thinking of Richard Niebuhr in this regard, and Fowler sent me to William Cantwell Smith. This internalization of what I already believed has made me all the more certain that nurture *in faith* is more basic to religious education than instruction in the *content* of the faith. I do not mean, as I have never intended, to underplay the importance of knowing how one's particular faith content interprets life and provides a meaningful frame of reference for faithing. In fact, I believe that one way of being led to faith is to understand *the* faith. Nevertheless, emphases such as John Westerhoff's on the crucial nature of the faith community take on new meaning under the impact of Fowler's theory.

What developmental theory has done for me is to provide a framework for holding together the bits and pieces of understanding I previously had acquired. Never mind that such theory is still in process; the basic principle seems absolutely sound to me, and thinking is always in process. Faith development theory in particular provides an explanation of our life journey in a way nothing else has. Life *is* a pilgrimage, and some people stop along the way and are quite happy at not having reached the "goal," while others continue to strive and recognize that the nearer they are to the goal, the more elusive the goal becomes. Incidentally, I find no contradiction between this psychosocial theory and my theology: The journey is possible only because of the prior grace of God that accepts us regardless of where we are along the journey. Faith *is* ultimately a gift of God through others and through other gifts God has given us that make our quest possible and uphold us as we move along the way.

In the midst of my discovery of developmental theory, I also came in contact with a still little-known theory of "patterns of personality." J. W. Thomas, a psychological consultant to management, began to develop a theory in the 1960s based on the fact that the business executives with whom he was working demonstrated different, describable, and fairly predictable ways of reacting to human situations. At this time he did not know of Carl Jung's theory of personality types nor of others who had posited similar points of view. He is an innovative thinker and based his theory on what he observed happening in the lives of business people and on his own intuitive thinking as he took his cues from observation. An important aspect of his theory is that basic patterns are genetic; environment affects but does not change basically the inborn pattern.

I became involved in conducting seminars in the early 1970s for students and church people concerning human understanding and growth, using what Thomas had come to call "The Bi/Polar Way of Understanding People." I became so intrigued with his ideas that I eventually wrote a book based on the system, *How to Become Your Own Best Self,* published in 1979. Thomas's basic premise is that human strengths are always bi/polar: Thinking and Risking; Theoretical and Practical Thinking; and Dependent and Independent Risking. The particular mixture of these six strengths provides the basic personality pattern out of which a person acts.

I recognize that both of these approaches—the developmental and the personality pattern—can be abused. The tendency to categorize people, to "put them in boxes" where you want them to stay, is an insidious one. Both, however, if used more as *indicators* than as *categories,* can be extremely helpful in understanding one's self and others and in relating to other people. Much that these "systems" say to us we have known. For example, Piaget was not the first person to recognize that children must be taught through using concrete experiences, stories, and objects. Thomas was not the first to recognize that people have different "temperamental" tendencies. Erikson did not originate the question, "Who am I?", as a crucial one for adolescents. Their contributions lie in the evidence they present, the refinement of vaguely understood concepts they provide, the means they suggest for assessing persons and shaping the way one approaches them in individual and group relationships.

In particular, James Fowler helps me understand why many people are so uptight about their beliefs: They have become equilibrated on a faith stage (usually Stage 3) where certainty and clearly stated propositions are their way of faithing. He helps me understand why seminary students sometimes get in trouble with their congregations because of their need to provide elaborate explanations of their faith symbols (Stage 4). He has provided evidence for a principle to which I have long held: that neither a single conversion experience nor a gradual process of nurture is adequate in our life pilgrimage. Life is not a steady process upward and onward but a series of forward movements, reverses, reappraisals, crises and reaction to crises. "Stages of faith" are identifiable steps along the way, the result of both inner forces and outer ones (what Gail Sheehy calls "marker events"). How does one become a Christian? One may start as a child and move through a series of faith commitments (conversions); or one may start as an adult through a more dramatic conversion experience, and move through a series of new experiences that bring new insights and wider and deeper commitments. How one reacts to life generally, as indicated by the Bi/Polar System, also effects the precise way in which one's journey from faith to faith occurs.

Thus, I have returned to a definition of Christian education I wrote in 1958 under the influence of neo-orthodox theology: It is preparation for and follow-up from "encounter with God." Perhaps "encounter" is too much related to that period of theological thought to be used; I have not yet found a better word. I have no objection to using either "conversion" or "born again" provided one recognizes that not one but many such experiences are a part of the Christian journey. Whether such experiences occur within a stage of faith, or whether they involve movement from one to another, or whether they involve both, I think is not clear. My hunch is that there are many kinds of *converting experiences*, and that the type, intensity, and content are related to both where one is on the journey of life and to one's personality pattern.

In short, what I have said in this section is that I have been open in my search for an understanding of the person—at times perhaps too open—

and that a variety of rich, new resources are available now to provide content for the search. The process of fully internalizing these new findings remains for the future.

The Cultural Context

I am surprised and somewhat embarrassed by the fact that I have not taken the cultural context of our common work any more seriously than I have. I do not mean that I ignore the larger context of teaching; it is rather that I think few of us in Christian education take into full account the radical changes in our world during the past decades. There are exceptions: Letty Russell, Malcolm Warford, William Kennedy, to name only three. I suspect that most of us are still functioning in a culture dominated by white, relatively affluent, nuclear families. Nowhere is this more apparent, in spite of efforts to the contrary, than in most curriculum resources for congregational study.

Once I moved beyond the social gospel—which I recognize now as being both naive and fairly middle-class—I have tended to become unduly concerned with the individual and her or his primary communities. I know that television, the Third World, the ethnic and women's revolutions, and many other social forces have changed our world. But has my thinking/action really taken them into full account? I know that the liberation theologies both in the United States and in Latin America call for change, but the fact that I did not mention that approach to theology in the theological section is not an oversight. I have read such theology but have not internalized it. How adequate liberation theology is as a mode of theological thinking is not the point; what such thinking represents is more important than the adequacy of the product.

The chapter on culture in the 1961 manuscript to which I have referred previously is by all odds as I read it now the least satisfactory. I was concerned then about such forces as depersonalization (David Riesman, William H. Whyte, and Vance Packard), the "domestication of religion" (Will Herbert, Roy Eckardt, and Martin Marty), technology, estrangement, and secularization. I suppose I could still affirm all of these characteristics of twentieth-century culture, but they seem almost irrelevant when one looks at the revolutions through which we went in the 1960s and later. We have made adjustments in regard to ethnic and religious pluralism; many of us have sought seriously to remove sexism from our speaking and writing; but by and large these are token changes that are necessary but not adequate.

The revolution which I suspect impinges upon Christianity in general and religious education in particular more than any other concerns the family, including the changes in sexual patterns. How do we deal with single-parent families? Two pay-check families with children? One-sex marriages? Live-in companions of the opposite sex? And so on. Some of these movements are probably temporary. In history a period of sexual permissiveness has often been followed by one of sexual repression. Quite frankly, one of the reasons I have not dealt more constructively with these aspects of culture is that I am not as certain as some people are concerning what to accept and what to reject in the name of Christian faith. In our confusion we often ignore what is happening and go on as if the household with two parents and one or more children were the only pattern.

Another aspect of our culture with worldwide implications is the resurgence of fundamentalism, conservatism, and evangelicalism in religion—Christianity, Islam, and others. The religious consensus—not agreement, but a general stance—which has prevailed in the mainline Protestant churches for a century is probably no longer viable. I sometimes say to students that it will be up to them to deal with this and other cultural phenomena. In a sense that is an accurate statement, but it is not enough—and I know that it is not.

It should be obvious that two things are different about this section in contrast with the two previous ones: It is considerably shorter, and it does not say how my mind has changed but confesses my ambiguities and uncertainties. I know that is not enough, and I know also if I continue not to deal constructively with these changes I will thereby contribute to the increasing irrelevance of the church's teaching ministry for a large number of people in our world today.

General Education and Learning Theory

It should be clear by now that I consider Christian religious education a branch of practical theology rather than of general education. That is, when I speak of Christian religious education ("the teaching ministry of the church"), I refer to *faith* education. The discipline ("organized field of knowledge") which deals with it in an academic setting I consider to be a branch of practical theology. There *is* a legitimate academic discipline of religious education, which in my scheme deals with education and religion—with teaching *about* religion in the public and private school and with general education from a religious perspective. I consider the works of Philip Phenix to be among the few which are true *religious* education. He is a philosopher of education with a Christian perspective, and his works are the best that deal with this discipline.

I do not mean that I have rejected educational theory as a source, and an important one, for church-centered education. It is true that I tended to repudiate much of the work of George Albert Coe (a great educator), William Chave, and other early twentieth-century religious educators (but not that of Harrison Elliott) because it seemed to me that they were primarily educators with a religious orientation rather than church persons with an interest in education.

Under the influence of mid-twentieth-century theology, my first mission in both seminary and in church meetings, I believed, was to establish the theological credibility of the discipline and the practice of church education. Unlike James Michael Lee, who rejects the control of religious education by Roman Catholic theologians, I rejected the control of church education by *non*theologians and deplored the general lack of interest in theology and the type of theological thinking which they had borrowed from others.

I do not mean that I rejected all educational theory. For some time I found helpful the classification of educators as classical (Robert Maynard Hutchins), progressive (John Dewey), and essentialist. (I later substituted "relational" as the third approach, under the influence of Rueul Howe and, both through him and directly, that of Martin Buber.) This fairly simple approach later proved less useful than I thought, and I began to speak instead of *issues* in education, instruction/nurture, content/experience, education/impartation (Sherrill), and so on.

I was also concerned for many years with learning theory. I seriously tried to make sense out of the various theories, but not very successfully. After a student evaluation report in which there was widespread belief that the time we had spent on learning theory was the most wasted time of the semester, I gave up a systematic approach to learning theory and instead began to consider issues involved in understanding how people learn. For some years I tried to reject all forms of behaviorism, only to decide finally that it was a necessary but questionable concept—necessary because so much learning occurs through behavior modification; questionable because of the power it gives the teacher over students. I eventually came to the conclusion that it does not matter much where one begins in teaching—with cognitive input, with affective relationships, or with changing behavior—so long as the teaching-learning act embraces all three in some effective juxtaposition, including also the conative, or the changing of "willing" or motivation.

There came a time, however, when I realized I had been so preoccupied with theology that I had neglected the social sciences, including general education. In one attempt to rewrite the manuscript of 1961, I tried the approach of philosophies of education. Frankly, I found that as confusing and as unproductive as I had found learning theory.

It was in the midst of this search that James Michael Lee's writing came to my attention. Here was a religious educator who took the social sciences seriously, who knew those disciplines, and who used them in his religious education theory in relation to teaching a Christian lifestyle. Here was one also who had a "high" view of the teacher—not as a "leader" (a common term among church educators) but as one who structured the learning environment. My first enthusiasm has been somewhat tempered because of questions about his "behavioralism." The offsetting influence of John Westerhoff, on the congregation as a whole and on liturgy in particular, has led me to the conclusion that we need both the structured teaching of Lee and the enculturation, both unconscious and deliberate, of Westerhoff. I still continue to appreciate greatly the emphasis which Lee has had toward a more serious consideration of the teaching process.

It was not until my young colleague, Jack Seymour, then of Chicago Theological Seminary and now of Scarritt College, introduced me to his typology of religious education theories that I was able to construct for myself a satisfactory classification of teaching theories. What Seymour did, and what I have adapted from him, is a way of looking at religious education theory from a combined educational and theological perspective. The six on which I have most recently settled, like but somewhat different from his, are socialization/enculturation; religious instruction (in both "content" and lifestyle); interpretation (a correlation of Bible/theology and life); developmental (personal development); formation (spiritual development); and liberation/mission (education for social responsibility and mission). I do not place utlimate value on this, or any, classification; what I do find is that it helps me in understanding the considerable pluralism among contemporary religious educators.

This is where I now am with regard to education. I obviously continue to draw on educational practice—for teaching approaches, methods, techniques. But, because of my increasing orientation in practical theology (to which I now turn), I am not much closer to being a religious *educator* than I was thirty years ago. I am still a religious professional interested in and concerned about sources we can draw upon for *faith* and for education *in the faith* within the church.

Practical Theology

In 1970 we initiated a new curriculum at Perkins School of Theology which attempted to relate the various ministries to one another and to the world. One of the required courses in the sequence was practical theology. The integrated program lasted for only a short time, and we returned to the teaching of separate disciplines in ministry. A few years later we added a seminar in practical theology to our Doctor of Ministry program, taught first by my colleague in systematic theology, John Deschner. That course, offered alternately by several of us, has proved to be an integrative experience for D. Min. students and a source of great interest at least for those of us who teach it. Out of these experiences I have come increasingly to think of Christian religious education, along with other ministry specializations, as one aspect of this larger discipline. I have also come to believe that Schleiermacher was right, that practical theology is the capstone (a better word than "crown") of all theology.

I prefer to the term "practical" theology to "pastoral" theology, a term used especially in Roman Catholic circles. In brief, the concern of this discipline is the critical reflection on the life of the church as it relates to the world, in the light of, as my colleague Schubert Ogden puts it, the Christian witness of faith. In this process of reflective thinking the other theologies (biblical, historical, systematic, philosophical) are utilized as are the "human arts and sciences" (philosophy, psychology, the social sciences) in the analysis of and plans for re-forming the church and its ministry, general and representative. From this overall perspective, one then moves to his or her specialized ministry and the academic disciplines which support it. One does not always proceed in this order, of course; in reverse order, one seeks to see his or her own particular interest in the light of the total life of the church.

Two ministry specializations have especially needed this kind of integrative thinking, Christian religious education and pastoral care. In the early days of the Religious Education Movement, educational ministry sometimes seemed to exist alongside the life of the church rather than as an integral part of it. This was true in local churches where the "Sunday School department" was often semi-independent, a result partly of the fact that the earliest Sunday Schools often arose outside the organized church. It was due also to the kind of independent perspective which many of the pioneer theorists advocated. Interestingly, this same process, beginning in the 1950s, occurred with regard to pastoral care. The "Pastoral Counseling Center," often only loosely related to organized religion and occasionally not at all, has become the end result of this kind of highly specialized and particularized thinking about pastoral care.

There is a sense in which I have found in practical theology a rationale for the manner in which I have thought of Christian education throughout my professional life. I do not know that this perspective will prevail, but I believe that it should do so. What the discipline of practical theology does is to provide an integrating principle and process for all ministries, and what it does in the theological school is to provide an overarching discipline through which specialized disciplines can be seen in relationship. How this should happen is not yet clear. One course in a Doctor of Ministry program is considerably different from a total seminary curriculum. It does not seem desirable that the benefits which have come with specialization should be lost; how those benefits can be integrated in an overall view of ministry remains to be seen. It may be that the general perspective is all that can be provided. In any case, this discovery of what Schleiermacher was aiming toward 150 years ago has become one of the growing edges in my own thinking.

Historical

I will discuss only briefly a final area where I have had a great deal of interest but have found it difficult to interest *others*—the history of the church's concern with teaching. Kendig Cully has rightly observed that religious educators have been far less interested in their history than they ought to be. I find it somewhat absurd that it was after I had completed graduate school that I discovered St. Augustine's two superb essays on educational theory, De Magistro and The First Catechetical Instruction.

Lewis Sherrill's The Rise of Christian Education introduced me to pre-Christian, early Christian, and Medieval church theory and practice, and over the years I have read in both primary and secondary sources. Through Sherrill, and by reading the primary sources of the early church, I early discovered the relevance of the first centuries of Christian theory and practice. The church in a pagan society, not altogether unlike ours, found ways of communicating both faith and the faith without benefit of many day schools. Its use of the Liturgy of the Word and intense catechetical instruction for those being prepared for baptism, and its dependence on the family (as William Barclay rightly concludes) for the faith education of children provide clues for us today. Its scant use of classroom teaching provides substance for those who, like Westerhoff and Illych, believe we have come to depend too much on formal settings for Christian teaching. I do not mean to suggest, as liturgical scholars often do, that we should follow in detail the pattern of the early church—only that it may provide clues for future directions of the church's teaching.

The Reformation tended to set the pattern for Protestant teaching, with its emphasis on communicating the Word and the words of the faith. I have concluded that one of the problems of Protestantism is that its beginning coincided with the invention of movable type. As a consequence we tend to believe that better printed materials lead to better teaching, that a plethora of words both written and spoken will lead to faith. The Orthodox and Roman Catholics still depend more on the visual, on smell, on the tactile, on drama, and pageantry.

This has led me to the conclusion that a period I long neglected as virtually useless may be that which we need to attend to most carefully at the present, namely the Medieval period. Lewis Sherrill makes a great deal of the fact that teaching was largely symbolic during this long period—the visual symbol in architecture, mosaics, stained glass, and statuary; the dramatic in the Mass, in the miracle and morality plays; and life interpreted symbolically through the church at the center of the town with its open door drawing people in to worship and out to live in the world. I am not sure what we can make of this, but I am interested in exploring it further.

In any case, speaking as a Protestant, I believe that we need to reassess our more recent history in the light of that which went before. The Protestant Sunday School has had an exciting two hundred years of history, and, unlike I once believed, I think we must seriously try to adapt it to the present situation. To depend on it as the primary, or only, agency for teaching, however, is both to forget the more distant past and to ignore the kind of psychosocial data which was noted in a previous section. As religious educators, I believe we must discover our past as we look for ways of pointing to the future.

The Congregation

Throughout my life, including that time spent as a teacher in a school of theology that is part of a university, I have been essentially a church person. I have spent my professional life on the boundary between the academy and the church, always tilted somewhat toward the latter, with the result that I have not participated as fully in the life of the university as I might have done. The security that I have found in the womb of the church has also kept me from as complete a participation in the maelstrom of the world as I now recognize would have been desirable. I have prized my ordination, not because it set me apart from the general ministry, but because of what it gave me by way of opportunities to learn and, in turn, demanded of me by way of pastoral concern. I believe that I have had the best of two worlds, the university and the church; but I have missed much of the dimension of God's larger world that I might have enjoyed had I been more active in it.

I acknowledge the gifts which lay people have brought to me, both in my personal and professional life—and the two are so intertwined that I have not been able to separate them in this essay. In particular, I have profited from teaching off and on for more than thirty years an adult Sunday School class. During my first year of seminary teaching, a group of young adult "rebels" asked my wife and me to be their sponsor–teachers. Only two of the original charter members remain in the class, and we have grown old together, but the class has been and continues to give me a forum for a discussion of my and their concerns, and they have been an important support group in many personal ways.

There are many other groups which have contributed to my personal and professional life: children, youth, and adults. Many of these groups have been a part of First United Methodist Church of Dallas which has

served as my laboratory. My faith has been nourished by its three pastors—Robert E. Goodrich, Jr., and Ben Oliphint, now United Methodist bishops, and Walker L. Railey, whom I knew as student fewer than
ten years before he became my pastor. Members of the congregation's
educational staff have been both mentors and students: Estelle Blanton
Barber, who served as director of Christian education from 1931 to 1981;
Lila Coffey, whose devotion to children has been exemplary; and Jo
Biggerstaff, who is now both student and colleague.

Nor can I fail to acknowledge the debt I owe to colleagues at Perkins
School of Theology. I have already named a few of them; there are many
others, both living and dead, who have enhanced my professional life
and, often without their knowing it, my personal life also. How can I
forget the prodding of Joe Matthews, later of the Ecumenical Institute/
Institute of Cultural Affairs of Chicago? The graciousness of my senior
colleague in early days, James Seehorn Seneker, who studied under
George Albert Coe? My religious education colleagues, Charles Johnson, Wayne Banks, and Richard Murray? And many others that I do not
name?

A Concluding Postscript

I said at the beginning that I am eclectic, by nature and design. What I
have said in this essay must surely make it redundant to repeat the
statement. I have sometimes wished I were more like John Westerhoff or
James Michael Lee or Morton Kelsey, with a clear, unequivocal statement to make. Such persons have influenced me, but sooner or later I
managed to integrate their clarity into my mix of ideas so that, to them, I
am sure I seem to have betrayed their cause.

The present situation in religious education is the most exciting I
have experienced—even more so than the renaissance which occurred
in the 1960s, when the synthesis generated by George Albert Coe was
being replaced by that of Miller, Smart, and Sherrill. The greatest
change that has occurred is that Roman Catholic writers are adding to
both the pluralism and the depth of current thinking. Indeed, I am
sometimes apologetic to students because I seem to assign too many
Catholic writers! Evangelical Protestant writers are also being heard in
larger numbers and greater depth. Thanks to James Michael Lee and his
Religious Education Press, the breadth and depth of serious religious

education writing is available for all to read. In fact, I suspect that Religious Education Press is one of the most important developments of the past decade.

It *is* an exciting time for church educators! *Religious Education* magazine continues to provide an invaluable source; Religious Education Press, Paulist Press, and others have provided a wealth of materials for teaching and reading. How different it was when I began to teach in 1949!

I do not pretend to be able to discern the future. One thing is sure: The future of religious education is in good hands, and for that I am grateful.

Chapter 7

Toward Accountable Selfhood

C. Ellis Nelson

I did not start out to be a Christian educator. My childhood interest was aviation. In junior high school when I was asked to write an essay on "anything of interest," I usually wrote on the history of aviation. This was during the late 1920s; and, since the first flight of the Wright brothers had occurred in 1903, the essay was not very long!

I was influenced by Charles Lindbergh. I can still point out the exact spot where I was standing when the town whistles blew and the news was spread that Lindbergh had landed safely in Paris (1927). But it was the machine rather than the pilot that fascinated me. This interest, plus the friendship of my Boy Scout master, Irwin Neville, who was an engineer, led me to the decision that I would be an aeronautical engineer. However, aviation was so new at that time that I was advised to take mechanical engineering and then seek employment with a company that made airplanes.

I graduated from high school at age sixteen in the midst of the depression. My father was employed by the Magnolia Petroleum Company in Beaumont, Texas. The policy of this company was to share the available work rather than to lay off employees. This policy provided family security at a time when many other people had no jobs and little hope. When I was ready to go to college, my father was working only three days per week, so there was no money for college.

Skepticism About Numbers

I entered the local junior college where tuition was cheap. One of my required courses was physics. This course consisted of two parts: lectures by the professor and a weekly laboratory session where we did experiments to illustrate the lectures. The laboratory work was done in teams

160

of three or four students and under the supervision of Dr. Anderson. I had had a very good course in physics in high school the previous year, conducted the same way. The purpose of the laboratory was to do a "hands on" project so we could understand the formulae which explained actual phenomena. The experiments were about things such as how the speed of sound would vary according to the temperature.

I soon fell into the habit of going into our kitchen each Sunday afternoon when the family was out of the way and working out next week's experiment. We were allowed a 2 percent error, so I would decide on the amount of error and then work the formula backwards and arrive at the data. I would then write up the data sheets and take them with me to the laboratory session. During the laboratory session, our little team would check out the equipment and fool around as long a period of time as we thought necessary, turn in our data sheets, and then go to the corner drugstore and loaf. Our team was always the first one to complete the assignment. We got caught one day because I had done the Sunday calculations on the basis of warm temperature; but the weather turned cool and the heat in the laboratory room was hard on my predetermined data. Our laboratory team was too lazy to recalculate the problem, so we opened the windows to cool off the room. As soon as the room got near our predetermined temperature, we turned in our data sheets. Unfortunately, our zeal to have a cool laboratory, of course, alerted others to what we were doing. The data sheets were signed by a laboratory assistant and turned in to Dr. Anderson who scored them on the basis of 1 to 10. Our team had always gotten a score of 9 or 10, but that week our data sheets came back with a zero. We went to Dr. Anderson in protest, asking, "What is wrong with our data?" "Nothing is wrong," he said; "there is never anything wrong with your data, but your grade on this experiment is zero." The next week our grade was back to 9. We knew that he knew what we were doing; but he was not going to penalize us because, if we knew how to work the experiment backwards, we surely knew how to work it forward!

I don't want to load too much on this experience of a sixteen-year-old college freshman engineering student, but it will serve to illustrate my appreciation for—and skepticism about—numbers. This attitude was given some respectability when I took a graduate course in statistics from Dr. Gray and a course in tests and measurements from Dr. Manuel at the University of Texas. I learned that one must always examine the *source* of numbers, as well as the *inference* that is made from numbers.

On a number of occasions during my career I have been involved in surveys, studies based on questionnaires, interview scoring, evaluations, and research designs of various kinds. I have found that many claims of certainty about human conduct based on numbers become somewhat shaky when the method of obtaining the data is examined critically. So I sit still and listen when educators and psychologists present empirical data, but I also sit loose to the conclusions until I know exactly how they got the numbers they are displaying.

Congregational Nurture

My goal of becoming an aeronautical engineer changed while I was in college. It takes a bit of history to give a proper explanation.

I was born a Lutheran, as most Swedes are. My mother was an American but born of immigrant parents in a small, homogeneous Swedish Lutheran community north of Austin, Texas. My father was an immigrant. They met in Galveston, Texas, where my mother was church organist, choir director, and Sunday School administrator. Soon after I was born, they moved to Beaumont, Texas.

My earliest memories of church are associated with a small Lutheran church. It was some distance from our home, so we had to get ready rather early on Sunday morning and go together as a family on the streetcar. I cannot recall attending Sunday School in this church, but I do remember going to church with my family. When things got dull, Mother would reach into her purse and supply me with cookies. Christmas in this church was always celebrated by the whole congregation with a Christmas tree, gifts for all the children, and an informal worship service. My mother was the pianist and choir director of this little church, and my father was the treasurer. Apparently, the human relations in the church were very good because our family visited other families in the congregation. This Lutheran church was part of the Missouri Synod; and, according to what I was told, that denomination did not allow its members to belong to fraternal orders. My father did belong to such a group; so the choice was made to leave that small congregation and to join the Westminster Presbyterian Church. This came about because the pastor, Dr. T. M. Hunter, had called on my family when they had first moved to Beaumont and had kept in touch with our situation.

My family became deeply involved in this Presbyterian church. The church was large enough to have a full Christian education program, and it was located within walking distance of our home. Our family attended church on Sunday morning and evening, and we were all involved in Sunday School classes. In those days there was a Wednesday night "Prayer Meeting," and we seldom missed that informal Bible study session. Our mother often taught Sunday School classes and for a rather long time was superintendent of the Junior High Department. My father was an elder in the church.

My childhood memories of that church are of more than Sunday School teachers. My memories consist of individuals who knew me and called me by my name, of the events when we gathered for celebrations or for funerals, of leaders of the business community who were also leaders of the church. At that time I did not know that this congregation was a fairly good cross-section of the population of the town. We had wealthy store owners, managers of the major industries, workers, salesmen, clerks, and many professional people. We had members who were known to be "poor." We even had a few professional baseball players and one deaf "hobo" who wintered in our town! I now realize this heterogeneous congregation that nurtured me was largely the result of the ministry of Dr. Hunter, the man who was pastor during my formative years.

Dr. Hunter was an unusual person. He had an aristocratic bearing, a good education, a sharp mind, a ready smile, and a sort of "no-nonsense" approach to life. He was mainly a pastor, and the whole city was his parish. The wealthiest oil man in town was not religious by temperament, but he respected Dr. Hunter, gave him a car every Christmas, and sent his daughter with armed guard to the Presbyterian Sunday School. He also requested that Dr. Hunter conduct his funeral. Dr. Hunter's only known recreation was baseball. He attended all of the home games of the Beaumont Exporters, a farm club of Detroit, and that is why we had a few professional ball players in our church. One of Dr. Hunter's habits was to get up early each morning and make the rounds of hospitals. Medical doctors often said that, when they went into the hospital in the mornings, they often met Dr. Hunter coming out!

Dr. Hunter's winsomeness and the congregation's alertness to the Gospel created an atmosphere that attracted a number of young people to the ministry. In my time six young people entered the ministry, and all of them continued in that vocation throughout their careers. There were others before my formative years and others after I went away to college who decided to become ministers. So, that congregation had a special spiritual quality which is difficult to describe or to define.

One aspect of that special quality while I was active in the church was involvement. As young people we were involved in the church and in the mission of the church as well as in our Sunday School classes and youth groups. We were looked upon as a part of the congregation—individuals who could do significant things as well as receive what the congregation had to offer. Some of the young people sang in the choir, some ushered, some helped lead in worship from time to time, and some were involved in education and evangelism. This last activity needs explanation.

In those days—the 1930s—it was appropriate to start Sunday Schools in rapidly growing areas where there was no church. Our congregation did so, and we young people did most of the teaching. Edward S. Bayless was the person out of our inner circle of young people who was most attentive to this work when I was a youth in that church. Ed and I worked with others in such an "outpost" until we went away to college. Later, the "outpost" became a church. Ed was important to me because he was a few years older and was one of the best all-around persons I have ever known. We were closely associated at summer conferences for young people. Once, while still in our teen years, we set up, promoted, and managed a week-long camp for junior highs with almost no supervision from adults.

Now, back to the vocational decision. After two years at our local community college, I went to Texas A&M to continue my engineering training. There I came up against the real world of engineering—its people, its values, and its problems. Since it was a military school, the study of engineering was perhaps more abstract and depersonalized than necessary, but I soon became aware of my greater interest in people, the church, and society than in building machinery.

A&M College at that time was overcrowded. We were housed three to a dormitory room designed for two people. If anyone became ill, that person was treated in the military hospital. During the fall of my first semester at A&M, I had a mild case of the flu and spent about a week in the hospital. During that time I did a thorough assessment of my situation and decided that I was called to the ministry. After consultation with the Reverend Norman Anderson (pastor of the college Presbyterian church), my friends, my family, Dr. Hunter, and others, I decided to start the Presbyterian process of preparation for the ministry. I transferred to Austin College, a Presbyterian liberal arts college, where my sister was enrolled.

Once, about thirty years after these events, I was back in Beaumont to visit my family. Dr. John R. Hendrick was then the pastor of our church. Dr. Hendrick, who has a doctor's degree in Christian education and is a specialist in adult education and evangelism, has now gone to Austin Theological Seminary as a professor. Dr. Hendrick knew the Beaumont congregation—its lore and its people—and he had read my book, *Where Faith Begins*. He asked me if my nurture in that congregation was an important factor in the theory of Christian education found in that book. I said that I was sure this was true, although I had not consciously copied that congregation as a model. Dr. Hendrick had an important point, because *Where Faith Begins* is a justification, from the standpoint of the Bible and of social science, of the idea that the Christian faith is lived by a congregation. A congregation is the normal and natural way for faith and belief to be communicated.

This basic idea is simple and profound. It means that the interaction of the people in the congregation is curriculum of the most meaningful kind. What the congregation decides to do in its worship and work is considered "right and true." Persons who associate together because of their beliefs also provide an "expectation" of each other; they support each other and in innumerable ways provide the kind of human hope and love which reinforce beliefs about God, life, death, and moral values.

I have had no special problem in retailing this idea about the communication of Christian faith except among some professional religious educators who say that I have made everything educational so that nothing in particular can be labeled education. This criticism would be true if I had taken the position that participation in the life of the congregation is *all* that is required. That is not my position. Education in the sense of systematic study, age-group activities, and other means of intentional instruction is necessary for good congregational life and for the development of a person's faith.

So I have no argument with religious educators who want to define education in precise terms or who specialize in teaching methods. I only want to say we are to love God with the heart, soul, and strength as well as with the mind, and the elements which relate to the affections come through, and are made meaningful in, and community of believers.

Church and Society

Austin College (Sherman, Texas) proved to be just what I needed. It was a small, church-related college. Ed Bayless and Marion Reynolds, ministerial candidates from my home church, were there as well as a few others who were preparing for the ministry. I majored in history, partly because I liked the subject and partly because the senior professor was a perceptive person who enjoyed history. I happened to take a good course in American literature that paralleled my American church history readings. So I began to understand the interrelationship of historical events, religious beliefs, and the church as an institution and the literature emerging out of each historical epoch.

Austin Theological Seminary (Austin, Texas), where I did my preparation for ordination, is just beside the University of Texas. Some of our courses were taught in the university. Although the seminary was small, the instruction was good. The professors were active in the church, and Dr. T. W. Currie, the president, was deeply concerned about a variety of social matters, especially improving race relations. He worked out a plan with the Texas legislature whereby black people could obtain higher and professional education. The goal of the seminary was preparation of persons for ministry, and—since that was my goal—I was pleased with my training.

During these years I continued to be active in church youth and college student activities. The demonomination provided excellent adult leaders—Wallace Alston and Nelle Morton, for example—who personified the finest in the Christian faith and who also had a deep concern for social issues. At that time, social issues were primarily race relations, war and peace, economic justice, and the right of workers to form unions. Through these adult leaders, readings, and seminary courses I had a powerful ongoing education in the way the church should relate to society. These experiences were supplemented by attendance at many conferences in the United States and at the first World Youth Conference in Amsterdam in 1939. At these conferences I received a firsthand experience with young people and adults from social and political situations that had previously been unknown to me. In fact, in touring Nazi Germany after the Amsterdam conference with a German-speaking friend, I found I was in the middle of the most tense political situation of our time. The ship on which I returned from Europe was in New York harbor the night of August 31, 1939; and the next morning we heard on the radio that Germany had invaded Poland, thus starting World War II. Theology, church and society and human events were living things, not static subjects, to me. Although sociopolitical conditions have changed, the relationship of these elements to each other continues to intrigue me. I ponder our current situation both as to what it means and as to what we church educators can do to influence the quality of human life. In fact, I test theories of Christian education, and I evaluate theological systems on the basis of what their ultimate outcome will be for our common social and political life.

Psychogenetic Personality

My fieldwork during seminary years was with students at the University Presbyterian Church in Austin. After graduation and ordination, I was called by this church to be the first full-time director of what today we would call campus ministry. The seminary asked me to teach one course in Christian education, so I began teaching my first year out of seminary. I accepted these positions because I was interested, but I expected to move on to become the pastor of a church in a few years.

Because I had lived in a university environment for three years, knew some of the professors at the university and was now teaching a course in Christian education, I thought I should learn more about education. I enrolled in the University of Texas for an M.A. degree with educational psychology as my major and sociology as my minor. This was my first experience with what might be called secular social science, and I found it fascinating.

I came into this area of study at a time when cultural anthropology was being developed by Margaret Mead, Ruth Benedict, and others who had studied "whole" cultures. They asked questions about the role of culture in human development and formulated answers which transcended the fields of psychology, sociology, and anthropology. Thus, in the late 1930s and on into the 1950s there were many efforts to understand human life from a cultural perspective. The University of Chicago formed the Committee on Human Development, an interdisciplinary group, and many of my professors at the University of Texas were from Chicago.

Dr. Ralph Tyler, chairman of the University of Chicago's Human Development Committee, sponsored several community-wide studies of human development that sought to apply to American life the research methods of cultural anthropology. *Elmstown Youth* by A. B. Hollingshead is but one example. Dr. Robert J. Havighurst, another member of this Chicago Committee, had a special interest in character. He and members of the research team carried on studies of character development in the same communities where other teams were working. *Adolescent Character and Personality*, written with Hilda Taba, was one of the studies which came out of that era.

There were so many studies of this nature that at one time it was suggested that all social sciences would be blended into one general field. Such was the excitement of the 1940s as thoughtful researchers asked broad questions and received different answers from professors who had studied life in a more restricted way.

I was also deeply impressed by the studies sponsored by the American Youth Commission. Dr. Robert Sutherland, the director of that project and the author of the summary volume, *Color, Class, and Personality*, came to the University of Texas to become head of the Hogg Foundation for Mental Health and professor of sociology. I knew him personally, was related to the work of the foundation, and took a course with him. Through him and other professors I was introduced to the efforts of some social scientists to integrate psychology and sociology. Books such as *Children of Bondage* (John Dollard and Allison Davis), *Social Learning and Imitation* (Neal E. Miller and John Dollard), and *Deep South* (Allison Davis and G. Gardner) illustrate that effort to integrate the social sciences around issues related to human development. Somewhere in one of these books the term "psychogenetic" was used to describe the many factors working to influence an individual's personality—factors such as race, social class, child-rearing practices, economic resources, and so on, and these factors were researched to account for personality. The term did not stick, mainly because Erikson came along in a few years with his well-worked-out "psychosocial" model which took the whole life span into consideration.

About that same time, the Progressive Education Association, through one of its commissions, published books such as *The Adolescent Personality* (Peter Blos) and *Emotion and Conduct in Adolescence* (Caroline B. Zachry). These books related psychology to the cultural situation into which adolescents were coming of age and provided an educational illustration of the central ideas I found in the social sciences.

Out of all of this I came to understand and appreciate what culture does to shape our lives. Yet I did not become a social determinist, because I thought the role of religion was to stand against culture and shape it toward more acceptable standards.

While I was being exposed to a good deal of sociology and cultural anthropology, I took a summer at Massachusetts General Hospital to do clinical pastoral training, which was sponsored by Andover Newton Theological Seminary. There I had the experience of dealing with people in crisis situations and having my work with patients supervised by experienced chaplains. The weekly seminars by psychiatrists and others opened up the psychological side of life in an intense way. On weekends I went to the hospital library and read—mostly Freudian psychology. I remember reading all of Brill's *The Basic Writings of Sigmund Freud* rather slowly. Although Freudian psychology has undergone severe criticism and has been amended by the neo-Freudians, some of the basic ideas stuck. I tend to like Freudian orientation in psychology better than that of Carl Jung. Jung's psychology is a bit too idealistic and vague for my taste.

In retrospect I am thankful that my introduction to a serious study of the social sciences came after I had finished college and seminary. I had experienced enough diversity of life in different sections of the United States to have honest questions as to why attitudes and values were so different in different places, yet I was secure enough in my understanding of Christian faith and of myself to be open to new explanations. And throughout my career I have received help from social scientists who do an honest job of describing human life and who try to formulate reasons for what they see. Although I know that people can and do change as they go through life and although I believe that some development takes place over the years in our understanding of God, I am also convinced that much of what we are and become is laid down in early childhood. This basic importance of early psychosocial influences is what separates me from the "structural-developmental" school of thought in the moral realm.

Conscience and Moral Development

After serving for a term as the national director of youth work with the Board of Christian Education of the Presbyterian Church, U.S., I was called back to Austin Seminary to be professor of Christian education. Accepting that position was also an acknowledgement that Christian education was now my vocation. In the early 1950s, when it was my turn for a sabbatical, I enrolled in Columbia University and Union Theological Seminary (New York) for a Ph.D. degree. It would be impossible to state in a few paragraphs my development during those years. There were great professors in Union Seminary and Teachers College. All of them helped me develop a better understanding of theology, education, society, and human situations. But in the midst of it all I began to give special attention to the moral aspect of personhood.

When I was called to be a professor at Union Theological Seminary in 1957, I found that—after agreeing to teach the required course—I was allowed to offer whatever courses I thought desirable. I was tempted to offer a course in moral education, but I resisted this temptation because none of my readings in that field was satisfactory to me as a Christian educator. After a few years I came to the conclusion that conscience was the concept that I was groping after. Conscience is a concept embracing many of the areas in which I have had an interest. The content of conscience is social, as Emile Durkheim has shown; but the dynamics by which it grows and operates is psychological. Also, one's theology and ethical standards are all intertwined in conscience. So, I began to offer a seminar in conscience and moral development and to do some writing in this field.

I have great respect for the first scientific study in moral development by Hugh Hartshorne and Mark May, *Studies in the Nature of Character* (1928) because they brought a calm, dispassionate spirit of inquiry to what had heretofore been considered to be too subjective to assay. Their study opened morality to the same careful methods of investigation that were being used in other areas of human life. That they may have overdone the "situational" aspect of forming moral behavior is understandable in view of the prevailing ideas of the time—that moral conduct was a part of moral ideas or religious beliefs. Hartshorne and May opened the gates and many have entered the field of moral development.

My dissatisfaction with most of the researchers in moral development is that they have been too rational (the Farmington Trust approach and Lawrence Kohlberg), too idealistic (Robert Havighurst and the Bloxham Project Research Unit), too confident that classroom or psychological methods would change moral behavior (Ernest Ligon and the Values

Clarification Approach). Moral behavior and its motivation is an extremely complex matter. This is especially true for Christian educators: We must attend to the known factors such as the development of the mind, the quality of interpersonal relations, the psychological status of a person, and we must also be attentive to people's concept of God—no easy matter in itself. Given the state of the studies of moral education, I continue to consider conscience a more useful concept for Christian educators to investigate.

(Note to reader. Remember my first point—a certain skepticism about statistics? Let's pause here for an illustration. The Hartshorne and May study was a giant step forward in social research. The statistics from that study supported the assumptions of the study: Morals are learned in specific social situations and therefore how a child would behave in a different social situation is unpredictable—i.e., the trait of honesty as a general factor is rather weak. The statistical data in the Hartshorne and May study were recalculated in recent years with more sophisticated methods, and the results showed more of a general factor or trait than the original calculation of numbers had shown.)

The Accountable Self

I am now in the last phase of my career. After seven years as president of Louisville Theological Seminary, I am back to full-time teaching and research. The term as president of a seminary required me to be actively involved with local congregations, judicatories, church politics, and practical planning, and it put me in close touch with leaders in business and government. These experiences have broadened my outlook and have forced me to test academic work by its long-term effect rather than by its novelty or its strictly rational procedures. I continue to be as concerned about the way the congregation carries on its educational task, the way individuals develop their faith in God, and the Christianizing of conscience as I ever was. But I am now asking what may be a more basic question. Put negatively it is, "Why do we not have a sense of God's presence, a conviction about God's desire for our life, and motivation to increase the rule of God in our world?" Put positively it is, "How can we develop a selfhood that is accountable to God?"

To be accountable is more than to be responsible. The responsible self is a well-developed, mature person who feels a responsibility for self and society. To be accountable for one's life is to go beyond one's responsibility. It means that one is under demand to live a certain way and to accomplish certain purposes. One is clear enough about these things to know how well he/she is getting along and is concerned about God's approval. Such a conception, of course, is charged with theological problems, but I wonder if we should let these problems prevent our thinking about what the Bible describes so clearly. The experiences of Moses, Isaiah, Paul, and Peter with God—and the results in their lives and the changes they made in society—are well documented. We have others in the history of the Christian church who were touched by the spirit of God and whose lives were forever different because they became conscious of their accountability to God. This experience is sometimes termed a "calling."

At the moment, I think the best way to get at this religious experience is to use the theophanies in the Bible as models. Theologically, the problem is revelation; psychologically, it is religious experience; culturally, the problem is how to change values and attitudes in a society while living in that society. All of these matters are expressed in the literary form of theophany.

Brevard Childs, James Sanders, and other biblical scholars are now well into constructing a theological view of the Bible which takes seriously the meaning of the text as tradition formed and shaped it. This approach is quite different from the older critical method which assumed that, when the first strata of writings were found, we would be nearer to the truth. This contemporary view assumes the tradition that formed the canon of the Bible was a living faith which shaped the stories according to the people's own experiences with God; therefore, the account has integrity in the form in which we now have it. Given this approach to the Bible, I find that it is a wonderful paradigm of what revelation is like when experienced in a specific social setting. I hope to develop this idea in my next book.

Where Faith Begins explained how religious faith is handed on from one generation to another through the congregation. That was a study in continuity, but it left unexamined the other part of our Christian tradition—namely, discontinuity. The Bible and Christian history also affirm that God leads believers on to different beliefs or to radically reinterpreted older ideas. This, too, is part of what we Christian educators must heed. Caught as we are in extremely rapid change, we need to give more attention to the way God changes our common life and how we educators can foster such change. But please note that I am saying something different from classic conversional theology—I am suggesting a theology of theophanies. Experience with the God described in the Bible always leads a person to a form of life and a schedule of work that he/she wants to present to God as a "living sacrifice, holy and acceptable to God" (Rom. 12:1).

This is a different matter from a mere sense of forgiveness for sin. The theology of theophanies is a description of how God calls persons to create something different, with the person thus called feeling accountable to God for the results. How this discontinuity can be sought and honored as a part of the continuity of our tradition is my present concern.

Chapter 8

In Quest for the Connection:
Toward a Synapse of Theory and Practice

Harold William Burgess

Practical Problems Lead To Theory

On a January day in 1968, the dean of the Christian liberal arts college at which I was the newly-named "Director of Religious Affairs" asked me, on six days notice, to become the teacher for a required freshman-level religion course entitled "Christian Foundations." With a kind of smiling, naive joy I began, certain that I could help the students—most of them products of midwestern Sunday Schools—on to a vibrant investigation of their faith. It did not take long for the naive smile to become reshaped into a gray-spirited expression, marked in public by a stiff upper lip. There was a flurry of "drop slips." I thought it would be informative to read at least one of them to myself. "Reason for dropping this course: *BORING.*"

As the course progressed, some instinct for survival heightened my awareness of how students were responding to my pedagogical efforts. 1) A number of them were indeed genuinely interested and they involved themselves deeply in the educational process of the class. 2) Other students—a sizable segment of the class—were willing to memorize anything, nod supportive agreement when it seemed appropriate, or jump through any multiple-choice hoop so long as these things seemed likely to lead to a good grade. 3) A third group simply slumped in their seats and stared back at me in a most incredulous, blank, and uninvolved manner; their papers and oral participation duplicated their body language.

It was the third group, the blank-faced, unresponsive, mostly silent students who captured my interest. "What had been done to them?"

"Why was it that these products of growing Sunday Schools—schools that prided themselves on being true to the historic Christian faith— seemed so tuned out, so turned off, so spiritually lifeless?" And yet, I suspected that these well-meaning schools were congratulating them- selves on having turned out yet another crop of highly motivated Chris- tian students into the Christian college of their choice.

Looking back, it is my judgment that this "Christian Foundations" teaching assignment, and more specifically my response to it, was a major turning point in my career. For some reason that I cannot now explain in any completely satisfactory manner, I was convinced that a significant factor in the total picture was that many of the students in my course had not been well taught in their churches. Furthermore, I was not at all sure that they were being well taught in "Christian Founda- tions,"—at least if the quality of their involvement in the life of the Christian community was in any sense a measure of teaching effective- ness. Thus it was that my desire to have some better handles on under- standing the dynamics and consequences of church education, and an accompanying desire to have better tools for myself as a teacher of the Christian religion, led me directly to a reconsideration of the founda- tions of my understanding of Christian education. This essay is some- thing of a record of my personal journey in respect to this professional matter.

There appeared to be a number of approaches for reconsidering these foundations of educating young Christians. For the purpose of this discussion, I mention only two. First of all there was the possibility of reconsidering the nature of the theological and experiential foundations of the particular Evangelical expression of the Christian faith to which I was a fourth generation heir. As a matter of fact I did this, and, in the process I found myself affirming, even rejoicing in, my own faith and the somewhat pietistic tradition of which it was a part. I chose then (in the late 1960s and early 1970s), and I choose now to understand the Christian faith through the "lens model" that our present generation commonly labels "Evangelical." In passing, though, I must confess that I am not personally pleased with a certain spirit of triumphalism some- times connoted by the descriptive term evangelical. In the fuller and really more accurate meaning of the term, the Christian religion itself is at heart an expression of *Good News* and therefore is itself, by definition, evangelical.

A second approach to reconsidering foundations, the one which

eventually appeared to have the greatest promise for my particular
needs, was to examine the interaction of fundamental theoretical components in the actual process of teaching as a dimension in Christian
education. As I look back upon the process which led me to this approach, and from examining notes made to myself from time to time, I
believe that even prior to any formal studies in religious education I had
come to a tentative personal judgment that Sunday Schools, to say
nothing of such educational institutions as colleges and seminaries, did
not always succeed in teaching what they thought that they were teaching. Indeed, it seemed that results were many times antithetical to the
obvious aims. By way of example, I recall a certain theology professor
who, during his lectures, continually bewailed the number of graduates
who had become enemies of the institution in which he taught. Even
while in his course I had made a mental note that the teaching process
he employed seemed calculated to insure that that particular result
would be obtained. I do not think that the possibility ever crossed his
mind that a significant outcome of his rather aversive, dogmatic teaching was that some (admittedly not all) of us learned that his discipline
was, at best, a discipline to be endured—to the glory of God. To this day
I am quite certain that it was not this particular teacher whom Robert
Mager had in mind when he wrote:

> A teacher with insight once turned
> To a colleague and said, "I've discerned
> That if I'm aversive
> While waxing discursive
> My students detest what they've learned.

Interestingly enough, it was not from individuals associated with my
own tradition that I received the greatest help. Early on in my efforts at
examining what had happened to my "group 3" students, and what was
in fact happening to students whom I was teaching, I chanced to come
across D. Campbell Wyckoff's *The Gospel and Christian Education*.
The timely selection of this provocative book was in some sense a
"library accident." To be perfectly honest, I suppose that the appealing
title of this small volume was misleading as I decoded its possible meaning and promise—given my particular field of experience. Nonetheless,
three sentences from Wyckoff gave me my earliest grip on the handle I
was looking for: "The most critical problem that faces Christian educa-

tion, however, is the need to understand itself—to gain deep insight into what it is about. It needs to see how it is related to the cultural situation, to the church's life and thought, and to the educational process. This problem of self-understanding is the problem of theory."

Not long after my somewhat chance, but highly meaningful, encounter with Wyckoff's thought, it was time for me to think about completing my academic training. Because I happened to live close by the University of Notre Dame, my first step toward academia was an interview with the chairman of the Theology Department there. I listened carefully as he stated his departmental objectives. Even as he talked I was consciously beginning to realize that the classical program he had in mind had almost nothing to do with my particular growing awareness of need. The issues with which the chairman was concerned were far removed from theory as it related to Christian education. It was a fruitful interview, though, one of those "aha moments" on life's journey. I came to know for sure that classical theology was examining different questions than I was asking at that time. In addition I came to know that I could not be true to myself if I did not search further in other disciplines for the leverage to gain understanding of how the Christian religion might not only be better explained, but better taught. Wyckoff had given me hope, but I did not know quite where to continue the search.

Having deliberately made a decision not to study classical theology at that time, it was again a chance reading event which enabled me to move up to another level in my personal search for a more effective way of teaching the Christian religion. I happened upon a brochure describing the University of Notre Dame's Religious Instruction Program. The first paragraph scratched me exactly where I was itching: "The Notre Dame program concentrates on the *teaching* of religion, the process whereby a person can most fruitfully be *taught* to become a worthy son of God. Thus the program fundamentally is not one of either basic or applied theology, but rather one of the teaching–learning process." Within a matter of hours I had arranged for an interview in the Department of Education which housed the program described in the brochure. Once accepted, I signed up for "Foundations of Teaching," a course taught by James Michael Lee.

Early in this course, an issue raised by Lee made solid connection with my earlier reading from Wyckoff: "I firmly believe," to state this issue in Lee's words from his *The Flow of Religious Instruction*, "that one major cause for the relative inefficacy of much of contemporary religious instruction lies in the fact that most religion teachers hold one theory of religious instruction while at the same time they utilize pedagogical practices drawn from another highly conflicting theory. Consistency in the relationship between theory and practice is absolutely indispensable for the effectiveness, expansiveness, and fruitfulness of a practice in any domain whatsoever."

In other reading, however, I found that Christian educators historically have not been committed to examining foundation issues theoretically. Influenced, it seems, by the prevailing popular attitude toward theory (i.e., that it is not very useful), it has been more usual than not for practice to be elevated above theory. Some statements in the literature of the profession are indeed startling in this regard. Witness, for example, the following passage from the "Introductory" to the first issue of *Religious Education* (April, 1906): "Religious education has no academic problem. There are plenty of philosophers who will take care of the theoretical aspects of the subject. The Religious Education Association stands for practice rather than theory, experience rather than speculation." This same sentiment was echoed in a very wide range of literature. And, since I am a practical individual in many ways, this emphasis on practicality sounded very good indeed. After all, the concern which had led me into the field of Christian education as a serious area of study was a practical one. Because it seemed that the payoff from any effort at seriously reconsidering foundations from the perspective of theory might be slow in coming, I was faced with a temptation to attempt a quick, practical solution to the problem of how to teach those "group 3" students in my "Christian Foundations" course—or at the very least to get them to move into a more comfortable posture. I felt sorry for them, slumped in their seats as they were. There was plenty of support for such a decision from writers of almost all points on the theological spectrum. But, and this was fortunate, I could not think of any purely practical solution that was certain to work. So I continued on with the process of personally reconsidering foundations, theoretically.

It was yet a third reading event that brought the theory–practice relationship into a more usable focus for me. That was the reading of Charles Melchert's article, "Hope for the Profession," in the September–October 1972 issue of *Religious Education*. Melchert pinpointed the "bias toward the practical" as a fundamental crisis in the field of religious education attributable to the lack of theoretical and conceptual clarity on the part of religious educators. Thus in the field of religious education a decision to change a practice generally means little more than that it will be done differently. This change process leaves little room for consideration of theoretical grounds which might justify either the change or the new practice, and so contributes almost nothing to the fund of knowledge by which practice could be guided. A summarizing statement from my own writing is expressive of the point of view which I eventually adopted: "The problem with practice not based solidly on theory is that it has no sources which would encourage educational enrichment, change and reconstruction on a basis more solid than whim and fancy. Furthermore, too close a tie to practice typically results in a myopic perspective with reference to objectives. Consequently, evaluation of results is difficult. 'Consistent Christian education practice must thus,' in the words of Wyckoff, 'be based upon an informed and responsible theory.'"

As my journey progressed, Wyckoff's perceptions and Lee's analysis of issues proved crucial at a number of points. It was primarily from following their insights relating to the ordering of Christian education theory that I hit upon the notion of employing a system of investigative categories as a means of facilitating the analysis and description of the several ways of thinking about Christian religious education that were becoming more obvious in my reading of the literature. (It is important to record that during this period I continued to teach the course "Christian Foundations" and that my search for "handles" thus continued to have a certain sense of urgency. Furthermore, my teaching was improving to the point where I was awarded the first award for excellence in teaching given by the alumni association of the college at which I was teaching. Since this aware included a substantial check, I literally found attention to theory has cash value.)

For the better part of the early three quarters of the twentieth century, writers in the field of Christian education had been employing category systems as a means of pursuing theoretical considerations. Early in the century George Coe suggested that 1) definite societal goals, 2) an awareness of the original nature of students, 3) careful attention to the character of educational experience(s), and 4) understandable evaluative measures were necessary facets in discussing Christian religious education. Indeed, it occurred to me at some point during this stage of my professional journey that a significant reason for the long-term influence of Coe was directly related to the cogent presentation of his views made possible by the careful ordering of his theory according to its elements. In those writings of Wyckoff with which I was familiar during the early '70s, I found him to be working with six basic units (objective, scope, context, process, personnel, and timing) as a means of understanding and expressing theoretical issues. Wyckoff's contention that the employment of such categories was a necessary step in the development of Christian education as a discipline became an encouragement to my intuition both in my scholarly search and in my growth as a teacher in the classroom. Lee's synthesis of religion teaching in terms of four categories 1) environment, 2) teacher, 3) learner, and 4) subject-matter added shape to my personal quest for helpful units in which to think.

In pursuing the study underlying my writing of *An Invitation to Religious Education,*—the book which up to the present time is my most significant contribution to the field—I elected to employ the following categories as analytical and descriptive tools: 1) *aim,* including such notions as goal, purpose, objective, and the like; 2) *content,* the nature of this category I found was conceived quite differently by writers from the several schools of thought (Is content, for example, primarily a message or is it a set of constructs associated with the teaching act?); 3) *teacher,* the role (and method) of the teacher as an instrument in the teaching of religion, 4) *learner,* especially the way in which the learner acquires and in turn manifests religious learning outcomes; 5) *environment,* particularly the manner in which the environment functions as a controllable variable in teaching religion; and 6) *evaluation,* the way and the extent to which one might know the degree to which aims are, in fact, attained.

To carry my thought, which was becoming focused during my professional studies in the early '70s, just a bit further, four major approaches to theorizing about religious education seemed to emerge quite naturally from the literature. In the first place there was that historic approach which viewed religious education as being primarily concerned with the communication of a divinely ordained, individually salvific and life-ordering, message. Second, there was an approach, very much the antithesis of the first, which proceded from the assumption that experience as interpreted by scientific methodology was normative for religion itself as well as for religious education theory and practice. In this second approach, then, a "divine message" was replaced by "human responsibility." Theologically, the attention shifted from individual salvation to social salvation. In the third place there was a much less neatly bounded approach that placed a primary emphasis upon the organic relationship between Christian education and the Christian community, the church. This approach, in essential harmony with, for example, the thought of Reinhold Niebuhr, recognized the sinfulness of man and viewed salvation, individual and social, as being very much bound up with the ministry (including the teaching ministry) of the church. Finally, there was that approach, most evident in the writings of Lee, that centered its attention upon the teaching–learning process while attempting to maintain a value-free, yet dynamic, relationship with theology.

It should be obvious that while these four approaches (the traditional theological, the social-cultural, the contemporary theological, and the social science) appear to be distinct and significantly different, that it is misleading to imply that in and of themselves they are necessarily discrete. The actual boundary lines between them are sometimes not absolutely clear and, more importantly, there are often areas of correspondence between (and among) them. One helpful way of looking at these four approaches, first suggested by Carroll Tageson (one of my professors at the University of Notre Dame) is that while all four approaches are significantly different from one another, there is considerable evidence that the social-science approach is, in fact, generically different from the other three approaches. This is so, according to Tageson, because the normative decisions for the other approaches appear to be ultimately determined by theological considerations whereas for the social science approach, normative decisions seem ultimately related to the facts and laws of teaching–learning.

It is well beyond the scope of this chapter to further follow my personal vision 1) for the establishment of a system of *agreed upon* categories to promote the articulation of the relationship between, and the meshing of, theory and practice; and 2) through the employment of such categories to nurture a communicating environment among religious educators which would be supportive of the development of a body of validated information which could be used alike, for example, by Evangelical Protestants, Mainline Protestants, and Roman Catholics.

Theory into Practice

To record another dimension of my personal journey in "reconsidering foundations"—especially in respect to extending theory into practice—

it was yet another series of reading events which contributed to the development of my convictions. Johann Huizinga's celebrated study of the play element in culture, *Homo Ludens* and Herman Hesse's *Beneath the Wheel* were significant readings in opening certain attitudinal channels regarding what one might call "the spirit of the classroom." Huizinga, for example, notes the curious history of the word "school" which originally meant leisure, but has come to mean something quite the opposite: namely "a daily life of severe application from childhood onwards." In *Beneath the Wheel*, Hesse's young theology student, Hans, made empathetic contact with my mental images of my "group 3" students (remember them, the ones who slumped in their seats and stared back at me "in a most incredulous, blank, and uninvolved manner"). As Hesse dramatically records the spiritual and intellectual death of Hans at the hands of his teachers, I could hardly help wondering whether some such experience was behind the posture and attitude of certain of my "Christian Foundations" students. It seemed possible that for all of their recording of numerical growth some Sunday Schools might well be practicing a variety of "Christian education" that was resulting in a kind of unconfessed murder of inquiring minds. I thoughtfully considered my own teaching too—it was not easy to own up to some of the possible results. Both Huizinga and Hesse thus contributed significantly to a developing conviction on my part that a properly playful attitude might well contribute to a healthier climate for the teaching and learning of religion—and perhaps even of theology. This playful spirit, by the way, also seemed to pervade the writings of a number of individuals who, for me at least, were representative of the better expressions of Christianity: C. S. Lewis, Tolkien, and Bunyon, for example.

Obviously, though, some organization of the playfulness (or to use Huizinga's image, "rules of the game") would be necessary in a setting appropriate for the teaching of religion. Thus I began to read in the broad area of the philosophy of science (Toulmin, Kuhn, Wartofsky, among others). Not only did these authors help a great deal with matters relating to the "rules of the game," but they also revealed that a certain spirit of playfulness operated in the sciences. In particular, this "spirit" seemed to be an essential element in the processes and pattern by which the several scientific disciplines made practical application of an acquired knowledge of theory in progressing toward goals. Beyond this, the whole of the process was aided by the willingness of scientists to communicate freely with other scientists, even with those who were working within opposing explanatory frameworks. In sum, then, the scientist makes his predictions (sometimes this is very much in a playful spirit—Einstein, for example, liked to watch the figures in his investigative equations dance) based upon the results of previous experience—especially controlled experience which has been made public through its publication—and tests the results of those predictions in practice. Could it be, I wondered, that some such process might work for teaching religion in the church—or even in the college classroom?

James Michael Lee's writings and personal influence contributed very much to this phase in my reconsideration of foundations. Following his lead I began to investigate how the teaching of religion—even an Evangelical understanding of it—might profitably be viewed as hypothesis making and testing. "To teach," Lee writes in his *The Flow of Religious Instruction* (*The Flow* is Lee's understanding of "the rules of the game," so to speak), "is to predict. A teacher elects to employ pedagogical technique X rather than pedagogical technique Y because he predicts that X will be more effective than Y in producing a desired outcome in the learner." Lee argues that such an approach, based upon an awareness of the antecedent-consequent relationship, will be generative of pedagogical invention that will enhance the development and employment of more and more effective pedagogical practice.

Eventually the time came to try out something of this hypothesis making and testing in the classroom. This I attempted to do in the "spirit of playfulness." To do so necessitated laying out new game plans with my students—devised for each situation. I found that this way of teaching tended to liberate a free and inquiring spirit in my students. As an Evangelical, my heart was strangely warmed (to borrow an image from John Wesley—albeit a bit out of context) as this liberation brought a new mental as well as physical posture to the class. Class sessions began to be much more fun for me. The level of enthusiasm began to rise on the part of students. Indeed so far as the one particular course to which a number of references have been made, we began to realize some of those objectives which were a part of my original dream for "Christian Foundations." We began to become involved in a vibrant investigation of our faith. As I was able through observing better "rules of the game" to take my students more seriously as persons, they were, in turn, somehow able to take "the evangel" and the responsibilities of the Christian faith more seriously.

I am a typical teacher; it warms my heart to hear from former students. And so I do, regularly. Although it has now been five years since I last taught "Christian Foundations," seldom a month goes by that I do not hear by letter or by telephone from former students with thanks for some aspect of that course which has contributed to their Christian life. In many such cases I realize that a theoretical insight derived from, or incubated by, the likes of Wyckoff, Lee, and Melchert is at the assumptive base of the teaching even which had a resuscitative effect upon the faith of that particular student.

An Exercise

The concluding section of this essay is a kind of theoretical exercise addressed chiefly to Evangelicals. Others, of course, are welcome to read it. As I mentioned earlier, I am by personal faith and heritage an Evangelical. I happen to belong to a smaller denomination (the Missionary Church, for the inquisitive) with roots in Anabaptism and the Mennonite movement. Interestingly enough, we were expelled from that movement somewhat over a hundred years ago by an uptight bishop who had not read Huizinga's "rules of the game" passage. A proper "spirit of playfulness" might well have contributed much to the bishop's quality of leadership; indeed, it might have healed a developing church split. The actual charges which he laid against the early leaders of my particular denomination were three in number: 1) allowing public testimonies, 2) allowing public prayer meetings, and 3) allowing "protracted" (i.e., revival) meetings. To these three sins, once we were on our own, we added a number of others, including the establishment of Sunday Schools. We have some excellent ones, too. I had the privilege of growing up in some of the very best that the Missionary Church has to offer. My early Sunday School teachers not only studied the lesson, they also learned to know something about me as a person. My very first teacher, Mrs. Hattie Schoenhals, learned to know me well enough that on one occasion, when she was more than ninety years old and totally blind, she recognized the sound of my voice even though she had not heard me speak to her in more than ten years. My life is the richer for what good Sunday Schools, genuinely interested teachers, and a live Christian education program have contributed to my life. Sadly, though, not all who have grown up in Sunday Schools have come through alive—to revive Hesse's image.

For the sake of the present exercise, then, it is not necessary to enumerate in any complete manner all of what might be called "foundation elements" in a typical understanding of what many Evangelicals chose to call "Christian education." Such a list, though, would commonly include some rendering and division of the following items: 1) that the core subject-matter content is a divinely revealed and ordained, salvific message to be transmitted by the teacher to the student, and 2) that numerical growth is directly related to Christian education as an evaluative measure. Evangelical churches are supposed to grow, and, in some sectors, growth comes close to being an article of faith.

It is not my purpose to raise issue with the underlying rationale of the above elements. I would raise for consideration, however, the possibility that an unfortunate interaction between such components may result from a "myopic" attitude toward theoretical considerations, and that this attitude might well contribute to unhappy results in practice. (It was this unhappy situation which first impressed itself upon me while I was reflecting upon my experience in teaching "Christian Foundations"— and in particular, reflecting upon the bored, incredulous segment of the class.) Suppose that a well-meaning Sunday School teacher, laboring too tensely under the double burden imposed by the two theoretical components described above, casts about in his mind for some "effective" means of drawing individuals into his classroom 1) where they may be counted, and 2) where they may respond to the message. By eagerly seizing too uncritically upon some, possibly gimmicky, practice drawn from a theoretical framework quite out of harmony with his own convictions, it seems possible that this teacher may cause his students to become inoculated rather than evangelized, indoctrinated rather than educated, brought under bondage rather than set free.

One obvious way that such an evangelically intentioned teacher might thus myopically seize upon a practice drawn from a theoretical framework outside of his own is to employ reinforcement methods rooted in the stimulus-response paradigms of behavioral psychology. Students in Sunday Schools are quite often positively reinforced for attendance and for memorizing verses from the Bible by being given tickets, trinkets, candy bars, hamburgers, and even bicycles. (Remember Mark Twain's image of Tom Sawyer winning his Bible with red, blue, and yellow tickets). The above teacher should, at the very least, be conscious of a possible conflict between: a) his own theoretical framework which probably suggests that it is the reception of the evangel which changes the student from within, and b) his actual practice which is rooted in a theoretical viewpoint which understands change to be produced totally through environmental factors. There are times when I have been tempted to wonder whether B. F. Skinner, for example, has been given adequate credit for the growth of some Evangelical Sunday Schools. A second obvious possibility for an Evangelical teacher to select a practice potentially unsuited to his aims would be to uncritically employ a social-interactive teaching method rooted in the theoretical viewpoint that I have labeled "the social-cultural approach." Theorists who have worked from this perspective have typically found the individualized salvific goals common to Evangelical thinking quite unacceptable. George Coe, for example, wrote: "Our generation has come to see that the redemptive mission of the church is nothing less than that of transforming the social order itself into the brotherhood or family of God. We are not saved, each by himself, and then added to one another like marbles in a bag." Consistent with this perspective, more recent social-cultural theorists have given serious thought to developing methods that harmonize with their goals of social salvation. For example, methods of transmissive indoctrination, which they perceive are likely to be productive of conformity, are to be rejected in favor of democratic procedures (social-interactive methods) which (theoretically) tend to produce creative kinds of behavior. It seems clear that the teacher, or curriculum planner, ought to be aware of the intended outcomes of the methods which are selected.

There is yet a third theoretical framework which I wish to mention in the present exercise since it also seems problematical to Evangelicals in terms of selecting their Christian education practices. This is the framework I have designated "the contemporary theological approach." Without going at length into a matter that I have discussed at length elsewhere, I believe that a major difference between Evangelicals and a wide range of other Christians has to do with differences in their understanding of the nature of revelation. For the Evangelical, then, some formulation of the notion that the core subject-matter of Christian education is given through a once-for-all, the one-way revelation is a primary component of his theoretical perspective. From the "contemporary" point of view, on the other hand, revelation conceptualized as a here-and-now occurence within the Christian community, is a key element in theorizing about the procedure of teaching religion. Pedagogical procedure itself is accordingly looked upon as a potentially dynamic vehicle of Christian revelation. A review of the literature indicates, appropriately, that theorists of this viewpoint typically have a high degree of interest in "relational methods" of teaching. It is common for them to suggest that religious education takes place primarily within the Christian community—especially in the process of interaction between persons. Lewis Sherrill, an earlier and very competent writer of this school of thought, argued that the objective of method was to facilitate effective, spiritually uplifting, two-way communication between selves (see his *The Gift of Power*). My judgment is that it is possible for an Evangelical teacher, with the very best of intentions, to select a "relational method" that is indeed out of harmony with his or her own theory of revelation. The results of employing such a method may well prove confusing to the teacher who has not given adequate theoretical consideration to the outcome.

One further possibility for explaining the bored behavior of certain "group 3" students is related to the possible failure of Evangelical educational theory to distinguish sharply enough between evangelism and education. Could it be that one reason why "graduates" of Evangelical Sunday Schools are sometimes so "tuned out," so incredulous in their outlook, is that they have experienced a kind of inoculation effect through having received the same (sometimes inadequate) dose of evangelism over, and over, and over throughout their life? It seems possible that many Evangelical Sunday Schools are so committed to telling and retelling the old old story—so committed to the accession of individuals into the institution—that they have not made adequate theoretical (or for that matter, practical) room for the growth of the individual either as a Christian, or as a person. It seems to have been exceedingly hard for Evangelical theorists to build more adequate structures upon the Sunday School, in part, at least in America, because it has so long perceived itself largely as a evangelistic movement and medium of church, as distinguished from personal, growth.

It should be apparent that it is not my intention to denigrate any of the several theoretical frameworks I have included in this brief exercise. Indeed, the same exercise might well be profitably conducted from the perspective of any one of them. I do argue, however, that an awareness of the theoretical underpinnings of the particular pedagogical procedures we elect to practice will enhance our efforts to fulfill the awesome responsibility of teaching our Christian religion.

Chapter 9

The Formation of an Evangelist

Donald M. Joy

At the age of twenty-seven, as one of the newest ordained members of the Texas Conference, I waited to speak to Bishop Leslie R. Marston who was presiding at our annual business sessions. I had spoken with him now and then since I was fifteen or so, and now I had an offer to make to him: Would he like to ride with me to Shreveport where his next conference chairmanship would be and where I had been hired as the guest minister with youth during the annual family camp of the Louisiana Conference?

Bishop Marston said yes, and we drove from Baytown, Texas across into Louisiana the next Monday. He was then completing *From Age to Age a Living Witness*, our denominational history updated. So we discussed his observations, and he drew on some of my youthful perspectives. I'm afraid he was also making mental notes.

Within the year our family was moving to the denomination's headquarters at Winona Lake, Indiana. Bishop Marston had engineered my appointment and made possible subsequent appointments which, by August of 1958 would see me installed as the seventh Editor of Sunday School Literature, successor to distinguished editors with long tenures who had either been elected bishops or died in office in generations when there was no "retirement age." I was twenty-nine.

During the next thirteen years I would take responsibility for developing the Aldersgate Biblical Series, for designing and facilitating denominational planning for the Aldersgate Graded Curriculum— serving seven denominations, for supervising two lines of denominational curriculum development, revision, and publication. In short, I was to hold in my hands the teaching tools by which the theological and social ideals of my denomination would be shaped. Beyond that, by furnishing the influences of the chair and by virtue of my role in curriculum design, my name and my values would come to bear on six other denominations. Today, ten years after leaving that post to engage in seminary teaching, I am recognized by name in the unlikeliest of places—because of the privileges and responsibilities of those years. My sons were unable to ride on public transportation during their college years without being spotted by the telltale mark of their father's name.

At twenty-nine, however, my formal preparation for entering the professional world of Christian education and curriculum development was minimal. My masters-level work in education and counseling was not yet secured by the approved thesis at Southern Methodist University. My brief career at public-school teaching had been, I thought, only an in-between stop to earn money to sustain my voyage through theological seminary. Those three years of teaching public school music and junior-high English in Minneola, Kansas, had forced me into emergency study in education simply to maintain my temporary credentials from the Topeka office. From the age of sixteen, I had had a clear summons from the numinous tugging at my insides; I was to be a man for others, a minister, a missionary, a prophet. Oddly enough, the education courses at Greenville College, during the summer of 1951, and the extension courses from Emporia State Teachers College and Kansas State University across those three years were transported instantly into an orientation for ministry and the care of persons within the kingdom of Christ's summons to me.

When our family loaded into the Allied van to move from Kansas to Kentucky, the indelible mark of "educator" was superimposed on my previous visions of ministry. It was here at Asbury Theological Seminary that Dean W. D. Turkington's "The Teachings of Jesus" and Harold Mason's several explicitly "education" courses continued the ferment and the consolidation into vocation. The Asbury spirit of evangelism and of prophetic preaching combined during that time to send me out to Texas to a ministry that was a synchrony of evangelism and education. The Rockwall Free Methodist congregation was not exactly a place to establish a twelve-tiered "university system" of elective education. But house to house, and family to family, the practice of ministry combined the hope of Gospel with the means of nurture, and both I and the congregation experienced radical change and growth.

The Rockwall chapter cannot be written as easily as can my own. It is especially complex since there are so many persons involved. My debt to the people there is certainly greater than any obligation I may have created by my ministry among them. It was there that Bishop Marston found me, and, for reasons he never explained to me, it was his initiatives which moved me to the religious education specialization which now follows me and consumes my energy.

I managed to get my wits about me when I was negotiating the final arrangements for taking the interim "assistant to the publisher" slot in 1958. "If," I reasoned with the representatives of the Board of Administration, "I am to assume responsibility for the denominations curriculum directions, how can I do that with integrity when I have never had any training in curriculum development?" They easily consented. It was eight years later before the weight of responsibilities could be adjusted and I could begin doctoral level work.

Where would I look for curriculum development training? I had had the good fortune in the winter of 1959 to attend a conference of denominational editors meeting at Spring Mill State Park, near Mitchell, Indiana. Rachel Henderlite led stimulating Bible studies. D. Campbell Wyckoff was the guest resource person in curriculum. My host was Dr. Albert F. Harper, then serving the Church of the Nazarene in a post parallel to mine in the Free Methodist Church. He invited me as the fledgling curriculum executive of a sister denomination. My own governing board had forbidden my denomination's participation in any committee structures related to the National Council of Churches; hence I was in no sense a "member" of that conference group, but was a welcomed guest. I would return from that conference to read Henderlite and Wyckoff in the days ahead, but I turned a corner soon that would take me away from further graduate theological education and toward a great public university.

I began, in the early sixties, to read Norman Cousins editorials in *Saturday Review*. I also followed John Lear's science section in the *Review*. My wife and I subscribed to the *Chicago Tribune*. I wrestled with the black and civil-rights issue. The Free Methodist Church had been conceived in 1860 in abolitionist sentiment, but by 1960 it was all but "lily white." Our "Freedmen Societies" in Kansas had by then been abandoned as blacks moved to the cities. The underground tunnel still connected the basement level of the Aurora, Illinois church to the river nearby. But we were essentially racist. Our editorial staff consulted, then bought John Howard Griffin's serials which preceded his book *Black Like Me*. I was taking cues from A. W. Tozer, whose editorials in *Alliance Witness*, while provocative, were pale compared to his hard-hitting appeal for realism in Christian writing. It was Edmund Fuller who, with Tozer at a Wheaton writers' conference, had urged all of us to read John Updike. C. S. Lewis died in 1963, just as I discovered *Screwtape Letters*, and I phoned in an order to my bookseller buying up every Lewis title that sounded remotely interesting to me. It was to be his *Miracles* which carried me through my mid-life faith crisis which was yet to come.

The cross currents of the times in the mid-sixties and the books I was reading—which included all the James Baldwin's books I could locate as I searched for the black perspectives—generated an almost chemical ferment. I examined the books and articles which were coming from the seminaries and the graduate schools of theology. While much of what they said was comprehensible to me, most of it was "common sense," I was troubled by the fact that my limited experience with secular educational resources had created in me an appetite for fruit "fresh from the tree." I could observe that the occasional religious education writer who cited research into human development tended to be three academic generations behind what was then current in the secular journals. For that reason, I studied catalogues looking for universities which offered majors or degrees in curriculum development. I located three: Columbia University, the University of Chicago, and Indiana University. It was then 1965. I drove for interviews to Bloomington. Shirley Engle interviewed me while my family waited beneath a tree outside. A month later he phoned to ask me to come to campus for another interview. I made the second trip. Only then did it dawn on me that he was looking me over very closely. "You are thirty-six years old," he said. "It is not always easy to place a graduate who is turning forty." It wasn't easy to get into his program in curriculum development, and when the committee had approved my dissertation and my degree in 1969, as chairman of my committee, Dr. Engle shook my hand giving congratulations. "You are the fifth degree earned here in curriculum development," he said.

Where Did I Come From?

Doc Adams took me with forceps from my mother just two blocks from Boot Hill in Dodge City, Kansas. I was eight pounds and more. It was a difficult delivery. Dad was there to help, since it was a home delivery. During the spring of 1928 my parents moved from Terre Haute, Indiana, where mother's roots lay in the nearby Clay County farm family of Quillow Royer. Dad had been born in a granary quickly built as the first "above the ground" home of the Charles Joy family on their Cave community homestead farm. They had lived in a cave house, burrowed on the southern exposure of a bank as a protection from the blizzards and high winds of duststorms which often blew in from the northwest. Cave community, southwest of Dodge City, was to sustain the evangelistic and Christian education impact of my grandmother, Carrie Joy, who almost single-handedly carved out a Sunday School in the Cave school house. She conspired with other earnest Christians in the community to bring a Kentucky Methodist evangelist to the schoolhouse for a revival meeting. She was chagrined to discover that he used tobacco. Yet Grandpa Joy was converted in that meeting. To her great relief he stopped chewing tobacco and even promised each of his five sons a gold watch at age twenty-one if they would never use tobacco. That revival meeting led to the organizing of a church—the Cave Community Free Methodist Church. Virtually all of my early experience in the congregation was centered there. I eventually served as pastor of that small rural church at the same time I was teaching school at Minneola in 1949–52.

Grandma Joy was the first Sunday School teacher I remember. Of the half-dozen other children near my age, I had the privileged status. Only I was her grandson. I sat on her lap a lot. And I knew that in the next hour when the entire congregation knelt to pray I could raid her purse to find the carefully planted Wrigley's gum. While the pastor and others would lead in prayer, I would enjoy the gum, its stimulating flavor, and would inhale the extended delicious odor from the foil which had, only moments earlier, contained the chewing gum. The giant Providence Lithograph pictures, hanging from their giant stand are still imprinted on my memory. Grandma always gave each of us a tiny replica of the giant picture to take home with us. B. L. Olmstead was editor and writer of my curriculum pieces; I would later be his immediate successor. Helen Hull bought the manuscripts and art which leaped at me from *Primary Friend* and *Story Trails*. I would later find her on the editorial staff I was to lead, and would learn much from her. Helen introduced me to Norman Cousins and Wheaton writers' conferences and to some truly fine novels before her early retirement. But she had spanned my childhood and had tutored me as her "senior editor." I never remember making "paper airplanes" out of the Sunday School papers, but I have vivid memories of reading stories and poems from them. I wrote letters to pen pals whose addresses I found there. Eventually I wrote poetry that got published at Winona Lake. Something in me died when Louise Tenney put Oliver Haslam's name to one of my poems as the author and printed it in *The Free Methodist*. She would be nearing retirement when I handled the magazine after the sudden death of Dr. J. F. Gregory for whom she worked as office editor. I never mentioned the pain of her editorial error.

I have no other Sunday School memory between preschool and junior high. During those years I was a child of poverty; the dust-bowl era was cruel, and survival in Western Kansas was, in itself, a kind of miracle. I had friends both at school and at church. But it was the church friends with whom our family shared meals. We wept with them at tragedy and loss. I went skinny dipping with friends on Sunday afternoons, and shared everything with my cousin Rex Hoffman. Rex's father was a high-spirited and devout man; his temper and his fervent public praying created a paradox in me which has fueled a lifelong quest which today treasures assertiveness and piety, though Uncle John baffled me for a long time. Sunday afternoons were often on the Hoffman farm where Sabbath rest precluded everything but evening milking and feeding the livestock. Rex and I had the run of the farm with its horses and its rattlesnake-infested pasturelands.

When I turned thirteen Mrs. Schmidt was my Sunday School teacher. Eunice Gardner was the only girl in the school. Clayton, Ed, Chuck, Quentin, with Rex and me, turned the class into a lively, sometimes physically active circus. We met on the raised platform, behind the pulpit, with a sort of choir curtain pulled from one side of the pulpit alcove to the other to screen us visually. But our sound contamination must have bled out into the sanctuary where three different classes were in session. Uncle John was one of the teachers. Lula Gardner was another. I could follow them in their intricate biblical interpretations, especially those theories they espoused with great feeling. But it was Mrs. Schmidt who won me, somehow. She gave each of us the most beautiful wall plaque at Christmas that first year. She had painted each frame by hand. She had used an art technique by which foil was adhered to the glass and the words she wanted us to burn into our lives were somehow lifted out of the foil. Through the bright colored foil came the stark but appealing words: "God First." It wasn't easy to contemplate what life would be like at thirteen if God were "first." But I knew then that it was a task that I could not avoid—making God the top priority of my life. I still treasure the small framed art piece; it remains aspiration and often accuses me in a gentle way.

What Happened to Me?

I was a man at thirteen. I grew more than twelve inches in height that year. At school my best friends turned me into an "instant" basketball player—simply because I was tall enough to play center and could jump better than most people. When I was four years old, my Grandma was sometimes calling me, "My little preacher boy." My peers in high school, sometimes in derision, dubbed me "preacher" at a point in my life when I was interested, instead, in a dance band of my own. Oddly enough, at seventeen, my vocation appeared in a moment's mental vision which remains indelible—one in which I am serving as the instrument of liberation to one person, a peer of my school days whom I hardly knew and did not particularly admire. He was the victim of what I now regard as "religious abuse" by his parents and his congregation.

My vocation was confirmed by the decision makers in the small rural church I was later to serve as pastor. They issued me the first of a series of licenses which indicated their endorsement of me and, in some special sense, their "responsibility for me—forever." Today, my ordination and its summons to a vocation in the care of persons is firmly bonded to my daily life as much by those people of the high plains and the authority they vested in me as by the hands of the bishop or other elders who laid holy hands on my head symbolizing the transfer of ecclesiastical authority.

My structural view of reality has undergone some major reconstructions since the age of seventeen. During my sophomore year of college, confronted with the physical and human sciences as if for the first time, I found myself also immersed in a men's dormitory-living environment with newly returning World War II veterans and with several non-veterans who were the products of troubled homes. Something or Someone evoked within me an enormous sense of a) respect for the value of every person, and b) hope that every one of them might rise above trouble and tragedy to peace and fulfillment. In some deep radical sense I became an "evangelist"—one who articulated that optimism to others. It was the "underworld" crowd on my campus which elected me student president. In adult life, criminals and delinquents have consistently sought me out.

At thirty-five, with two masters-level degrees behind me, each put in place with gigantic amounts of reading and writing, I was still in search of a basic theory of humanity to match what I was experiencing. By this time, I was holding eagerly to the life and teaching of Jesus of Nazareth who I regarded as the original and prototype Evangel. I was well saturated in C. S. Lewis. I was a well-read and well-informed Methodist in the Wesley tradition. Much later, nearly fifty, I discovered Herman Hesse's "A Bit of Theology." The decisive catalyst for me at mid-life was William Lynch's tip. I was trying to nail down my research problem at Indiana University. "Have you looked at Piaget's *The Moral Judgment of the Child?*" Somehow I had entirely missed Piaget in undergraduate and even graduate education at SMU. The center half of that 1932 title was to weave together a high-fidelity pattern which organized my life experience in a highly satisfying way. His observations of children playing marbles and dealing with rules led him to articulate perceptions of adult constraint, unilateral respect, moral realism, and to trace the consequences of cooperation in the changing views of justice. I have painted the main lines of that satisfying pattern into two chapters: "Life as Pilgrimage," and "Moral Development and Christian Holiness: John Wesley's Faith Pilgrimage." They appear in my *Moral Development Foundations: Alternatives to Agnosticism.*

So, here I am, found at last by a research and theoretical base-line on which I was already intuitively ministering and developing curriculum. My research published in 1969 on *Effects of Value-Oriented Instruction in the Church and in the Home* was paralleled by the launching of the Aldersgate Graded Curriculum. It was put into service in more than a half-dozen denominations in September of 1969. The training manual for volunteer lay staff had appeared in the early months of 1969, *Meaningful Learning in the Church.*

Today everything I touch is left printed with my belief that the human adventure is dynamic, relational, aspirational, epochal, and cumulative. I regard this more general human pattern as especially responsive to the grace of God who has given us his image, creating us male and female to run the essential minimum spectrum of that image. The divine image has implanted in us the indelible/imprinted marks of justice/righteousness and attachment/affection. These potentialities may be captured for the good, the ennobling, for the common welfare; or they may be seduced for evil, the destructive, the common dissipation.

Reflection: Apology

The editors' instructions for this chapter were clear. "The chapter should not deal with the *personal* odyssey of the person (whether farm boy or city lad) but rather should deal with the *professional* odyssey of the individual." I have failed to comply. My professional effectiveness today and my commitment to concrete experience as the primary source of any theory or theology (after all, God acted before men wrote!) is rooted in my life experience first and in professional and theoretical sources only a pale second. I can read the "sources," and I try to heed the pitfalls which historians point out, but I have little patience with the dullness, the ineptitude, and the commonsense redundancy which plagues much of the literature in the field of Christian religious education.

Chapter 10

Visions and Realities

Eugene F. Hemrick

A Context

Some call it legacy, others heritage or background. No matter how you phrase it, the words suggest we are not a composition of self unto self. Rather, we are composed of innummerable outside influences. Why certain influences take hold of us more than others I leave to the wisdom of a Sophocles. What follows is a mosaic of inspirational moments, the persons who were behind them, and how they influenced my thinking in the world of catechetics. Before starting I believe a need for con-textualization is in order.

Reflecting on this chapter has made me conscious that my approach to catechetics has been very unlike that of my peers. It has developed from a feeling that if the catechetical world is to be changed, the use of reflection is the best way to achieve this. It is this action of reflection which seeks to understand essence, causes and relationships—in short, to define existence. In contrast to many of my peers, I have not focused on the content of theology in order to develop a new theology, or to develop new models and programs. My content, on the contrary, has been the operations within catechetics. These consist of such processes as teacher training and evaluation, administrative policies and pro-cedures, and learning outcomes. I have approached religion teachers with two simple questions, "What are we doing to the students?" What are the students doing to us?"

I feel that although one cannot totally measure the depth of a person's faith or fully understand the effectiveness of catechetics, an assessment can be made of the means we employ to cooperate with God's grace. There is a responsibility for good teaching and administration and cre-ative approaches in catechetics. The effectiveness of these processes can be identified, analysed, and through analysis improved.

It is also my belief that the tenets of faith are not as much a stumbling block to catechesis as are the poor pedagogical procedures that are employed in transmitting them.

This desire to analyze the causes of impact have led me to picture my lifestyle as one continuous experiment after another. I further find I am greatly fulfilled when I pass on the findings of these experiments to others for application to their particular situation. I hope this brief explanation will help the reader de-complicate the complicated writings of this author.

The Period of Inspiration

If a child's heart is reached by storytelling, then I was, and still am a child at heart. My first memorable contact with formal catechetics came not in the classroom, but rather from the pulpit. (I say "formal catechetics" because I believe the foundation of of catechetics is not found so much in institutionalized religion as it is at our parent's knee.) On Sunday we were often treated to wholesome homilies by my pastor. He was a master storyteller. During those ten or fifteen minutes our minds would weave in and out of the Holy land. He had us talking with Hebrews, St. Paul, and of course, Christ. He knew how to personally draw you into the theme and be "there."

As I drew closer to my pastor I came to better understand his gift of preaching. He had traveled throughout the world. From these travels he had gathered an inexhaustible list of lived experiences. They provided exciting ancedotes. He was a copious reader in more than one language. His presentations were very orderly, reflecting long hours of preparation. But most of all, he loved to preach. I would often visit him on a late Saturday evening and watch him relish polishing an idea to be presented the next morning.

Years later, when studying the derivation of the words *educator* and *scholar*, I came to realize this man was both.

In Hermann Hesse's book *Magister Ludi* there is an opening episode in which a young talented musician, Joseph Knecht, performs his first duet with the grand music master of the country. There then follows a description of the rhapsodic excitement Knecht discovers anew in music; how he sees the "world of Mind behind the music, the joy-giving harmony of law and freedom, of service and rule; and how he vows at that moment to unite his life to this higher order." This sacramental union, as Hesse calls it, was what I sensed between my pastor and the liturgy of the Word. I also believe that a similar union was being forged within me at that time.

Recalling another type of catechesis I received, I remember particularly a church history teacher, much like my pastor, who taught me a love for history. He too, was well-traveled and employed imaginative ancedotes in his classes. Most appealing of all was his logic, a beautiful road map with many exquisite details. He started from a set-point and methodically led to a well-rounded conclusion. Because of his orderly presentations he seemed to be in continuous control of the subject matter, and thus be one with it.

In addition to these two men, later there were retreat masters, professors of theology, Scripture, and philosophy who had that same engaging gift of touching the imagination.

As I reflect on my major seminary days in particular, I feel my attraction to imaginative thought is a very healthy stage of growth all youth undergo. At eighteen my mind was feeling its muscles for the first time. The surge of new ideas and the exhilaration of power in manipulating them was intoxicating. Looked at through the pedagogical categories of process and product, one might say I was enamored with the process of mental gymnastics which was operating in a philosophic-theologic product atmosphere. I don't know what I loved better. On the one hand there was the enjoyment one finds in gaming with ideas, turning them upside down, combining them and creating new insights. On the other hand there was the feeling of adventure in entering the historic world of the church, of ancient Greeks and Romans, and vicariously experiencing their golden ages of creativity.

I must admit that a seminary environment, in which much of this inspiration was born, helped immensely. There were no distractions. I was young, very idealistic, and I felt a definite calling. The spiritual exercises, the hours of silence, the absence of newspapers, magazines, radios, and television in one way deprived us of the sensations most people live on daily. And yet, the deprivation was compensated for with a sense of oneness with self and the higher order of learning.

Many who go through the seminary disapprove of this type of trade-off. They abhor the isolation of the seminary and consider it an unreal world which ill prepares us for the real world in which our priesthood operates. They contend it desensitizes us to family life and social-justice issues and thus dehumanizes us. Personally, I never felt this way. It is this strong positive feeling about my education that has influenced me to bank on it when writing on such topics as "burn-out." In these articles I find myself encouraging DREs to develop a love for reflection and to create a space similar to that which comes from prayer and silence. My enthusiasm for history and philosophy prompts me to advise them to combine the wisdom of the present age with that of the ancient philosophers and spiritual writers.

Leaving the seminary after ordination I received my first opportunity to emulate my heroes of the word. Whether it was a honeymoon experience, or people just being nice to a newly ordained priest, I do remember the thrill I received when first preaching and teaching religion. They were good first experiences.

I also experienced a wholesome support system in my first parish. The pastor encouraged me to continue my studies. The other priests in the rectory worked hard on their homilies. Frequently they taught religion in our elementary school. The Sisters were into the newest theology and loved to challenge us. This community spirit and the challenges it presented were an ideal setting for a beginning.

The Period of Specialist

The experiences recounted in the last couple of pages motivated me to study more intently the dynamics of good preaching and teaching. I had always wanted a specialty. I thus began to gravitate toward an area I enjoyed, and in which I was receiving strong support. I believe the desire to analyse the art of communication was what first caused me to think about research and its connection to the field of catechetics. I felt if I could somehow identify and quantify the particular variables that were operating in an inspirational class I would cultivate one of the most valuable qualities of my priesthood. I wanted to be able to imitate those teachers who captivated me as a youth!

The scientific aspect of this pursuit likewise caught my imagination. (I often wonder if my awe for working in a laboratory setting might have stemmed from the seven years of a quiet seminary setting in which the library or the study were considered the fonts of wisdom?) To picture myself analysing and conducting field experiments had great appeal. Through such a discipline I proudly thought of myself making a great contribution to religious education.

After five years of parish life and graduate studies at Loyola in Chicago, I pursued a doctorate in education at Notre Dame. There I had the opportunity to test whether research was for me and the world of catechetics. I was again blessed by a strong support system. Thanks to persons such as James Michael Lee, Walter Doyle, William Tageson, Raymond Whiteman, William Friend, and the Holy Cross Brothers I received the needed encouragement to complete my doctorate in the specialized area of my choice. I chose as my specialized area the study of teacher behavior as it affects religious education. I say "my choice" because so often a person studying for a doctorate ends up doing a dissertation on a topic far removed from his or her area of personal interest. Sometimes this is caused by a self-serving director. Often it is the fault of the student who has no specific vision of where he or she is going. I often wonder if we, in higher academia, might serve graduate students better if we required them to specify some type of present and future vision prior to their entering our programs. In any event I experienced great freedom at Notre Dame not only in the choice of my dissertation, but in all other academic phases as well.

Beginning in 1970 at Notre Dame, until the present, my heart's desire to be a specialist found its fulfillment. I have videotaped not only religion, but also college, business, and television presentations. In each analysis I have searched for those particular gifts of communication, which if captured, could create a Knecht connection.

In the effort to identify the essence of effective communication I have discovered a variety of fascinating models. Some examples of these are the Abba Eban model in which exact wording, perfect diction, and exquisite logic are a hallmark; the Vince Lombardi model in which clarity, details, contextualization, visual aids, and a well-ordered presentation are prominant; the Johnny Carson model which utilizes intermitent humor to loosen the atmosphere for better dialogue; the Lawrence Oliver model which emphasizes demonstrative sentences to create emphasis; and finally, there is Mother Teresa whose poverty of spirit transcends any model and goes directly to the heart.

During my research on teacher behavior in religious education I have likewise developed a list of favorite skills. These, I believe, greatly improve teaching. A good story well told is a winner always. No matter whether the story is told to a sophisticated group of scientists or a mother's club, people love the ancient art of storytelling.

An observation on storytelling is in order here. I have found, after studying religious education programs, that teachers often will rely more on a film than on themselves to tell a story. Films do make a strong impact. But I wonder sometimes if they are not relied upon too heavily, which robs us of that extra-special personal touch. It is enjoyable to listen to a violin or piano concerto on the latest stereo equipment with all the flaws screened out. And yet one does not really experience music until the artist himself or herself is experienced. There are so many added dimensions in a concert hall a record cannot duplicate. So too is it true regarding audio-visual aids and the artistry of the teacher.

I am realistic enough to know that today's religion teachers compete against the overwhelming odds of attractive television programs and marketing techniques. These have a way of calling one's best teaching skills into question. They also entice one to use modern media. To employ the latest technology, and yet maintain personal contact, seems to be a problem of our electronic age we have not fully faced up to in religious education.

Other winning qualities I have found within a presentation or dialogue include the use of concrete, colorful examples, narratives within a narrative, and the timely use of details, similies, and contrasts. A good sense of humor is a must, as is the ability to listen and accept other opinions that need sounding out. Finally, there is the need of a sixth sense to understand an audience's disposition and the mood of the times. These qualities are what I feel to be the *crème de la crème* of an artistic teacher.

In working with teacher training I have learned that the best way to improve the pedagogical procedures of religion teachers is not found, however, in superimposing on them a list of skills. Rather, teachers should be studied first by observing how they teach. These observations should then be carefully analysed to identify those particular qualities and skills which are their unique, par-excellence, style. Feedback should follow which aims at reinforcing what is effective in that pedagogical style, and improving those areas that could be more effective. Hence, I start with the teacher's qualities, rather than preconceived lists of desirable skills. If and where possible, new skills are encouraged only after existing ones are solidified.

For a moment I must comment on one of the greatest frustrations I have encountered in training catechists. I have found that some people take to teaching religion like a duck takes to water, while others take to it like a fish out of water. The reason why some can teach and others cannot lies hidden somewhere in the parable of the talents. As I mellow with age I accept as fact that you cannot fashion a person into a good teacher. If a person has innate talent in teaching one can improve it. If talent is lacking the best one can accomplish is to help a person become less dangerous to himself or herself. These remarks are not meant to sound a note of negative fatalism. Rather, they come from the feeling that persons who lack teaching talent should be channeled into those areas of catechetics that do not require teaching.

A word must be said here about the volunteer religion teachers who have good will, but are not effective teachers. Many parishes rely on volunteers who are unprepared. Even if they were prepared, they should not teach. These parishes rely on such people because they have no one else.

It is true, good will and zeal often are better witnesses to the faith than polished pedagogy. And yet we are told "the blind should not lead the blind." St. Teresa of Avila felt that priests who were poor confessors did more damage than good. Having analyzed well-meaning, but poor, teachers, I have seen many so overmoralize their students as to demoralize them. They take the very health out of religion.

If a person is good hearted however, should we not let our heart be overruled and accept them? Is there not a justification which says in such love community is born and God works in his own mysterious way for the good? Is it not also true that some parishes, and especially missions, have no choice?

I have a hard time accepting the proposition that one can get backed into a corner and have no choice when it comes to catechesis. Programs can be designed to utilize well-meaning persons who are not teacher types. Sometimes a little extra effort in screening or recruiting can avoid the dilemma before it arises. I believe reflection and ingenuity can overcome the paucity of talent. If we cannot fill our classrooms with good teachers perhaps another model of teaching should be employed that utilizes nonteachers as part of a team under a qualified teacher. If a parish has no creative talent to develop new models, perhaps it should combine its programs with another parish that is more fortunate. There are many "if-this-is-not-so-perhaps-that-is" possibilities that offer hope.

This realization has led me to several related conclusions. I believe religious education cannot rely on a classroom model solely, which in turn relies on good teachers. Talented educators are not all that available. Some religious education programs are fortunate to have one good teacher. Other support systems must be brought into play. These systems might include good homilies and liturgies, the example of works of charity, parish sensitivity to social justice issues, community spirit, and the witness each person gives.

Closely related to this is my response to the question, "What are the most important areas of concern on which a DRE should focus for success?" Having specialized in teacher training my first tendency would naturally be to say teacher training should receive priority. Good models of teaching have deeply influenced my understanding of the faith. I have experienced the power of the well-spoken word. I like the professional feeling that comes with being a specialist. And too, for DREs to specialize in one area and not be distracted by many others is much better for keeping themselves under control. Yet, when I reflect on the environment in which my professors taught and the support I received from the surrounding environment of my experiences in the seminary and the university and my first parish, I am now more prone to tell DREs something else. "Include the teaching model but look beyond it." I feel they should attend more to the community spirit of the pastor, associate pastor, parish committees, parents, and the faculty. Do those youths or adults we are trying to instill with the faith sense a healthy spirit of teamwork and collaboration from the instillers? Is there a strong effort by the staff to create a sense of personal responsibility among all parishioners concerned, rather than only being concerned with the catechists and a school model? Is there a fear of loss of control if the attempt is made to involve those parishoners whose personal involvement can speak louder than the spoken word?

No doubt the holistic approach recommended here requires of DREs a new style of management. More systems must be included within the system and, thus, more personnel employed. Burn-out is a threat. And yet, if the concept of "division of labor" is employed and DREs adhere to the principles of community-building, I believe they have an adequate arsenal ready to meet the challenge of this approach. Is it really too much of the "Brave New World" thinking to suggest that DREs consider one of their roles to be that of a "systems analyst"?

The Period of New Vistas

During the same time I was involved with communication and pedagogical behavioral skills another type of influence was affecting me.

For many, the effect of Vatican II was to experience a new liturgy and a new way of perceiving church. For me, it was a time of extensive travels, speaking both figuratively and literally. I, like Joseph Knecht, after listening to homilies and classes in which the pastor or professor had been to the Holy Land or visited famous cities, promised myself to do likewise. I made good on that promise and traveled to Europe and Central America.

During the same time I was also on another type of trip. The field of catechetics was enjoying a renewed vigor. I had the good fortune to return to graduate school at Loyola in Chicago and imbibe the newest trends in theology. I found myself once again reading copiously about living faith, commitment, form criticism, salvation history, the Omega point, the anthropological approach, and of course, pre-evangelization/evangelization/catechesis. What was more exciting, we not only read the works of great scholars, but many were our professors.

New ideas brought about by travel and graduate school gave me a sense of openness I never experienced before. As I reflect on this now in relation to my involvement with research I wonder if the desire to create openness and new interesting possibilities in religious education is another reason behind my present involvement with research. Travel throws one into foreign worlds and customs. At first it is like a bolt of lightning to discover that not everyone does things the way we do. It is also shaking to find how dependent we have become on the American way of life. Another shock wave hit me when I learned my pre-Vatican II education had to change to accommodate a post-Vatican II church.

Once these traumas normalized however, a fresh thirst for adventure and challenge arose. To become too dependent, too settled in, too complacent, and to seek a stagnant stability now seemed most distasteful. In retrospect, I believe these feelings and my propensity to come at the catechetical world through a research approach have a common denominator. I see research as a wholesome educational catalyst for stirring religious education into considering new challenges and adventures. So often I come across religion teachers and DREs who are discouraged, frustrated, and burnt-out, and I ask why? What is responsible for destroying these persons? Do we expect too much of them? Are they working against overwhelming odds? Are there helpful models of success that can be transferred to them?

I feel these and even harder questions about institutional policies and responsibilities must be asked continuously in order to motivate DREs

and religion teachers and open them up to new and refreshing possibilities. I further believe that if real change is to happen, then con-
science-pricking questions must be asked along with the many pat
answers that already exist.

My own personal background, the Vatican II period and its connection to research in religious education, has led me recently to espouse
what some might consider a radical position. For me, disciplined reflection, the ongoing quest for deeper understandings and the insightful
questions needed to obtain them must be as much a part of religious
education as are textbooks and the new ideas and models of theologians.
Textbooks and theologians challenge the system of religious education
from within. But the system must step back periodically and take a new
look at its operations lest it continue without effect. Too many youths
attending religion classes are saying they have heard it before, while at
the same time crying for a value system to interpret a sometimes hard-to-
understand world. Too many adults are into every imaginable cult, save
the most important one. As present models, policies, and institutional
practices serve religious education, someone must be at their service.
That person must ask, "Are present models out of date? Is there a need
for policy change? Are we really listening? Have institutional practices
become too mechanical and lost their punch?"

I am aware, as travel so well teaches, that everytime there is a jolt to
the system there is also the risk of shaking its balance and possibly never
regaining it. Looking back on the impact of Vatican II and some of the
freightening, but at the same time exciting, learning experiences I have
had with foreign travel, I believe we wouldn't risk as much as we think
we would.

A Period of Contribution

After having received a B.A., two M.A.s, and a Ph.D., and traveled all
over the world, my mother's reaction was sobering. I told her how
fortunate I was to get a well-rounded education. Her reply was, "When
are you going to work?"

Although I had been an associate pastor, worked in the diocesan
office of religious education, taught, and was chaplain, she had a good
point. When would I start to make a noticeable contribution directly
related to all this specialized education?

The opportunity came in 1971 when Robert O'Gorman asked me to co-direct a summer institute in evaluative methods at St. Louis University. For the next four summers I feel I had one of my "finest hours" as an educator.

We were expected to design a course in evaluation, systems analysis, and to introduce students to various styles of supervision. I went to St. Louis with no preconceived ideas. I had developed skills at Notre Dame in assessing verbal dialogue using the Flanders Interaction Analysis system. I was also familiar with various schools of counseling I had studied at Loyola in Chicago. Having been taught the Rogerian method, and being conversant with Gestalt therapy, Jung, Freud, Maslow, and schools of administrative theory such as MacGregor, Follette, Drucker, and Etzioni I felt I could meet the challenge of the summer institute. However, what we needed most was not theory, but a method for making Flanders, Rogers, and the others operational. Would a student have, in addition to cognitive understanding, a good experiential grasp of our goals? It was because of this question I experienced a new outlook on teaching.

As we began to design the course we first looked at the total number of hours it entailed. Then we asked ourselves how many of those hours should be spent on input by us. Should there be a series of lectures and discussions with a final paper due, or should we opt for a different outcome? We chose the latter. It was decided that one-third of the course should explain how to evaluate teacher behavior, a parish religious education program, and utilize supervisory skills. Another third should give students time to team with each other in order to practice these skills. The final third should be used to go out into a real situation and perform these skills.

The most exciting pedagogic experience for me was to learn that a well-structured course which encourages students to test their cognitive learning in a real situation is far superior to the lecture, storytelling presentation I first had cherished as the model of teaching. To systematically structure a course so that a student can feel the emotional anxiety between his or her learning and its practical application was a new concept in teaching for me. It is one thing to read a foreign language and feel you grasp it. It is quite another to speak that language with a real foreigner and experience the sense of being the foreigner. Such experiences have a way of bringing out the "real you." Once exposed to this experience two possibilities exist. You learn much better or you withdraw from the course.

Some might take exception to my desire to create an emotional anxiety in learning. Is this not adding yet another weight to those already shouldered by students? As Shakespeare put it, "Knowledge maketh a bloody entrance." It is my feeling too many so-called educators come in from the wrong entrance.

After this awakening I now try to build into any course I structure a process which allows a student to experience learning in an operationalized manner. When, for example, Scripture is taught, I feel it is more important for students to go to primary commentaries, to experience the struggle of the library hunt and to fumble around reconstructing the information they find. This I advocate over lecturing or dialoguing in a classroom setting. I believe if graduate students properly learned how to find information and were encouraged to reconstruct it on their own this process would be the most valuable learning they could obtain. The less a student relies on the teacher and can develop his or her own criteria for finding information or experiencing a new learning, the better the teacher we are.

I am always amazed in teaching religious educators who may already have an M.A., or even a Ph.D., to find, when an assignment is given, that they cling to the professor. They seem to fear developing their own standards of assessment, to go beyond what the writer says, to touch life and author it. They will call at all hours of the night to confirm whether they are on the correct wavelength. This does wonders for professors with a guru complex. But can it be called real education? The desire to develop religious educators who are independent thinkers, who can go into a situation and take it upon themselves to construct their own way of understanding and coping with it has led me to one of my most cherished *desiderata* for religious education.

Much is being written about the right administrative or teaching model for religious education. It is argued that a good model will create a professional image. At present most administrative models come from the commercial business world or the medical profession. So often we attempt to copy these models. Business consultants from prominent firms are brought in for DRE seminars. They expound on the latest school of thought at Harvard or the Wall Street technique. This has value. I believe, however, that religious education leadership must go beyond the copy-adaptation stage. Unless the field of religious education creates a distinct model which coincides with the specific nature of its work, the spiritual, as well as the secular motivation behind the work, and its eschatological goals, I am afraid it will cling to familiar apron strings and have a diminished image.

From Specialist to Founder

As so often happens to persons who start out specializing, I became an administrator. I continued to videotape religion classes and design courses according to the new insights I had received in St. Louis. Eventually, however, I felt a need to establish a school of catechetics for my diocese. In retrospect I believe I was beginning to long for a home where I could pass on the findings of my work in religious education. The idea had occurred to me while at Notre Dame that we had a rich resource that was under-utilized. The resource was a Benedictine college which had departments of theology, history, philosophy, English, and education. These could provide a first-class faculty to train catechists and DREs. After consulting with the college president, Daniel Kucera, and receiving his backing, my first move was to visit pastors and DREs and conduct a needs assessment. I asked them if a certification program at the college would be desirable. Would they send candidates? What did they think would be the advantages and disadvantages in sending parishioners to the college catechetical school? Finally, we discussed the length of time and number of courses a person should be required in order to receive certification.

In addition to parish visitations I dialogued with the college faculty to assess who would teach, what would be taught, an equitable stipend, and the best time to have these courses.

After securing a commitment from parishes and the faculty, the goals and curricula were formulated and defended before the faculty senate.

Finally, there was the need to advertise our school of catechetics to all parishes within our diocese and those that surrounded us. As one can surmise from the above activities the establishment of a school of catechetics requires as much diplomacy as it does skills in curriculum development.

When the catechetical school opened one of the first novel policies I formulated was to have new candidates tour the campus with special interest directed toward the library. The librarian had agreed to give a mini-lecture which was aimed at making prospective candidates confortable with a college setting and the use of a library card system and systems such as ERIC's microfishe.

It was my hope that after they felt a sense of belonging on a college campus they would feel comfortable coming to the college library at any time. Here they could do their own specialized studying, independent of a teacher or course. If I could help those religious education candidates feel more self-confident in independent learning, I believed this would cultivate a stability in them. I argued that being one's own teacher generates more enthusiasm and endurance in religious education interests. I was working against the burn-out syndrome in which teachers take all types of seminars and courses, but often do not experience the freshness of growth. Instead they wear down. I believe this is one reason why there is so much turnover. Somehow we fail to demonstrate to our students the beauty of a sacramental union between self and the pursuit of knowledge.

Here I came upon one of life's imponderables. For some, the step from classroom and teacher to assertive independence and leadership was a natural sequence of growth stages. For others, it was like that frightening moment when a baby attempts to let go of mother and take that first step alone. Could it be that my belief in individual self-assertiveness is unfounded? Or that I should see student dependence as more the rule than exception? Although students vary, I still feel today that it is a duty of a professor to encourage them to step out on their own. Whether they do or not is their problem. At least the responsibility of education has been shifted to the right person.

Another ideal I attempted to build into the catechetical school was that it should not depend on a training model only, but should go beyond this and provide formation. Beside learning subject matter, I felt days of renewal should also be an integral part of the curriculum. By praying together a balance would be struck between the intellectual and spiritual. I find it strange as I reflect back now on my own training that we never had a day of renewal. Moreover, a national survey of catechetical programs I conducted found a great lack of days of renewal very prevalent. When time schedules get hurried there seems to be a tendency among catechists, as well as among others, to neglect the time and space needed to reflect and pray. And yet, I wonder, is it a question of priorities? Could it be that one person cannot legislate or encourage others to pray—that this must come from the group, and only when it is ready? Another imponderable to ponder.

Since we were close to the parishes where our student catechists and DREs worked, we also built into our curriculum on-location-observations to assess whether our program was having an impact at the parish level. It was felt the college should establish a closer union with parishes other than just offering them courses.

I must admit I did very few on-site visits. Once I got involved with the college I tended to center-in there. Most visits which entailed travel were short-circuited. Some would call this living in a world of my own. It became for me a means of survival. I had only one administrative assistant and a faculty of twelve. To teach and administrate were enough to keep my hands entirely full.

The on-site visits my assistant and I made, however, were very enriching experiences. There is nothing like watching cars deposit hordes of children; to endure the pandemonium that ensues before those restless creatures settle down; to see how little time is actually allotted to teaching, and to come to the realization that something more has to be given to religion teachers than the ability to be independent thinkers. I often felt, after those on-site visits, that parishes were fighting a losing battle. Unless they switched to a different structure which fostered order and a setting where a teacher's lesson preparation could be effective, the process seemed to be a useless exercise. Here is where I deeply believe parish leadership should strive for learning environments other than a classroom model. Also, there has to be an endeavor to enlist as many people as necessary to form a strong support system around teachers. Harking back to what was said earlier, I feel very strongly that religious education leadership must make the cultivation of support systems a number-one priority. This of course implies that DREs and parish teams are thinking along the lines of structuring the learning environment. At present I feel there is too much concern with class schedules, textbooks, and teaching aids. There is less concern with providing an environment where teachable moments can be facilitated. I am realistic enough to know that what I am advocating requires an engineering similar to that I experienced in St. Louis. I also know this consumes time and resources. But it can be accomplished and once accomplished it becomes easier and more economical to repeat.

Reviewing my first experience as an administrator, I encountered a problem I believe most DREs have. Once I had developed a specialty I felt I had to maintain it. After the catechetical school was in full swing I therefore, went back into the classroom. I tried to be both teacher and administrator. The work of administration in itself entailed budgeting, recruiting new faculty, promotion, P.R. work, attending to registrations and records, and being available to everyone involved. This role alone is enough to fill all twenty-four hours of the day. It also raises the question, "Should administrators both administrate and teach?" I often hear this same question from DREs who feel they have to keep in touch with teaching in order to understand their teachers, and to maintain their own acquired teaching skills.

I believe one cannot do justice to both. Proper preparation and the energy it takes to teach one course are big tasks in themselves. Attempting to structure a course as we did in St. Louis, would require full control over the content, plus managerial skills that are very time consuming.

I also believe that although administration gives one power, it is more of a thankless job than teaching. When a teacher reviews his or her progress there is usually the feeling of having touched someone with an idea or helping to form a heritage. Most administrators' memories are consumed with problems of replacement, schedules, and budgets, all of which seem impersonal. And yet, good administrators are a support system to many. They can be the catalyst for new programs. Could the lectures they give and the meetings they hold not become their classroom? Here they can employ their best teaching techniques and keep their skills sharp. Do not their listening powers generate as much in-service good for teachers as any course? Nor should they ever discount the power of presence.

If DREs see this unique value I believe they would realize one can't teach and administrate at the same time and do them equally well. To be a good administrator means to devote full attention to administration. It does not mean being less of a specialist. Most of all, one need not be depersonalized by this role. I must admit personally it is hard to let go of teaching once you have done it. To leave it and concentrate solely on administration is like losing a language or musical skill after having put so much time on them and experiencing that "higher order."

The National Scene

In 1974 I had occasion to be in Washington D.C. While there, I visited Wilfrid Paradis and Mariella Fry, who were directing the National Catechetical Directory (NCD). I asked them how they envisioned the implementation of the NCD's recommendations. The reply was, "How would you implement it?" I responded that surveys might be conducted on a regular basis. On the one hand they could track the NCD's progress. On the other, the items on the surveys could act as catalysts and become an educational tool. I commented that sharply constructed questions enliven thinking. They also provide categories, or a construct which can help religious educators see the whole and its parts.

I do not know whether it was this conversation, my writings, or having established a catechetical school that influenced Wilfrid Paradis. In 1975 he invited me to become coordinator of research for the Bishops' Conference's Department of Education. When the offer came a close friend told me that I would not last two years. He contended the bureacracy would "chew me up." At that time I also had been reading *The Education of Henry Adams*. I have never read a more incisive, realistic, and pessimistic account of politics and work at the national level.

After weighing the negative with the positive I opted for D.C. I felt it was a challenge. I needed a change. Most of all, I believed I had something unique to offer. This offer was the promotion of creative thinking, better use of existing ideas, and support to church ministries through a research approach. Both Wilfrid Paradis and Bishop James Rausch, the General Secretary of the Bishops' Conference, shared this vision. I might add here that my background also made me feel prepared for a new challenge. I had been rector of a small group of seminarians. While directing the catechetical school I was in charge of the formation program of permanent deacons and was likewise in campus ministry. At the college I taught Scripture, liturgy, and teaching methodology. In retrospect I felt like a "Man For All Season" and probably would have burnt out or had a heart attack had I continued to nurture this messianic complex.

During the first two years at the conference I conducted a national study of parish catechetical programs. I also directed a national symposium on catechetics. The study assessed the position of DREs and the various responsibilities they undertake. The symposium brought together catechists and experts in psychology, sociology, and research to address all areas of catechetics. Here again I experienced the value of a support system from the people at the conference, the Boys Town Center for the Study of Youth Development at Catholic University, and the National Conference of Diocesan Directors (NCDD).

Thanks to the success of these projects and the confidence of Wilfrid Paradis and Bishop Thomas Kelly, the new General Secretary of the

Conference, I was made director of research for the entire Conference in 1977. This promotion cast me into an entirely new role. I now found myself conducting studies on the permanent diaconate, campus ministry, SEARCH programs, migration trends, inner-city schools, and social justice. In addition to conducting these studies I also became deeply involved with the world of computers.

During the last six years the various experiences at the conference have deeply affected my understanding of catechetics and catechesis. Living in a staff house with a black and a Hispanic priest and men from every part of the country I have become more cosmopolitan in my thinking. This growth has been enhanced by the wide range of dialogue I have had with every part of the country. As a consequence, I have come to believe that catechetics must be more universal in its approach and appeal. It cannot be directed to one class of people or one type of lifestyle. Rather, there must be a sensitivity among its leadership to adapt the Word of God to multi-cultures and local situations within local situations. Translated on the parish level this might mean two or three catechetical programs instead of one to which all are expected to adapt. It also means writing textbooks which are attuned to ethnic differences. I believe the argument that this is not economical both financially and personnel-wise is unfounded.

I have also learned that the concept of catechetics goes beyond parish boundaries. There is catechesis in campus ministry, when a deacon visits a hospital or jail and works to promote social justice.

This may sound simplistic. In retrospect, I must admit that in embracing a speciality, I overstressed one area of concentration and often was oblivious to other worlds. Working on a national level I have come in contact with the pain of foreign refugees. These people have no country, have difficulty in being understood, and suffer unspeakable humiliations. On vacations I have bicycled through Europe and have become very conscious that this continent is on the brink of a nuclear holocaust. I have spoken with exiles from the Orient and heard of unbelievable misery. I shall never forget those eyes I looked into which expressed a hopeless longing to return home.

These experiences have led me to believe that catechetics must include, but go beyond, the teaching of doctrine or moral values. We must attune our people to the human cries of man's inhumanity to fellow man. Before further developing a theology of liberation I wonder if we should not first develop a philosophy of awareness. How easy it is to be provincial and unconsciously become an isolationalist.

I have learned other lessons on the national level. Often interest groups look for national studies to solve local problems. Because a national office provides a cosmopolitan response, the response is sometimes of little value to a particular local situation. One needs only read Rahner's distinction between principles and prescriptions to understand that national studies are limited by nature of their being national. A national study of catechetical programs can recommend that DREs have a role description. It can demonstrate the bad effects of not having one. But a national study cannot set a policy that all DREs must have one. This must be carried out by the local church. The lack of the control of taking a study from beginning to end and implementing its results has been a frustration to my specialist bent. In a laboratory-teaching situation, to which I was accustomed, I had full control over formation. I was the chief change agent. Perhaps I wasn't always successful, but at least I had the option. On the national level I must now be content with generating questions and ideas. If they are good I must then have faith they will be acted upon. However, others must take over as chief change agent. This realization has greatly sharpened my understanding and practice of delegation. It has also tempered my messianic complex.

Other changes in my thinking have occurred because of being in Washington. As a specialist I frequently find myself wanting to delve into a study in its entirety. Underneath this desire I believe there is a defense mechanism against becoming involved with the political ins-and-outs most national positions experience. I often feel a disgust with those who seem to be concerned about who's who, who is influential, or how someone reacted to this or that situation. Like Henry Adams, I have concluded certain types of people live off of political gossip.

And yet one cannot put one's head in the sand. If one is going to cause any type of change whatsoever, there must be a certain level of political awareness. I believe this principle has much to say to religious educators. It is not enough to seek out truth and design programs. People must be sought. They must be assessed. Persuasive techniques have value, especially where there is a true mission involved. At times there is a legitimate need to know how people are reacting to us, as persons. To know the political climate and to engage it honestly, is a prerequisite for pre-evangelization. To overly indulge in a drawing board atmosphere and forget to shake a few hands, make telephone calls, or market a program is to disregard a very important step of catechesis.

Apologia Pro Vita

Over the last eighteen years my relationship to religious education has gone from the desire to develop the specialized art of communication to that of taking a strong interest in other ministries and social-justice issues. Most of my interests have been generated through personal or national research. As I look back on the many hours devoted to question design and analysis, I sometimes wonder if that time might have been better spent focusing on the study of Scripture, which I cherish. Instead of being in a national office concerned with cosmopolitan thinking and national trends I might be in some university inspiring young minds with the Scriptures. Would this not be more in line with my vocation?

As nice as it would be to be a professor of Scripture I truly believe the world of catechetics, and the church as a whole, is moving into a new era. Whether we like it or not the age of the computer is creating a more profound sense of analysis than ever before. The better we use the tools of this age and analyse how our youth experience their faith, the values our society needs, and the means for making that faith strong, the better will be the world of catechetics.

The laws of philosophy, and especially logic, are considered the working tools of theology. I see the tools of the social sciences much the same. They attempt to define the terms, to justify the major and minor, to review the evidence and to defend a thesis.

Unlike theology, they cannot make a leap of faith, or conclude with a *de fide* proposition. Mystery is not in their vocabulary. Their inability to deal with eternal realities seems to create a lacuna.

Although the social sciences differ from theology in regard to their range of possibilities one cannot deny they offer a positive assistance heretofore underutilized in the field of catechetics.

Computers and new analytical methods are not in themselves the answer for solving the many problems of religious education. Much credit must be given to God's grace. But grace works off of nature. I believe it is the nature of our times to improve our reflective thinking powers. I further believe it is the nature of mankind always to be on the prowl for new methods of conceptualization. In taking nature for what it is, and working with it for what it desires, I feel I am somehow mysteriously cooperating in God's grace. I also feel I have been blessed in making my contribution to religious education in this manner.

Chapter 11

In Celebration of And

John H. Peatling

INTRODUCTION

In the late spring of 1952 my friend, classmate, and fellow Methodist Richard C. Stazesky was elected secretary of the Yale Divinity School Class of 1952, and across some twenty-eight years he has collected and published an annual class letter. While I have not always contributed, I have frequently acknowledged a simple fact: I seem to be persistently religious. That is, I have not had the faith-shaking experiences of some of my classmates. As near as I can tell, God neither died nor even took sick. The five parishes I have known were never intolerable, which is not to say they were perfect. Somehow, as I have changed and grown through the years, reality and religion have rarely suffered a strained relation.

Actually, that is a considerable mystery, for I know that my experience has been just that, mine. Some of my classmates, and a goodly number of my contemporaries, have had quite other experiences across those decades. Perhaps, like that election in 1952, it is but the prevenient grace of God. However, if that is so, the mystery remains. I can not make much of such a straightforward symbol substitution, even if the substituted symbol is most meaningful.

Frankly, this is an attempt to assay my course across a considerable number of years. Inevitably it is an introspective view. However, it is also a chance to seek answers to three puzzling, probing queries which are not too often posed, except in some forms of therapy. Those three questions are:

Who are you?
How did you become that?
What are you doing?

Not one of those three questions is simple. Still, I have come to relish a challenge and, even, to value complexity. So, I want to attempt answers to those three questions.

A FIRST QUESTION: WHO ARE YOU?

Way back in 1954, when I was a curate at St. John's Episcopal Church in Saginaw, Michigan, it seemed impossible to escape the thesis that Christian religious education was concerned for the pointedly personal form of this query. As I now remember it, we seemed to presume that to seek an answer was to theologize, and that to educate meant enabling others to so theologize. That certainly left a very great deal along the side of one road or another. Still, it was more than just a facile existential alternative to either kerygma or didache. Even so, it could be nought but a word game for the distracted and the distractable. Yet, it was (and *is*) a good thing to ask: Who am I? That is why I want to attempt two answers. One is simply history, for history is important. The other is a thing from that extended, non-Augustinian present we once spoke of ever so easily as "the now."

An Answer from History

On my father's side I am the great great grandson of a Methodist local preacher who lived in the vicinity of Boston, in England. I am also the great grandson of an immigrant who walked somewhat over five hundred miles from eastern Pennsylvania to northern Indiana, swimming rivers crossed by toll bridges because he was too poor to pay any toll, in order to homestead a farm just south of the U.S. Land Office in White Pigeon, Michigan. I am the grandson of a Methodist minister who spent much of his career in the villages and towns of southwestern Michigan, and died as the director of a Methodist home for the elderly. Finally, I am the son of a businessman who, as a young man in World War I, was part of an expeditionary force to northern Russia and, as a result of that proto-Vietnam, never owned a gun or (to my knowledge) ever hunted for sport. Other things in life held far greater appeal for him.

On my mother's side I am the great grandson of a captain of a sailing vessel on the inland seas we know as the five Great Lakes. I am also the grandson of an entrepreneur who sold meat and other supplies to logging camps and small communities in the extreme northern part of Michigan's lower peninsula. He died while I was quite young and, as a result, I am really the grandson of a remarkable lady who outlived her husband by many years without losing her sense of who she was. Lastly, I am the son of a kindergarten teacher who, late in life, completed a college degree her original life-certificate to teach never envisioned and, so, graduated from college a year after I left home for seminary. Growing children and education were important things to her.

I remember these things because of numerous tellings and retellings of stories about the people from whom I am descended. Memories are powerful. Family memories encapsulated in stories told by parents, aunts, uncles, and distant cousins are just as powerful . . . perhaps even more so. The stories I heard are part of me, just as surely as I am some genetic combination of those about whom the stories of my childhood were told and retold and, then, told one more time. In a word, I am because of that line about which I know and, behind that, lines about which I have not the foggiest idea.

I am the only child of a couple who almost lost me, except for a medical doctor who performed a then new surgical procedure to put my stomach and my intestines into relationship with one another. In a word, I was saved from starving to death as an infant. That, too, is a story I have heard many times. However, once I had a chance to live I seem to have had a reasonably normal childhood in Kalamazoo, Michigan. While I can barely recall going through what must have been the Oedipus complex, there are much stronger and more pleasant memories of growing up, school and friends, and a circle of my parents' peers, who were all aunts and uncles as far as I was concerned. In a word or two, I grew up in a nuclear family which had a quite extensive, somewhat informal but very real, extended family. I was fortunate.

Some of my earliest memories are associated with Sunday. It was a day we all went to Sunday School and church together. My memories of First Methodist Church, Kalamazoo, Michigan, are remarkably positive ones. I cannot, for instance, recall a time when I did not make communion when that congregation celebrated eucharist. Moreover, I grew through childhood to adolescence as part of a worshiping congregation which faced a central high altar, above which three lancet windows portrayed Saints John and Paul on either side of a risen, reigning Christ, robed as high priest and king. The only time I did not regularly see that colorful stained glass Christus Rex was at the very end of World War II, when I was in the U.S. Navy for a short year and a quarter. Our pastors were family friends and, I suppose, I regarded them as such. For me, Sunday was a good day, and our parish was a part of that good day. Looking back across all these years, I am almost embarrassed at how positive my memories are of that parish.

An Answer from the Extended Present

On the evening of October 15, 1979 I had the opportunity to present a paper to the Psychological Association of Northeastern New York. Because of the ingenuity of the program chairman, the meeting was held in a second-storey room of the Fort Orange Club in Albany, New York. After a meal and the organization's business, Professor Paul J. Centi of Sienna College in Loudonville, New York, and I spoke to the theme of the evening—psychology and religion. In my paper, "Psychology and Religion: Uncommon Partners?" I introduced my late-1979 self with these words.

Twenty-five years ago and some 550 miles west of Albany I learned the usefulness of personal introductions. Therefore, I want to begin with a few simple statements.

I regard myself as a "religious" person.
I am a Christian, and a priest of the Episcopal Church.
Fundamentally, I am an optimist about human posibilities.
I have described myself as a practicing existentialist.
I am an editor, a writer, and an occasional versifier.
By both preference and reputation,
I am an empirically oriented and a psychologically interested
    researcher.
I enjoy the detective work involved in data analysis,
    as well as the farther reaches of theory.
I am presently the associate director of a small research cooperative,
    the Union College Character Research Project in Schenectady.
Finally, I am a member of an endangered species,
    the researcher concerned with science, religion, and education.

Twenty-one months later, in mid-1981, I would only add to that listing the category of artist. I have returned to painting in oils as a hobby and am, once again, exploring that medium. In addition, I have in-

creasingly found it useful to regard research as a conceptual art, somewhat as really good science is an art akin to poetry. I think I owe that
insight to my encounter with the work of R. Buckminster Fuller, especially his slim little book *And It Came To Pass—Not To Stay*. However, I have found much the same thesis more recently in Gary Zukav's
The Dancing Wu Li Masters: An Overview of the New Physics.

The category of artist, let alone the subcategory of poet, is not something so obviously a part of empirically oriented and psychologically
interested research that most would regard it as self-evident. Yet I find it
useful and, I think, true. For instance, there really is a gestalt in which
the poetry of a Gerald Manley Hopkins, the art of a Monet or a Renoir or
a Winslow Homer (or a Maurits Cornelis Escher), and empirically
oriented and psychologically interested research are all a part of a patterned representation of knowable reality. Actually, the analogue between the art of Johann Pachelbel in the Canon in D Major, or Johann
Sebastian Bach in the Brandenburg Concertos, or Gustav Mahler in his
Symphony No. 4, and the research associated with good, artistic science
is so close that I am reminded of the nine times in the Christian Gospels
that the injunction "If you have ears, then hear" is given . . . even if
there is a pun involved in putting things that way. In addition, I find it
both intriguing and instructive that Fuller decided to close the Foreword
of his recent book *Critical Path* by reproducing "A Poet's Advice," by
e. e. cummings.

That, then, is who I am.

I am the one who heard all those tales of my families. I am the one
who grew up in spite of the high probability of an infant death. I am the
product of an informal extended family, the public schools of Kalamazoo, Michigan, and a Methodist parish. Yet, I am also all those
things I listed for the Psychological Association of Northeastern New
York, plus the category of artist. As near as I know, I am now those
things as surely as I am also the time-extended result of that child and
adolescent who grew up in southwestern Michigan. Those two sets of
facts lead directly into the second query.

A SECOND QUESTION: HOW DID YOU BECOME WHO YOU ARE?

As I started to explore this question, two things came to mind. One was a
recurrent memory of a minor character in Austin Tappan Wright's

utopian novel *Islandia* who was honored as a great artist because he made an art of life itself. I first encountered that idea in the mid-1940s, when I read Wright's story of John Lang's encounter with quite another culture, and it was firmly reinforced during the late 1960s when I came upon the novel again. The other is the memory of that true genius and gentle scholar, Edward Rochie Hardy, Jr., quietly suggesting that some question of history or liturgics was overly simplified by some structure I had discerned (and schematized). He was probably correct, for I *am* inclined to look for discernible structures; although now, thanks to that gently quiet suggestion, I do regard them as models.

Very, very generally the answer is simple: I became the person I am because of the books I read (and remembered) and the persons I knew (and remembered). Actually, that parenthetical phrase is quite important. It thoroughly and appropriately personalizes my experience of both reading and knowing. It also means that there are books and persons who, now at this moment of writing, I do not remember. In the words of a very old confession, "it is my fault, my own fault," that I remember neither more nor other than I do.

In addition to a peculiar memory there is another limitation on what could be nought but an exercise in attempted total recall. As best I can achieve it, this an answer to the query implicitly posed by that late 1979 description of the person who was invited to write this chapter. It is, therefore, only a professional biography, the tracing of a career path between where I once was and where I now am.

An Initial Caveat: I'm Not Sure I Started Out to Get Here

One of the interesting things about my career is that during my seminary training I had little intention of ever being a religious educator. I went through three years of seminary and a fourth year of graduate study convinced that I was preparing for the parochial pastoral ministry. Of course, I took the then required three courses in Religious Education (probably with Paul Vieth and Randolph C. Miller), but I spent far more time in Preaching (with William Muehl and Halford E. Luccock), Old Testament History (with Davie Napier), and New Testament Exegesis (with Paul Schubert, Eric Dinkler, and Halford Luccock). I managed to get thoroughly intrigued by Church History (with Roland Bainton), and to spend too much time learning what interested me. I found Systematic Theology (with Albert Outler), the History of Christian Doctrine (with Robert L. Calhoun), the *Summa Theologica* of Thomas Aquinas and

the *Church Dogmatics* of Karl Barth interesting and challenging. Somewhere along the line I also became very interested in Christian Worship
(probably with David MacClennen), Early Christian Art (with Eric
Dinkler), and Christian Small Groups (with John Oliver Nelson). I also
managed to pick up a course in rural sociology, and one in human
growth and development (with Hugh Hartshorne).

By the time it became possible for me to spend a fourth year working
on an S.T.M. degree, I had taken advantage of cross-registration with
the Berkeley Divinity School to learn some English Church History
(probably with Edward Hardy) and some Sacramental Theology (probably with the late Percy L. Urban). However, during that fourth year I
spent all of my time on theology and liturgics. My advisors for that year's
project were Edward R. Hardy, Jr., of the Berkeley Divinity School
faculty, and Robert L. Calhoun, of the Yale Divinity School faculty.
The reason for that ecumenicity was that I wanted to examine the
relationship of words and actions (or rite and ceremony) during the first
eight Christian centuries, and the liturgical and patristic knowledge of a
Hardy simply had to be used. It was, and I did the project. In addition, I
had a chance to do library research for Professor Calhoun on the doctrine of work during the early centuries of the church's life.

In many ways that record seems to leave a good bit to be desired as
preparation for either a practical ministry as a religious educator or for
the practice of research as a calling. That was not what I then thought I
was doing. Instead, I believed that I was preparing for a parochial or
pastoral ministry; and that *is* what I had when I finally left seminary in
mid-1953. In fact, in a thoroughly strange way that is basically what I
have had ever since, although a parochial ministry has not supported me
for some twenty-one years. For approximately three-quarters of my
career I bave earned my living "outside" a parish, although I have been
related to a parish all of those years.

When my career is described in that way, I suppose I have been a
worker priest for just over twenty years. That's strange, for I never
intended to be a worker priest. I thought I would be fortunate to follow
the career path of my paternal grandfather. Instead, I followed a different path to reach my current state of career.

From There to Here: A Wandering Pathway

When I finally had an answer to Halford Luccock's query—"Peatling,
what are you still doing around here?"—it was in terms of a United

Methodist parish in the far northeastern part of Detroit, Michigan. In mid-1953 I was assigned by Bishop Marshall Reed to Mount Hope Methodist Church on East Seven Mile Road. My senior associate there was recovering from a stroke, but during that assignment he taught me something about what a spiritual father might be. It was also at Mount Hope that I realistically faced the educational conundrum of translating what I had learned into terms early adolescents preparing for confirmation and communion could seem to understand. In fact, Paul Nicholas had the accute perception to recognize that I should be an Episcopalian, rather than a Methodist, and to help me recognize that fact and then do something about it. Paul, a Berkeley classmate (John Salles), and John Henry Newman's rationale for switching ecclesiastical allegiances all helped me during the early part of 1954. So, of course, did my wife (Jane Cobb Peatling).

The Parochial Episcopalian

I became an Episcopalian in mid-1954 and, with the aid of Bishop Richard S. Emrich of the Diocese of Michigan, translated my ministry ninety miles north to Saginaw, Michigan. I became a curate at St. John's Episcopal Church to Rexford C. S. Holmes, a gracious and good man who (as a result) was a fine supervisor of young clerics. He was a former Army chaplain, and through him I was able to hold an appointment as an assistant chaplain at a Veterans Administration hospital. That appointment taught me much more, I suspect, than I was able to do in the crisis situations that got me out of bed at 2:00 a.m. I was fortunate indeed, for I learned a very great deal while I was in Saginaw. However, much of it had to do with the Anglican ethos and the pastoral ministry, although some had to do with the practicalities of parochial religious education. Actually, I got rather involved with the diocesan department of religious education, attended an early Church and Group Life laboratory at the University of the South in 1954, and learned a great deal from a Conference on Adult Education at the University of Indiana in 1955. That all had much to do with my later career.

In mid-1956 I accepted a call from George R. Selway, the rector of St. Paul's Episcopal Church in Lansing, Michigan, to be that parish's director of Christian education. As the second priest on that parochial staff, I had not only a Sunday church school to supervise and a staff to train and support but, as well, an educational ministry to adolescents in a State Training School (an experience that made H. R. Weber's *The Communication of the Gospel to Illiterates* and Hendrik Kraemer's *The Communication of the Christian Faith* important statements for me). In addition, I had a share in a parochial ministry to journalists (the state's capital was directly across the street from the parish), the normal hospital and crisis ministries, and, because of where my office was located, a good bit of experience with transients looking for help or a handout. Once again, I was fortunate. George Selway was another good supervisor of young clerics, in addition to being a mature, caring person. In fact, when George accepted a call to be dean of the Cathedral parish in Phoenix, Arizona, I had the care of the whole parish until a new rector was chosen. However, he was not the man who hired me, and I think we both were relieved when, in mid-1960, I accepted a call to be associate secretary of the Curriculum Development Division in the Department of Christian Education of the Domestic and Foreign Missionary Society of the Protestant Episcopal Church in the United States of America.

The Denominational Episcopalian

I remained an employee of the Domestic and Foreign Missionary Society of PECUSA for eleven years. During that time, I did a number of things. I supervised the planning and writing of the Seabury Series curriculum materials with my friend and senior associate, Lester McManis. I headed a team which investigated the application of programmed instruction to religious education. I was responsible for planning children's work for a year. I became the primary investigator in a project to discover the relation of cognitive operations and the understanding of biblical material, after the department had been exposed to the person and the ideas of Ronald Goldman. For several years I supervised all of the research and development work of the department and so was one-third of a troika administration that included Robert Martin and Carmen St. John Hunter. In addition I represented the department and the Episcopal Church on a number of interdenominational committees, including the old Professors and Researchers Section of the Division of Christian Education of the National Council of Churches of Christ. Moreover, at various times during those eleven years, I worked with a Committee on Christian Education of the Department of Church Building and Architecture, a committee to develop a curriculum design for released time, and several committees of the N.C.C.C.'s Department of Research. I also functioned as a kind of representative to the Religious Research Association and, as well, was an early member of an informal fellowship of researchers known as the IDIOTS (an acronym which was designed simply to give comptrollers pause). As the 1960s moved toward their close, I was part of the group of Episcopalians who met with our counterparts in the United Church of Christ and the United Presbyterian Church at Columbia University's Greystone Conference Center to begin a process that eventually became the Joint Educational Development project.

About 1964 my responsibilities for the generation and supervision of research made it important to get further training. So I enrolled in the religious education program at New York University, which then had a two-person faculty consisting of Lee Belford and Norma Thompson. My responsibilities for the investigation of Goldman's ideas with a nationwide sample of Americans finally became my doctoral dissertation, although it took nine years of part-time study to see the thing through to completion. I owe a very great deal to both Professor Norma H. Thompson, who was my chairperson, and to Professor Philip R. Merrifield, who kept the research as psychometrically clean as it was possible and, in the process, encouraged me to learn much about statistics, educational psychology, tests and measurement, research design, and psychometrics. While it was a difficult experience, I am glad to have had Professor Fred N. Kerlinger introduce me to research design in the behavioral sciences, and his book *Foundations of Behavioral Research* has been a recurring help. I am also glad to have learned much about tests and measures and psychometrics from Professor Eleazur Pedazur, a fine teacher who managed to balance rigor and helpfulness. In addition I had the financial support of my employers throughout the whole process of graduate work, and I am indeed grateful for what both the Domestic and Foreign Missionary Society and the Union College Character Research Project made possible. With their assistance, I was finally credentialed in 1973, when New York University awarded me a Ph.D. degree.

During ten of the eleven years that I worked for the Episcopal Church I had the good fortune to also be a weekend assistant at St. Paul's Episcopal Church in Riverside, Connecticut. Part of that good fortune consisted in the fact that St. Paul's was our family parish. Another part was that I was responsible for adult education, assisted regularly with the parish liturgical life, and occasionally assumed some pastoral duties. Those ten years were good ones!

My three daughters grew up and were confirmed at St. Paul's. I had a chance to try all of the then-known options for regular, week-by-week adult education, and I was able to celebrate the Christian mysteries weekly with my fellow parishioners and fellow commuters. My wife was able to return to her profession (occupational therapy) and even to get quite involved in the Connecticut Occupational Therapy Association and, in 1966, participate in a world meeting in London, England.

She and I were able to see our oldest daughter enter Middlebury College before my wife Jane died within the Octave of All Saints Day, 1970. After twenty-one years together, the loss was quite disorienting. I know that now, but could not really understand it at the time.

The Oekumenical Episcopalian

All things considered, I was rather relieved to spend most of 1971 on an institutional sabbatical, and terminal leave, while I analyzed data from my doctoral research, went back to the very source of Goldman's work (Professor Edmund A. Peel of the Faculty of Education at the University of Birmingham in England), and looked for other employment. Finally, with neither diocesan nor parochial work available, I accepted a position on the professional staff of the Union College Character Research Project. Again I was fortunate, for Bishop Allen W. Brown of the Diocese of Albany agreed to accept me as a canonically resident priest and appoint me to my position at the Union College Character Research Project in exchange for my agreeing to be a weekend assistant at St. Stephen's Episcopal Church in Schenectady, New York. So, in mid-November of 1971, I moved myself and my two youngest daughters to Schenectady.

I have been there ever since.

However, shortly after moving to Schenectady and the Union College Character Research Project, I became aware of, began to enjoy the company of, and then realized I loved my colleague, Lucie W. Barber. We were married on Easter Day, 1972, and have worked together ever since. It was a second marrage for us both, and the two of us have learned a good deal about both the nature and the power of love, to our mutual benefit.

We have been fortunate. We are a two-career couple, but our careers are so related that we can and do reinforce one another, help one another, and only rarely lose track of what the other one is trying to do. While our employer has never been known to pay well, let alone generously, we have been able to discover possibilities neither one of us thought existed. As a result, we have been able to do some good, creative, and important things, simply because we were *who* we were and we were *where* we were.

On the whole, it has been a very good experience.

Even so, the historian in me found joining the Union College Character Research Project a surprising, often jolting and occasionally absurd experience of the realities so nicely described in Jacob Burckhardt's *The Civilization of the Renaissance*. It was like simultaneously existing in a thirteenth century Italian despotism and in a twentieth century North American small suburban town. Of course, as Fuller was at pains to point out in *Synergetics*, "experiences are nonsimultaneous."

Coming to recognize that fact helped. On the one hand it brought freedom from the serfdom of absurdity. On the other hand it brought a freedom for the possible, the discovery of heretofore unrecognized potentialities. All in all, the 1970s were a strange Renaissance experience which, quite naturally, contributed to what I could do and subtly formed the person I now am. For instance, I came to recognize the wisdom in Gertrude Stein's best known line, which has it that "A rose is a rose is a rose." I came to recognize that it *is* true that a person is a person is a person, *and* that a situation is a situation is a situation, *and* that a patron is a patron is a patron. Stein's affirmation has everything to do with is-ness, and almost nothing to do with ought-ness. It is a celebration of encountered existence, an affirmation of the perceived. In fact, it is a healthy objectivization of experience. That is, it is an acceptance of that which we can most surely say we know and, as well, a recognition that norms and standards and feelings of rightness and wrongness and fairness are applied to just such data.

While my gratitude for the 1970s may be part of that mystery which is unresolved by symbol substitutions that only rename ultimate causes, a firmer and more objective reason can be found in what I have been able to do during the decade I have been in Schenectady. Actually, when I set out to list the things I had done, I was surprised to find nine things on my list. That is an average of a thing every 13.3 months for a decade. However, that arithmetic mean completely ignores the fact that most of those things have been done only across several years.

The Forming of a Theory

The first thing on my list of things done during the past decade was what I know as Mathematical Group Theory. Actually, it was the one of

Ernest M. Ligon's many fascinating insights which led me to believe I could seriously think about coming to the Union College Character Research Project. It is, in fact, a very general way of describing mature, integrated human personality as a dynamic, interactive system which is the result of growth and development, even as it is also amenable to predictive analysis. Moreover, when I arrived in Schenectady, Mathematical Group Theory was only partially ordered, organized, or systematized. So I set out to do something about ordering, organizing, and systematizing that Ligonian insight. Because I was *where* I was, and because I was *who* I was, I could expend almost five years in that effort.

Early on in that effort, at the 1972 convention of the American Educational Research Association in Chicago, Illinois, I met David V. Tiedeman. As a result of that meeting, we joined his almost Quaker concern for the process of career development and my interest in systematizing Ligon's model of the human personality. The two of us spent approximately the next five years creating and, then, getting published *Career Development: Designing Self*, a book informed by our complementary interests. Surprisingly, our minor classic is still selling, although at a rate that reminds me of the first of the late C. S. Lewis' books. However, I am proud of what we did, and I am grateful for the opportunity its writing gave me to rediscover my concern for sheer blessed theory. I had forgotten that about myself before Tiedeman and I became co-authors and friends. In fact, that friendship has continued across the years as we have exchanged ideas, dreamed more than a few dreams together, and come to value and enjoy one another as persons and colleagues in the quest for a better, more humane humankind.

I think of that quest as the progressive process of sanctification, but my friend is uneasy with such theological constructs. Fortunately, because we are friends, we do not have to agree upon everything and, so, can easily allow one another to be just who we are.

The Publication of Creative Yet Rigorous Research

The second thing on my list was the journal *Character Potential: A Record of Research*. Once settled in Schenectady, I realized that the journal was close to dying. As an in-house journal, it was a burden to the staff and, frankly, not too attractive to anyone else. However, I thought that it might be really useful as an interdisciplinary forum where creative-yet-rigorous research into human growth and development from counseling, psychology, religion, and sociology could co-exist in an implicit dialogue across often not crossed disciplinary boundaries.

At the time, it was no great problem to get the job as editor, for I was the only staff member with a positive idea of what the journal might be, and (it seemed) the thing had no where to go but up. So I began to invite friends and acquaintances to take part in the effort to make *Character Potential* into a new thing. During the second half of 1973, I was able to collect articles from David and Margaret Steward, Merton P. Strommen, Delbert Schultz, Kalevi Tamminen, Earl D. C. Brewer, and Ross P. Scherer, and I was able to carefully edit Ligon's notes for an heretofore unpublished address at a meeting of the American Psychological Association in 1940. In February of 1974 those articles were published in Vol. 6, No. 4, of *Character Potential*, and a new thing was started. By the fall of 1974 I was prepared to begin Vol. 7 with an issue that contained articles from a symposium at the American Personnel and Guidance Association's convention in New Orleans, a report from Ingemar Fagerlind of the University of Stockholm on the Swedish experiments in religious education, a critique of research in religious education by John Wilson of the University of Oxford, and a first report of my dissertation research into the development of religious thinking.

Since becoming editor of *Character Potential*, I have been able to edit and publish 88 articles in 13 issues. Frankly, the journal has only slowly built a readership and a reputation, but I have begun to be able to publish an increasing number of good, important contributed articles. Even so, it is still subsidized by the Union College Character Research Project. That is its weakness, although it has come a long way from the almost certain quiet, unlamented death facing it in 1972–1973. Actually, I have been fortunate to have the advice and assistance of such consulting editors as William E. Chapman, Martin J. Coffey, Richard K. Gladden, James Michael Lee, Charles F. Melchert, Ralph L. Mosher, Norman A. Sprinthall, David S. Steward, Margaret C. S. Steward, David V. Tiedeman, Margaret J. Thomas, and F. Franklyn Wise from the United States, plus the international perspectives of Trond Enger (Norway), Andre Godin, S.J., (Belgium, Canada, and Italy), John E. Greer (Ulster), Brian V. Hill (Australia), John M. Hull (United Kingdom), Foeke H. Kuiper (the Netherlands), Peter J. Naus and Henry C. Simmons (Canada), and Kalevi Tamminen (Finland). Even more pleasurable than being able to give new life to a poor, dying thing has been the opportunity to use the editorial skills acquired during the 1960s to repeatedly offer creative-yet-rigorous research from this and other countries in a readable form. I am grateful for that opportunity.

Moreover, since 1975 the Religious Education Association of the United States and Canada has identified *Character Potential* as "an arena for the sharing and publication of research reports in the field of religious education." However, the editorial and creative independence of *Religious Education* and *Character Potential* have been carefully preserved. The two journals do very different albeit quite complementary things. While one is concerned just with the theory of religious education, the other is concerned with the idea that good research (regardless of where it may have been done) facilitates good education (regardless of where it may be done). In addition, eleven of the last thirteen issues have included articles from outside the U.S.A. by authors such as Ingemar Fagerlind (Sweden), Leslie J. Francis (United Kingdom), Ronald J. Goldman (Australia), John E. Greer (Ulster), Eugene J. Mishey (Canada), Eric F. Rolls (United Kingdom), and Kalevi Tamminen (Finland). In part, that is because I believe that religious educators need to be aware of research findings from other places, under other conditions and, often, involving not so subtly different assumptions. Unless that happens, religious education can be all too parochial, even though the parish is as diverse as the fifty United States. Thus, editing *Character Potential* has been a way to be ecumenical, interdisciplinary, and multinational during a period when this planet has become all three. I am grateful to have been able to publish creative, important research relevant to the growing need for informed yet humane persons as passengers and crew on this small planet, our island home. Deo gratias.

The Exploration of Religious Thinking

The third thing that I listed was an instrument originally developed for my dissertation research, *Thinking About the Bible*. It was intended to permit a large, nationwide sample of students to so detail their preferred interpretation of the biblical miracle stories used by Goldman with 200 English students that it would be possible to (i) assess the level of religious thinking in a large North American sample and, thus, (ii) test the hypothesis that the level of cognitive operation and the level of preferred interpretation so covary that they seem to be positively and inextricably linked. From the beginning it was recognized that if the hypothesis could not be rejected, then it would be important to take Piaget seriously (since Goldman's construct of religious thinking took its rationale directly from Piaget).

What I found was that Goldman's general hypothesis could not be rejected. However, what could be rejected were his specific results. North American students simply are *not* English students. Even so, what was far more important, Piaget turned out to be correct. Scientifically, that may not be surprising. Practically, however, it meant that there was no simple-minded way to transfer Goldman to the North American scene. Neither his results nor the materials influenced by them, nor his speculations, transfer across the Atlantic in any simple way. North American religious educators have been too anxious for a quick and simple "answer," when there was none at hand. We must do our *own* work, with our *own* students and, in that effort, we are better guided by the Swiss than by the now disinterested Australian.

Interestingly, I do not dislike Ron Goldman. My wife Jane and I were his house guests in the summer of 1966. He and his wife Julliette were our house guests in the fall of 1979. I do like the man, and I think I understand what he has done and is now trying to do. However, after some fifteen years of close attention to a subject that Goldman has not touched since the late 1960s, I have considered the religious thinking of sixty-five times as many persons as he had in that original English sample, and those persons have come both from several nations and several denominations. I think that I know not only more about the changes in the organization of religious thinking across time than Goldman but, as well, what I know is vastly more representative of human religious thinking than Goldman ever believed he had achieved or (for that matter) ever hoped to know. The difference between us is simply that I have continued to consider Piagetian cognitive operations and thinking about religion, while my friend has gone off after one or another fundable golden calf, a hardly surprising behavior for a knowledgeable, ambitious academic psychologist. He has chosen to be a successful academic entrepeneur, while I have been able to be a more persistent, scientific researcher. As a result, our career paths have rather noticeably diverged, as have our interests. However, a friendship based on a past we both share and value remains.

Actually, since 1971 I have had a collegial relation with a number of researchers interested in the assessment device *Thinking About the Bi-*

ble. That is how I have been able to consider the results of something like 13,000 administrations, most of which have been to children and adolescents. That is why I am grateful for such colleagues as Thomas B. Newton (UMC, 1971), Charles W. Laabs (LC-MS, 1971 and 1976), Sr. Lois Castillon (RC, 1976), Sr. Catherine Killeen (RC and Public School, 1976), Dean R. Hoge and Gregory Petrillo (RC, UMC and SBC, 1974), and Douglas Degelman (Nazarene, 1981) in the United States and such international colleagues as Kalevi Tamminen (Finland, 1974), Peter D. Taylor (England, 1978), John E. Greer (Ulster, 1979), and William K. Kaye (England, Ulster and Ireland, 1980–1981). Not all of those colleagues have used the device as I advised, but each has been a reasonable person investigating something they recognized as important. They were all independent colleagues who used *Thinking About the Bible* for their own purposes and, along the way, advanced my understanding of the relation between Piaget's cognitive operations and biblical interpretation that we call religious thinking.

I believe that I would not have had those collegial relationships if I had not been in Schenectady, New York, at the Union College Character Research Project. But I was. Moreover, while I am inclined to credit the prevenient grace of God, I know that only rearranges the labels: The mystery remains. Still, I remember spending hours in the rare book room of the Stirling Library at Yale reading the Early Puritan casuists. They had (as I recall it) a clear, compassionate yet realistic sense that a calling involved an interest, an ability, and an opportunity. During the 1970s, I was fortunate to have all three.

The Exploration of Justice and Moral Judgment

The fourth thing I listed was what I call *Thinking About Justice.* Actually, that is a symbol for my increasing interest in the investigation of what Piaget called the idea or sense of justice in *The Moral Judgment of the Child* and, later, referred to as the "feeling of justice" in *Intelligence and Affectivity: Their Relation During Child Development.* For most of the 1970s the investigation involved the progressive analysis of data from a fourth, nonbiblical story I had included in the original research edition of *Thinking About the Bible.* That story was based upon one Piaget used to study an aspect of the feeling of justice which concerned one's relation to authority, a relation which develops from submission to autonomy and eventuates in a regard for equity. Initially, I had only the data from my dissertation research (N = 1994). However, during the early part of the 1970s, I used the administration of *Thinking About the Bible* as an experiential introduction for a number of talks to religious educators about the development of religious thinking. In four years of doing that, I had in hand something over one hundred administrations to adults.

In the mid-1970s, with the help of the staff at the Union College Character Research Project, I began to analyze that adult data and, then, to compare it to the results from my dissertation sample of children and adolescents. During the same period, Kalevi Tamminen used all four stories from my *Thinking About the Bible* in a stratified, semi-representative sample of children and adolescents in the state-supported schools in Finland (N = 1368). Actually, my device was but one of a battery that Tamminen and his colleagues from the Institute of Practical Theology at the University of Helsinki used in but one part of a massive, sophisticated study of moral and religious development. Also during the mid-1970s Sr. Catherine Killeen used copies of my original research edition of *Thinking About the Bible* with a sample of students in grades 7–12 in both private and public schools in New Jersey (N = 206). Her study was part of a dissertation project at Rutgers University, and her real interest was in moral development. That is why she put my device into a battery that also included James R. Rest's *Defining Issues Test*, Gilbert M. Burney's *Logical Reasoning Test*, and Gorham's *Proverbs Test* (an intelligence test). The data from that battery which was shared with me was a veritable researcher's treasure trove, for it permitted me to compare and contrast two measures of cognitive operations, two measures of moral judgment, and a measure of intelligence. However, I have not yet tried to publish my independent analyses of Killeen's dissertation study data.

All of those experiences during the 1970s reinforced my intuition that the single aspect of Piaget's sense, idea, or feeling of justice that I used in my dissertation research was but one-fifth of what was to be learned. So, I began to think about a family of five aspect-specific devices. I did some design work in the late 1970s, and I had a second device in hand by the middle of 1980. At that point, I remet a former parishioner from St. Paul's in Lansing, Michigan, Professor Robert H. Scott of the School of Criminal Justice in the College of Social Science at Michigan State University. As a result of our getting reacquainted, he took both my initial device and my second device and collected data from the twelve students in his Values and Ethics class. That small body of data proved to be intriguing and important. So much so, that I spent much of the late spring and most of the summer of 1981 on the remaining three aspects needed to complete a family of five aspect-specific devices for assessing Piaget's idea, sense, or feeling of justice. As these words are written, that seems like a challenging and important "next" thing to be done. The interest and the ability are available; given the opportunity, that next thing could qualify for a calling, according to the criteria of the Early Puritan casuists.

Actually, whether that calling ever is actualized or not, I am grateful to have been in a place where my concern for moral development, and data, could be supported and permitted to grow. In other places, that concern might have been supported, but it probably would have been formed into the Kohlbergian model. That was not my experience and, as a result, I have been able to develop a way to assess Piaget's idea, sense, or feeling of justice that does not require the philosophical speculation of the North American cognitive developmentalists, nor does it need an "invarient sequence" to be educationally useful. While it could confirm a general developmental hypothesis, it could also be a way to help a person understand their present existence and grow toward a future possibility. That last is a developmental and educational ideal. But that ideal does not have to depend upon appeals to philosophical or ethical authority. It is an ideal that can be based upon empirical assessment.

Unfortunately, appeals to authority often masquerade as thought in moral education. Some of the entrepreneurial pronouncements of Harvard's prime cognitive developmentalist are clearly not only self-serving but encouraging of a kind of conceptual dependence. However, as both John Dewey and Paul of Tarsus argued, humans have the option to be free from a slavery to their past, and education has a part to play in that process. In many ways, Christian religious education has close to an indispensible part to play in the growth of those free humans we can recognize as brothers and sisters in Christ. Clearly empirical assessment of that growth can *help*, not hinder, education toward freedom.

The International Connection

The fifth thing on my list was the International Seminar on Religious Education and Values (ISREV). For me, the beginnings go back as far as my trip to the University of Birmingham in search of Goldman's roots in 1971. It was on that trip that I first met John M. Hull, an Australian transplant who was teaching religious education in the Faculty of Education at the University of Birmingham. I met John again when my wife and I flew down to Birmingham from Edinburgh for a day with Hull and his wife during a trip to Scotland and the Outer Islands in 1973. Following that meeting, there was a good bit of correspondence, and then Hull spent several days as our house guest during a North American speaking binge in 1977. At that time we compared notes and realized we had both reached the same conclusion: Religious education in our two nations was *similar enough* to make us wonder why we each didn't know more about what was happening in the other's place, and religious education was also *different enough* in our two places to lead us to believe it would be useful for the two to encounter one another. Thus, after some months of dreaming, we decided to see what could be done about getting persons from both sides of the Atlantic into the same place at the same time, and we settled upon a time in July of 1978 for a first try. Actually, some three dozen persons from eight nations showed up at the University of Birmingham for three days over the North Americans' July 4th holiday.

It was a real venture in faith, for neither of us knew if it would work. However, it did. At least, a second meeting was held at Union College in Schenectady, New York, in 1980 during approximately the same period in early July. Moreover, at the conclusion of that meeting, it was decided to meet a third time in the Netherlands in 1982 and, probably, to anticipate a fourth meeting in Canada in 1984. From the first, the North Americans have included persons with both a research orientation and a public school orientation, as well as a parish orientation, because there is nothing in the United States that comes close to a European religious educator's concerns without that kind of a mix.

In fact, it is exactly that sort of recognition that North Americans need to achieve if we are to benefit from contact with, or learn anything from, or be capable of speaking in a language understood by many of the rest of the world's religious educators. Without that recognition, the North American endlessly repeats the Ugly American syndrome. However, the reverse holds true, too: It is all too easy to encounter an Ugly European syndrome—one which makes North Americans just as uncomfortable, distrusting, and downright suspicious as any Third World national in a UNESCO conference. The Atlantic is not really a bond that binds; it is an ocean that separates and, therefore, needs to be overcome. Only romantics think differently. Only dour pessimists believe it neither should nor can be done. Hull and I are neither romantics nor pessimists, but experience has taught us to be flexible realists.

The Identification of Research Important to the Field

The sixth thing that went onto my list was a fairly recent project, the *Annual Review of Research: Religious Education*. It was an idea initiated by John H. Westerhoff, supported by Boardman W. Kathan and Herman J. Williams, and brought off with the support of an international network of friends and colleagues. The thing is an odd two-step dance, in which an overall integrated statement is published in the journal *Religious Education* late one summer, and then the next spring a book with all the supporting information is published by the Character Research Press of Schenectady as a contribution to the whole field of religious education. One of the most interesting things about the effort (to date) is how readily international scholars are willing to be a part of the project, and how remarkably reticent North American religious educators are to get involved. While that does not quite prove the case, it does fail to disprove the hypothesis that we North Americans are very, very, very parochial. I think that is sad. Clearly, a number of my colleagues in North America do not: They neither swarm to help in the process nor flock to purchase the result.

Frankly, I enjoy the opportunity to be in contact with scholars, educators, and researchers around the world. I think the project is a needed service to the field. I believe it must continue if North American religious education is to escape a narrow ethnocentric concern for only itself and its own state. I do not think that means becoming less confessional, less rational, or less organized. Copying others will always be a sign of immature dependence, even if it is done in the name of Isaianic servanthood. No one of us is called to slavery (dependence); rather, we are called to freedom (autonomy). That is just as certainly true of North Americans as it is of Africans or Asians, Slavs or Greeks, Arabs or Latins, Polynesians or Europeans.

Actually, in only three years this international network of friends and acquaintances has enabled the *Annual Review of Research: Religious Education* to identify something close to 400 instances of empirical research important to the field. Moreover, each of those studies has been vouched for by someone willing to say that they regard the results as trustworthy, as well as important. I regard that as a monumental accomplishment. I am also delighted to have been able to participate in bringing to attention works that might well have gone unnoticed. I hope the field of religious education will benefit. I know that research in religious education will; for disinterest, lack of acknowledgment, and simple ignorance do as much to retard such research as hostility or repression; or dumb, stupid, meaningless studies ground out by mere technicians. Fortunately, religious education has remarkably few such technicians!

The Exploration of Early Development

The seventh thing on my list was the *Barber Scales of Self-Regard: Preschool Form*. As their title indicates, those scales are clearly the work of my wife, Lucie W. Barber. However, I have both a colleague's and a grandparent's pleasure and part in them. The scales were built as an assessment of analytically determined prototypes (at the preschool age-level) of the theoretically posited interactions of that Mathematical Group Theory I ordered, organized, and systematized in the process of creating a book with David V. Tiedeman. Providing a theoretical base for the Barber Scales is my grandparent's claim to pleasure in them. My collegial claim is the result of months of listening to Lucie talk about her progress, checking her ideas against the theory, and thinking together about just what prototypic behavior (at the preschool age-level) could possibly be.

In addition, I have thought along with her as she analyzed her field-test results, and considered with her what those observed results might mean. It has been both fun and a real challenge. Finally, I joined with her in creating a technical manual for those scales in 1977. It is something that could only have happened in Schenectady during the 1970s, and I consider it a thing worth remembering from that decade. While those Scales rightfully belong to Lucie W. Barber, I am pleased to have had a part in their creation.

The Facilitation of Early Development

The eighth thing I listed was a structured small-group program for parents of preschool children, *Realistic Parenting*. If anything ever was, that program was a grace-filled confluence of an idea that my wife and I had for what we called assessment-based education and the concerns of two friends who were practical religious educators. John T. Hiltz is a secular priest of the Diocese of Toledo in northwestern Ohio, the director of that diocese's Department of Religious Education, and a former doctoral student of James Michael Lee at Notre Dame. Louise Marie Skoch is a Joliet Franciscan Sister who is the assistant director of the Department of Religious Education for the Diocese of Toledo. With their interest, encouragement, and help, a program of assessment-based parent education using the *Barber Scales of Self-Regard: Preschool Form* was completed and then field tested in the six dioceses of the Province of Cincinnatti in the Roman Catholic Church during 1977–1978. It worked well, and Abbey Press published the program for parish use in 1980. For the researchers, the fact that it worked well was both satisfying and confirming, for it suggested that our idea of an assessment-based education could be used to help others to themselves accomplish a genuine good. Throughout the process of creation and field testing I functioned as a ready consultant and editor, and I regard the result as a thing for which to be grateful.

Closely related to *Realistic Parenting* is a project that Lucie and I became involved in during the winter and spring of 1980. Largely through the advice of John H. Westerhoff, Edgar Hartley (the executive director of an Episcopalian conference center at Kanuga, which is outside of Hendersonville, North Carolina) got Barber, Peatling, Westerhoff, Doris Blazer, and himself together for just over twenty-four hours in Durham, North Carolina. The charge was to identify and design a program to help the church help the parents of preschoolers exercise their parental ministry and, if at all possible, to do so in a way that could have both national and ecumenical impact. As a result, during the spring of 1980, we put together a plan for the training of diocesan cadres of parenting educators which, by using the facilities of the Kanuga center, could impact every diocese in the Episcopal Church by the early 1990s and, as well, begin to affect other Christian denominations. It really was an exciting challenge. It also led to a plan for a Kanuga-Based Parent Education Program that turned out to be somewhat more than the board of directors of Kanuga were ready to put into place, or fund. However, the plan remains a real possibility for ministry to and through the parents of preschoolers; something which could, quite literally, remake parish-based religious education. The team of Barber, Blazer, Hartley, Peatling, and Westerhoff was nicely balanced, and the result of their work is still a lively possibility for the church and the churches. The plan is not yet dead, but certainly is in a coma. While its creation was a remarkable instance of grace, its accident-prone life to date is an example of the fact that, in this creation, grace often only informs and enables but does not control.

The Complexities of Cooperation

The ninth and last thing I listed was the Religious Education Association of the United States and Canada. Although I have been a member of the R.E.A. since the mid-1950s, it was not until the 1970s that I became either a member of the Association's Research Committee or a member of the board of directors of the association. In fact, it was not until 1976 that I became Chair of the Research Committee, a somewhat honorific and somewhat thankless task. The honor comes from following a Walter Houston Clark (1954–1971) and a Merton P. Strommen (1971–1976) in the position. The somewhat thankless part of the task comes from the fact that the committee has no funds to either do or support research. Thus, the task has devolved into one of trying to keep alive an invaluable and indispensible aspect of religious education during a period when the sources of funding seem to have dried up. Actually, the Union College Character Research Project has allowed me to expend time and travel on the work of the association and its research committee. For that, I am grateful. However, I also am frustrated by the inability of either the association or the committee to fund important, basic, rigorous research in the field. Not until the association's adult education committee was revivified by an academic entrepeneur was it possible to even approximate a research project of some scope and importance. Unfortunately, it is just such "attention" that turns researchers' interests into other fields and, so, leaves religious education poverty striken and parasitic.

A Reflection on a Wandering Pathway

The fact that I did not start out to be either a professional religious educator or a researcher is not too surprising. A fair number of career paths show something similar, much to the distress of rational career theorists. In a surprising number of instances, something like sheer dumb luck or, to be more theological, the retrospectively recognized prevenient grace of God intervenes in the course of a human life, and the end is not all what was imagined at the beginning. Another way of recognizing the same things is to simply acknowledge that few North Americans have careers that match the idealized nineteenth century Teutonic academic or civil career. Few of us wind up doing what we thought we would do with our lives; that is both the glory and the conundrum of our experience.

Actually, our experience probably has much to do with living in a relatively open society, one in which interest and ability are surprisingly often matched with opportunity. Thus, the fact that my career has followed the wandering path it has is probably more a simple contextual difference than anything else. It is an all too frequent pattern for me to make much of the fact of the wandering, or to be anything other than grateful that I have been able to follow that pathway to this present.

That last sentence is an existential statement. It is not necessarily of much help to anyone else for, in truth, my path has been just that, *mine*. My friends have had other paths. Some of those paths are clearly more rationally ordered than mine. Others are less rational than mine, and some have led straight into something like John Bunyan's Slough of Despond. However, there is that third question yet to be answered. Perhaps in the answering of it there may be some help for another.

A THIRD QUESTION: WHAT ARE YOU DOING?

The query requires only four words. The answers take many more. The practicing existentialist could be satisfied with one word—living. The optimist might consider only responding to the challenge of lively possibilities. The Christian would need words like serve, or help, or supple (an especially pregnant idea of Evelyn Underhill's). However, the artist and the detective would be unsatisfied; they look for a more time-extensive pattern from all those years. It is not that any of the other answers are false. It is just that the artist and detective have an itch to find a sensible *pattern* for what is, all too easily, no more than a series of occurances.

While I do remember Edward Hardy's quiet caution, I have sought for a discernible structure in the career I have lived. I know that what I have identified is only an hypothetical model, but it is something with which I feel reasonably comfortable. Thus, it may be of some help, even as locating it proved to be an intriguing exercise in conceptual analysis.

Background

Vacations can be many things. One summer in the early 1980s my wife and I spent ten days in the vicinity of Williamstown in the state of Massachusetts. We wanted to enjoy the collection at the Clark Institute of Art, as well as relax from our work. We took several things to read along with us, and I brought the basic problem of this present chapter along with me. During those days in the Berkshire Hills of western Massachusetts I worried that question, in between enjoying the Renoirs at the Clark and the good eating available in the area. As a result, I reached an insight vis-à-vis the details of my career. That is, I discovered a way to model it.

Actually, I began by building personally meaningful pairs of words that could be separated by the conjunction "and." Then I clustered those pairs into topics. After a while, I discovered that I had three such pairings for each of eight topics. At that point, the developmentalist asserted its concern, and I tried a rough chronological ordering of those eight topics. Next I asked whether I had a linear progression or, perhaps, something more like the spiral model of human knowledge in Jean Piaget's *Structuralism*. After trying it out, I settled upon the Piagetian spiral as a way to think about those eight career-related topics and, especially, about that pointed question concerning what I *am* doing.

Then I began to ask the natural questions a model stimulates. I particularly asked whether the spiral could help me identify something more about the eight topics, something about the predecessors, and something about the future not-yet. I found that the model was a help with the first and second queries, but was of little help with the third one about the future not-yet. Thus, I recognized that I had modeled my career as a thing known between two unknowns (the distant past and the future). Actually, both my practicing existentialist and my Christian priest knew that be an inevitable result. One really *cannot* know the complete, complex causal sequence from the far distant past, nor can one really know the caused next event which lies on beyond any present.

All one can know is that they are a result of an ultimately unknown past, and the one who will be in some only vaguely discerned future not-yet. Thus, my model reminded me that mystery is the context of being, and career.

As I think about that spiral model of a career, I realize that a full explication is beyond the limits of this piece. In part, that is because the meaning of the words I used are not self-evident. However, that is not too surprising, for very little actually is self-evident. Thus, I simply want to use topic-words as the quadrant symbols in a two-level spiraling which seems like a fairly good way of assaying the detail that I have already listed.

Spiraling Between the Once Was and the Not Yet

In September of 1967 I had an opportunity to do some field interviewing in parishes and missions throughout the Sacramento River valley of northern California. It was something my work at the national head-quarters of the Episcopal Church did not normally involve. Perhaps that is why I so clearly remember visiting a former Gold Rush town in the Sierra Madre foothills. On what was left of Main Street was the Assayers Office. It was close to the bank and, one could tell, it once was a center of that community. I remember the office and what it once meant to the people of that town as I try to assay the career I have described. The gold, if there is any, in that description will be in a discernible structure or pattern; it will not be in the mere accumulation of remembered persons, or remembered occasions or, even, remembered books once read.

A First Turn of the Spiral Through Four Quadrant Topics

The model of a spiral that I am using is described in chapter 12 of my recent book *Religious Education in a Psychological Key*. The model envisions an ascending spiral which moves from "earlier" to "later." The path of such a spiral through conceptual space can be segmented into as many portions as one can meaningfully define. In this use of that model, however, I am identifying only four positions per turn, and I am positing that they are analogs of the quadrants on a compass. In addition, I am using only two turns of such an ascending spiral to model my career.

A First Cluster of Words for Quadrant A₁—Symbol

My earliest cluster of word pairs consisted of (i) King and Priest, (ii) Master and Friend, and (iii) Word and Son. They come to mind as I remember that stained glass Christus Rex I saw for all those years at First Methodist Church in Kalamazoo, Michigan. Eventually, as I grew up, I recognized that the window was a symbol of the Christian faith preached, affirmed, and celebrated in its presence. Somewhat later that symbol became something to be understood. The symbol, however, was a beginning; it was where I started on the pathway that led me to today.

A Second Cluster of Words for Quadrant B₁—Theology

My next cluster of word pairings consisted of (i) Law and Grace, (ii) Didache and Kerygma, and (iii) Sin and Salvation. They came to mind as I recalled my late adolescent attempts to understand that symbol I faced each week. Actually, it now seems reasonably evident that the attempt to understand that stained glass Christus Rex as a symbol led me into theology. Certainly, within a Christian context, the six themes in my three pairings are basic to many robust theologies from the time of the Church Fathers on.

A Third Cluster of Words for Quadrant C₁—Liturgy

My third cluster of word pairs consisted of (i) Earth and Heaven, (ii) Time and Eternity, and (iii) Creature and Creation. For me, those words signify what it means to express a theology in an action or liturgy. Actually, other than the local parish liturgy with which I grew up, my interest in the topic blossomed during my years in seminary. My participation in the Anglican-Orthodox Fellowship at Yale during the early 1950s, and my long acquaintance with (and interest in) the Orthodox Churches, find expression in those three pairings. I suspect that my interest began generally with such books as Evelyn Underhill's *Worship* and William D. Maxwell's *An Outline of Christian Worship*. I know it became more focused when I encountered Dom Gregory Dix's *The Shape of the Liturgy* and James Herbert Srawley's *The Early History of the Liturgy* and *The Liturgical Movement*. Eventually, my 1953

S.T.M. project at Yale was focused upon the relation of words and actions during the first eight Christian centuries (i.e., up through the First Roman Order).

A Fourth Cluster of Words for Quadrant D_1—Ecclesiology

My fourth cluster of paired words included (i) Scripture and Tradition, (ii) Rite and Ceremony, and (iii) Service and Celebration. I think those three pairings represent what I regard as the organizing power or dynamic of a liturgy, a dynamic that almost inevitably eventuates in an ecclesiology. Although it is probably 20/20 hindsight, my translation of ministry from a United Methodist parish to a parish of the Episcopal Church in 1954 may have been little more than the working out of a nearly inevitable organizing interaction of liturgy and ecclesiology.

A Second Turn of the Spiral Through Four Quadrant Topics

In the ascending spiral model, as one reaches a second level there is a re-encounter with quadrant topics which is more than repetition or replication. Thus, although the quadrant in conceptual space is the same, the pathway "through" it is not identical to the pathway traversed before. As a result, the quadrant topics will not be the same, although there will be some positable similarity. As I have suggested in my book, *Religious Education in a Psychological Key*, this quality of the spiral model permits us to acknowledge re-encounter with themes, ideas and problems without presuming that nothing is ever new, or that change is but a fantasy. Re-encounter is not repetition; spiraling is not recycling.

A Fifth Cluster of Words for Quadrant A_2—Piety

My fifth cluster of word pairs consisted of (i) a Clear Head and a Warm Heart, (ii) Action and Faith, and (iii) Behavior and Belief. The first of those pairs quite clearly represents my Methodist heritage, especially as I came to know it from the *Sermons* and the *Journal* of John Wesley. While the second and third pairs do have their roots in the Methodism in which I grew up, they also represent a growing concern during my seminary years which, actually, was confirmed by my encounters with the doctrine of vocation or work. For me, then, these word pairs represent the internalization of ecclesiology which finds its expression in a piety. However, in this instance, that is a rather practical piety which finds expression in works such as Brother Lawrence's *The Practice of the Presence of God*, or Evelyn Underhill's *The School of Charity* or *Abba*, or that remarkable Russian Orthodox classic *The Way of a Pilgrim and The Pilgrim Continues His Way*. It is a piety which appreciates and approximates a Quaker concern.

A Sixth Cluster of Words for Quadrant B_2—Psychology

My sixth cluster of three word pairs consisted of (i) Formation and Development, (ii) Cognition and Affect, and (iii) Environment and Person. For me, those three pairs of six words represent the result of trying to understand what such a practical piety means for the nature of humankind, which is a way of describing a psychology. I suspect the process probably got started with my reading of Gesell and Ilg, *Infant and Child in the Culture of Today* as my oldest daughter lived out her first months. However, it eventually went on to include such books as Hall and Lindzey, *Theories of Personality*, and Raymond B. Cattel's *The Scientific Analysis of Personality*, and H. J. Eysenck's delightful *Sense and Nonsense in Psychology*, and Kurt Lewin's *Principles of Topological Psychology*. Although I have a number of Freud's works, I find Ernest Dichter's *The Strategy of Desire* much more interesting. Still, across the past fifteen or so years it has been the works of Jean Piaget which have proved most intriguing, interesting, and helpful. The Swiss genetic epistemologist has been a continuing instructor, and an inspiration.

A Seventh Cluster of Words for Quadrant C_2—Ethics

My seventh cluster of word pairings consisted of (i) Justice and Love, (ii) Agape and Eros, and (iii) Responsibility and Freedom. For me (and, perhaps, only for me) these six words represent the expression of a human psychology, or what we are more likely to term an ethics. These themes are very much a part of my present concern for research into the sequences of development characteristic of moral judgments and the feeling of justice. Very generally, they relate to such studies as Herbert

Butterfield's *Christianity and History* and Oscar Cullman's *Christ and Time*. More specifically, they have an obvious relation to such works as C. H. Dodd's *Gospel and Law*, Edward Leroy Long, Jr.'s *Conscience and Compromise*, and Sir Walter Moberly's short, pithy little study *Responsibility*.

An Eighth Cluster of Words for Quadrant D_2—Science

My eighth (and last) cluster of words consisted of (i) Practice and Theory, (ii) Probability and Possibility, and (iii) Data and Design. For me, these six words represent the organization of the concerns of an ethic into the themes of a science. This is where I am at the moment and, in fact, it is where I have been for some time now in my career as an acknowledged religious educator. In being in this place, I have found help in some fairly diverse places. For instance, I have been helpd by such books as Ronald A. Fisher's classic *The Design of Experiments*, William L. Hays' encylopedic *Statistics for Psychologists*, the report by Charles E. Osgood, George J. Suci, and Percy H. Tannenbaum on *The Measurement of Meaning*, Jean Piaget's *Logic and Psychology* and *Insights and Illusions of Philosophy*, G. Polya's *How to Solve It*, Michael Polanyi's *Science, Faith, and Society*, Claude E. Shannon's and Warren Weaver's *The Mathematical Theory of Communication*, B. F. Skinner's early *Science and Human Behavior*, and both Norbert Wiener's *The Human Use of Human Beings* and his *God & Golem, Inc.* In addition, I continue to find the work of R. Buckminster Fuller fascinating, intriguing, and frequently helpful. His *Synergetics* and *Synergetics 2*, as well as *And It Came to Pass—Not to Stay* and *Critical Path* are part of my workï¨g ʟbrary.

The Nature of the Quadrants Through Which the Spiral Turns

In Piaget's model of human knowledge as an ascending spiral that I am using here, the radius of the turns increases as the spiral pathway rises. Thus, the spiral not only re-encounters what I have called the quadrants of a conceptual space at a "higher" level but, as well, traverses a more "extensive" part of that quadrant. Conceptually, theoretically, intuitively that is why re-encounter or re-occurance is not repetition or an identical recycling. However, it helps to identify the quadrants of the space that is being modeled. In fact, without such an identification, the model is nothing but an abstraction.

When I asked myself what the quadrant symbols meant, I found myself looking for a set of general categories which identified the similarity of the quadrant topics in both turns of the spiral model. I was, specifically, asking what category includes both an A_1 and an A_2, or a B_1 and a B_2, given the quadrant topics already identified (and the clusters of word pairs used in that identification)? Moreover, I realized that the spiral model implied that those general categories (once identified) should themselves form a related sequence. If I could discover such categories, the model would have worked in yet one more way and, thus, would have evidenced a certain robustness that general models ought to have.

As I thought about the problem, I came to realize that the A quadrant topics (Symbol and Piety) represented a kind of basic data within my career. As a result, I was able to recognize that the B quadrant topics (Theology and Psychology) represented a certain structure which was, in fact, quite related to the preceding data. Then I found that I could consider the C quadrant topics (Liturgy and Ethics) as a kind of role that seemed like a result of the previous structure. Finally, I was able to recognize that the D quadrant topics (Ecclesiology and Science) represented a story which was an outcome of the preceding data, structure, and role. Thus, I found that I could look at my career path, wandering as it may have seemed, as a spiraling from data through structure and role to story that has made at least two turns thus far. Actually, that result seems remarkably reasonable.

The Dynamic Involved in the Spiraling Through Two Turns

Implicit in any model of humankind, such as my two-turn spiral model of my career, is the quite important question of the dynamic which explains "movement" within the model. Piaget and Inhelder, for instance, recognized this question in *The Psychology of the Child* when they posited that a process of equilibrium was an "internal mechanism of all constructivism." I considered that possibility, but came to the conclusion that it was a macro-level description of the quadrant topics, but not necessarily a micro-level identification of the transformation processes which provided the dynamic for my career's "movement" from quadrant to quadrant along that spiral pathway. Thus, I set out to see if I could identify a set of such transformation processes for the career being modeled. If that should be possible, the model would be both elegant and potentially generally useful.

The A Quadrant to B Quadrant Transformation Process— Rationalization

The clue I used to identify this transformation process involved the backward glance. That is, I asked how Theology (a B) was related to Symbol (an A), and how Psychology (a B) was related to Piety (an A). What I could discern was that, in both instances, there was an effort to understand, to make rational, or to rationalize the previous quadrant topic via that "next" quadrant topic. I suspect that is correct.

The B Quadrant to C Quadrant Transformation Process— Expression

When I used the same backward glance clue for this quadrant-to-quadrant "movement," I found that I was asking how Liturgy (a C) was related to Theology (a B), and how Ethics (a C) was related to what I had called a Psychology (a B). In both instances, it seemed to me that that later topic involved an expression of the previous topic. Thus, I suspect that the attempt to express—expression—is the dynamic involved in my career "movement" from quadrant B to quadrant C.

The C Quadrant to D Quadrant Transformation Process— Organization

Once again I used the backward glance as my clue. Thus, I found that I had to ask how what I had called Ecclesiology (a D) was related to Liturgy (a C), and how Science (a D) was related to Ethics (a C). When I asked myself just how one might arrive at a D here from a C there, I concluded that an answer was via a process of ordering and relating, or what we usually mean by the idea of organization.

The D Quadrant to A Quadrant Transformation Process—
Internalization

This is a transformation process which is peculiar to the spiral model. In fact, in my two-turn model there is only one instance of this progression, although there is the presumption that it lies "behind" my initial A quadrant topic (Symbol) and "beyond" my second D quadrant topic (Science). The clue from a backward glance again proved useful. Thus, when I asked how Piety (an A) was related to what I had called Ecclesiology (a D) I could recognize that the transforming process involved a kind of taking into oneself a known in order to "move ahead" to a not-yet-known next. That kind of process is what psychologists tend to call internalization. Actually, all things considered, that probably is the dynamic.

My Four Transformation Processes and Piaget's Terms

Since the ascending and expanding spiral really is a Piagetian model, I next asked whether there were four Piagetian operations similar enough to my identified transformation processes to be regarded as functional equivalents. I really did not have to think too long or too hard to discover four constructs that seemed like good functional equivalents for my processes of rationalization, expression, organization, and internalization. What I had termed rationalization actually seems very similar to what Piaget tended to call accomodation. It also seems that what I had called expression was quite similar to what he called conduct in *Intelligence and Affectivity: Their Relation During Child Development*. Moreover, what I called organization seems similar to what Piaget called construction in his book *Structuralism*. Finally, what I had termed internalization seems functionally similar to what Piaget called assimilation. Thus, I seemed to have found a potentially useful way of using Piaget's terms and Piaget's model to assay my career pathway. There is a certain elegance in that result which suggests general usefulness.

The Pattern Discerned in the Spiral Model of a Career

This essay is almost complete. A structure and pattern have been discerned in what, at times, has seemed all too like following the wandering pathways left by generations of sheep on hillsides. The spiral model of my career suggests that my professional life as a religious educator has involved two turns of the career spiral, one early on and one somewhat later. I have re-encountered themes and problems, but in different ways. Actually those quadrant topics rather define, in a very general way, my career: It apparently has been a spiraling between Data and Structure, and Role and Story. It is also likely that the four transformation processes have been operative throughout that career, so that I have "moved" from Data to Structure via a process of rationalization (or Piaget's accomodation), and from Structure to Role via a process of expression (Piaget's conduct), and from Role to Story via a process of organization (Piaget's construction), and then from Story to Data via a process of internalization (or Piaget's assimilation).

Actually, the pattern is quite general. But it could be nothing else, for it is a pattern that has taken thirty or more years to work itself out, to "move" through these two turns of the spiral. A good bit of detail has been given of my career. But the model may be of most use to another as a way for them to assay their own career, to determine where (if anywhere) they are on such a career spiral. That just might be the gold in this assay of a seeming wandering pathway from the long ago to the present.

What I am Doing

When I concluded my introduction to that 1979 paper for the Psychological Association of Northeastern New York with the words, "Finally, I am a member of an endangered species, the researcher concerned with science, religion, and education," I meant it. Thus, I am now concerned that the species not become extinct. I want to encourage other researchers, especially younger ones, and one way I can do that is to help them publish their results and recognize their work. However, as I wrote a younger English friends several years ago, being one of this species is very like becoming one of those early Franciscan mendicants. For most of us opportunity is added to interest and ability only when someone else pays the bills. Yet it is a calling, and it is important that the called be able to respond. Actually, as a researcher and religious educator, I am at a point in my career where telling the story is one of the things I can and should be doing.

AN AFTERWORD TO THE READER

Congratulations. You have persisted to reach these words. I honor you for that. I do wish I might have been more obviously helpful. However, careers are rarely what texts or theorists imagine. Certainly mine is not. Still, if you can use Piaget's formal operations, I may have shown one way a pastoral and scholarly concern, plus a personally pragmatic piety, can become that honorable and high calling I acknowledge. As Paul of Tarsus reminded the earliest Corinthian Christians—"There are varieties of gifts, but the same Spirit. There are varieties of service, but the same Lord. There are many forms of work, but all of them, in all men, are the work of the same God. In each of us the Spirit is manifested in one particular way, for some useful purpose." (1 Cor. 12:4–7, NEB)

That is a bold affirmation. It is also a common ground for religionists, educators, and scientists. Only a congenital blindness can keep us from seeing as much. Yet we who are religious educators have no need to be so blinded, nor can we afford it. Our calling is to educate human beings to see, to be free, and to be responsible sub-creators in *this* Creation . . . refracted (perhaps) but still real images of their Creator!

Chapter 12

To Basically Change Fundamental Theory and Practice

James Michael Lee

"He who rides the horse of revolution must always have one foot in the stirrup."

—Turkish proverb

Of necessity this essay will be quite lengthy because of the utter totality with which my personal life and my religious education apostolate are existentially fused. My religious education apostolate is not something apart from my personality and the life-events which shaped this personality. I breathe and eat and drink and sweat religious education throughout the day and night because I am my apostolate and my apostolate is I.

This essay will be highly personal and quite frank because this is the way I am. The views which I express in this essay are very individual and candid ones, and thus represent my own perceptions of the persons, events, institutions, and forces which I have encountered over the years.

In recounting my life as it directly relates to the development and refinement of my religious education theory, it is necessary to discuss certain persons and institutions. By virtue of what I regard as their commendable qualities, some persons and institutions have exerted a decidedly positive impact upon my overall religious education perspective. By dint of what I believe to be their failings and defects, other persons and institutions have exerted a negative impact upon my overall religious education perspective. I do not hesitate to forthrightly identify and describe those persons or institutions in terms of the positive or negative influence they have had on me. My sole purpose in such cases is simply to show the impact which these persons or institutions have exerted on the forging of my religious education perspective and theory. It is not my direct or indirect intention to extol or embarrass any person or institution by respectively revealing what I believe to be their good points or by exposing what I believe to be their failings. Having written this, I hasten to add that my approach to religious instruction is by no means a reaction to the positive or negative influences of the persons or institutions that I have encountered in my life. Rather, the positive or negative influences of persons or institutions have served as signposts alerting me to the inherent strong points or weak points of different kinds of persons or institutions. Having been thus alerted, I was able to delve more deeply than I otherwise would into the underlying causes as to why some persons and institutions seem to me to be exemplary and why others seem to me to be deficient. I then incorporated the findings of this segment of my research into my overall religious education theory.

BOYHOOD

My birth certificate reads James Lee. And I was baptized James Lee. My father did not give me any middle name, probably because he wanted to situate me unequivocally within the James Lee tradition. James Lee I, my great-grandfather, was a prominent New York political figure and civic leader, national rowing champion, and first honorary president of a baseball team called the New York Knickerbockers and later renamed the New York Yankees. James Lee II worked in the New York district attorney's office. James Lee III, my father, was a certified public accountant in New York City, where I grew up.

My father liked to remind me frequently that I am James Lee IV. He would tell me stories about the James Lee's who went before me. By doing this, he psychologically positioned me within a tradition which was truly living because it was a tradition of which he and I were a here-and-now part. I also learned from this process that while it is foolish for me to live in the past, still it is essential to realize that the past lives in me. I suspect that my abiding love of the historical dimension of reality and my deep sense of being both a part of history and a shaper of history stem from my father's existential placement of me within the ongoing James Lee tradition.

Parental Influence

The home in which I grew up was a milieu of deep love. It was a constant source of inspiration for me to see how deeply my father and mother loved each other and showed this love in their daily lives.

Both my parents were extraordinarily secure as persons. They gave me a great deal of love and support, together with a great sense of security and confidence in myself.

At home I was repeatedly taught to strive unswervingly for what is right religiously and what is best qualitatively, regardless of what others might think. My parents educated me never to look for approval and applause of others, or to be disappointed when such approval and applause do not follow an act which I regard as religiously significant or qualitatively admirable. They believed that human approval and applause are at best incidental to the worth of an act. In their view, approval and applause may well exert a corrupting influence in that the person eventually strives more for human approval than for the intrinsic and extrinsic worth of the act itself. This early education proved to be a great source of personal strength and consolation to me in later years, notably in the apostolate.

As an only child with very few relatives on either side of the family, I developed a particularly close relationship to my mother and father and was deeply influenced by them in virtually every aspect of my personality. This powerful influence perdures to this day, not just in my personality configuration, but also in my religious education apostolate.

My father was a wonderful person, though I did not appreciate him in my boyhood as much as I do now. He was deeply religious—not pious or frothy in his religion, but a man who greeted all reality quite naturally and easily into a deliciously integrated religious worldview. An idealist in all things, he ceaselessly saw each and every reality not just as it is here and now, but also the way it would be and should be if it were to genuinely fulfill the imperative of its own basic nature. He was a brilliant CPA, especially in developing significant new theoretical models and approaches for the field of accountancy. One of his most widely recognized contributions to his field was an important article he wrote for the *Journal of Accountancy* in which he devised a fiscal paradigm by which investment trusts would be able to save considerable money in taxes. He was fiercely independent and was in every way his own man. An incurable romantic who loved life to the brim, he was felled by a massive stroke when he was only forty-five years old.

Religion has meant everything to my mother, and together with her family life has been her deepest reality. Most people regard her as saintly. An extremely intelligent woman, my mother graduated at the earliest allowable age from all the schools she attended. She and my father were classmates at New York University's School of Commerce. I have always been very close to my mother, and as everyone who knows us can testify, she has exerted an enormous and abiding influence on my life and career. She is well known for possessing an extraordinary ability to make prodigious sacrifices for her ideals and for what she thinks is right or religious. She consistently maintains the highest standards of perfection with herself and others, especially her loved ones. I have never known a person who did not respect my mother for her great intelligence, incredible hard work, deep religiosity, perfectionist standards, absolute reliability, and an amazing ability to surmount any difficulty which might come along.

I have always admired my parents very much, and have been enormously proud of them. They have served as a source of inspiration and strength to me throughout my entire life. I am truly honored far beyond my worth to be their son.

My childhood was extremely happy. I cannot imagine how it could have been happier.

Early Milieu

As a boy who grew up on the streets of New York, I quickly learned to prize what is real and demonstrable. Conversely, I learned just as quickly to despise what is fake and amorphous, regardless of the high-sounding or even pious labels which might be attached to the fake and the amorphous. Like most city boys, especially those from New York, I acquired the tendency to be rather direct and to call things as I see them. The well-known fact that my approach to religious instruction uncompromisingly searches out the real and the demonstrable while simultaneously rejecting the fake and the amorphous no matter how these might be festooned with pious verbiage or ecclesiastical trappings can be traced at least in part to my growing up on the streets of New York.

The psychophysical environment of the apartment which I called home thoroughly imbued and in some way sublated the realistic core and flinty edges which I had acquired on the streets. Wonderful Oriental rugs covered the floors, even in the hallways. A large and splendid

English oil painting occupied the place of honor in the living room, flanked by two smaller oils executed by a continental artist. Three lovely original Turner watercolors graced another wall of this *petit salon*. Reproductions of renowned religious masterpaintings hung in the bedroom, and the entrance hall was decorated with some of my father's finest photographs, all tastefully framed. Dinner and party guests would often comment that the apartment looked like a small museum. My father had purchased the rugs and pictures during the depths of the Great Depression. The family could not at all afford to buy them because, like many CPA's, he was out of work for several years during that dark period. But my father regarded art objects as absolute necessities of life. My early development in a milieu of art provided me with an abiding felt awareness that, at bottom, the immediate realities of daily life on the street and in the office and in the religious instruction setting can only be genuinely appreciated, adequately explained, and optimally executed when they are performed artistically, that is to say when the beauty which each reality possesses in its basic nature and in its operations is fully released and masterfully orchestrated by the human person.

As a boy, I was very active in all kinds of sports. My greatest sports passion was stickball, a baseball-like game indigeneous to New York City. Our baseball team sometimes played its games on a grassy diamond situated right at the entrance to New York harbor. Watching the luxury liners and freighters from all over the world sail in and out gave me an awareness of the international which has remained with me ever since.

Primal Religious Experience and the Call

The call to serve God came rather early in my life. When I was six years old I had a religious experience which set into motion the basic direction which my life was to take. I am completely convinced that it is the enormous and abiding residual power of this early religious experience which has unfailingly continued to serve as the powerplant and gyro-stabilizer of my life-voyage from six years of age down to the present moment. This childhood religious experience did not consist in a single ecstatic moment of plunging headlong into the ocean of complete truth, or in a sudden soaring into blinding light amidst a romantic flourish of trumpets. It was, as I vaguely remember, a rather low-keyed occurrence which took place on and off for some time, possibly for as long as several weeks. I can no longer clearly recall, if indeed I could ever clearly recall, the specific details of its structure or substance. All I know for certain is that sometime during this extended experience and also as a direct consequence of this experience I irrevocably and completely gave myself to God's service. "Irrevocably" is an odd and almost ridiculous word to use for a six-year-old child's decision. Notwithstanding, this decision was irrevocable for me then in a six-year-old child's way. This irrevocability has remained with me at the core and the perimeters of my existence ever since. I can never remember a moment in my life since that time in which I was not personally and totally convinced that God had personally called me to be one of his apostles.

How does a person devote himself completely to God's service? For a six-year-old boy living in the Catholic Church of that day, the answer was virtually automatic: become a priest. The lay apostolate was even more neglected and disparaged by the Catholic Church in those days than it is today, if such can be imagined. Consequently, it was not by any design on my part that I inevitably interpreted my primal religious experience and its concomitant complete commitment to God's service as necessitating my becoming a priest; it was simply that there were no other viable options presented to me at that time.

My family subscribed to *The Field Afar*, a monthly magazine published by the Catholic Foreign Mission Society of America, popularly known as the Maryknoll Fathers. I was deeply impressed by the stories and photographs of the tireless and sometimes even heroic apostolic efforts made by the Maryknoll missioners to win souls for Christ in distant mission lands. The missionary apostolate held magnetic appeal for me, since it involved total and unselfish commitment, leaving one's homeland and family to go to an alien land to bring God's saving grace to others with little appreciation or applause. Even today, I believe that a basic key to my own self-definition as a person and as a religious educationist is that of a missionary.

The Maryknoll missions in those days were almost exclusively in China. My formative years revolved around the burning desire to spend my life for Christ in the China missions.

I still clearly remember being in my room one August evening in the summer house my parents had bought at the tip of Seaford Harbor on the southern shore of Long Island. I was eight years old. Suddenly and with no warning, I found myself in the midst of a very powerful religious experience. This one lasted only a few minutes. It was not accompanied by any visual or auditory sensations, but rather by a kind of deep movement through my whole person which fused my heart and mind and life. At the height of the experience I cried out: "God, if you give me eighty years, I will work night and day for you with everything I have." From an objective theological perspective, such a statement represented a childish form of religion, one which almost irreverently sought to bind God and ensnare him in the nets of my own desires and strivings. But it seems to me that this statement which I uttered when I was eight years old is eminently understandable and valid when viewed from the subjective perspective of a young boy. Any basically different kind of utterance from an eight-year-old boy would have been unreal, chimerical, or anachronistic. Naive, delusionary, and perhaps even impious as it might seem, I still somehow hold it fast within my soul that God heard and accepted that solemn promise I made to him that soft summer evening and for his part will fulfill that which I so ardently begged of him.

Coindre Hall

After three years at the local parish elementary school, my parents enrolled me at Coindre Hall, a small private boarding school which had just opened in a rustic picturesque spot on Long Island. The student body was international and interesting. Coindre Hall turned out not only to be a paradise for me, but also to be very important for my religious life. The Brothers of the Sacred Heart were fine teachers, and demanded a high level of performance from me. I learned a great deal from them. Most significantly, I learned to deepen my love for religion and its lifestyle by seeing how they lived with each other and with us. I shall always treasure who they were and what they did.

Sometime in the seventh grade I was confirmed. Confirmation was a momentous event for me, and during the three years prior to receiving this sacrament I frequently pondered long and hard on the name I would select. My parents were of great help to me in these deliberations. For me then and also now, a name is not simply a name. In my view, a name somehow embodies a person and proclaims his mission in life. Regardless of which saint's name I would consider, I always returned to the same one, Michael. This was natural, since I was born on the feast of St.

Michael, always felt very close to him, and greatly admired his mission. For a long time I believed that God had given St. Michael to me as my own personal guardian angel. Though I no longer believe that this is true, I still cling fast to the belief that somehow and in some way St. Michael is personally watching out for me and armoring me in a very special way. Throughout most of my life, when the going became difficult or the path a trifle unclear or the resolve battered, I have always devoutly recited the church's prayer to St. Michael which used to be said at the end of every Mass: "St. Michael the Archangel, defend us in battle. . . ." On affective as well as on cognitive grounds, I pay no heed to those who in this day or in others deny the existence of angels or of St. Michael. I was enormously proud to receive the grace of the sacrament and the name of Michael at the Coindre Hall chapel. I ardently hoped that I could thereby forever join St. Michael as a fearless warrior for God.

ADOLESCENCE

Brooklyn Prep

After graduation from Coindre Hall, I attended Brooklyn Preparatory High School, a Jesuit institution located not too far from where I lived. With the exception of my religion classes and a few others, the schooling there generally did not live up to my academic or pedagogical expectations.

The religion classes at the Prep were remarkably open. Though I not infrequently disagreed with the teachers' views and even sometimes with church doctrine both in class discussions and on written examinations, the teachers gave me very high grades because they appreciated the reasoning and the evidence which I brought to my positions. This fact made a deep impression on me, an impression which remains as forceful today as it was in my adolescent days. Religion in its objective and especially in its personal subjective dimensions can only be discovered and lived through honest and open exploration. The effective religious educator is one who encourages such exploration in terms of the learner's here-and-now existential situation. In my adolescence I was, as I am now, contemptuous of religious educators who label the views of certain colleagues or learners as "dangerous." In my view, the only real danger lurks in the closed, airless, and fearful mentalities of such educators. This holds especially true for a denomination's cadre of religious education administrators.

Adolescence is widely regarded as a period often accompanied by more or less serious doubts of faith. I never experienced such doubts, even in the slightest, during adolescence or at any other time in my life. Later on, when I taught at Notre Dame, some of the preachers at Sunday Mass would declare that a person was still burdened with a childish and immature faith if his faith had not been seriously rocked and then rebuilt. However, I have never felt religiously enfeebled because I have never been convulsed by doubts of faith. For me, my faith has always been as natural as breathing, and my breathing flow has not been shaken seriously thus far in my life. Perhaps all this indicates that my faith is indeed childish and immature. Be this as it may, all I know is that my religious life has been a gradual unfolding and realization of the seminal religious experience which I had as a six-year-old boy.

The Venard and Missionary Enthusiasm

In my junior year of high school I entered the Maryknoll junior seminary called the Venard. This seminary was housed in a wonderful stone building nestled in the hills of eastern Pennsylvania. As my fellow seminarian Donald Caulfield and I were wont to remark, the Venard was an ideal place for a young man to grow up. The setting was ideal, the food magnificent, the size right, the sports facilities excellent, the priest-teachers fine men, the students diverse—the only thing missing were girls.

The disappointingly low academic schooling provided at the Venard was more than offset by the burning religious idealism and the enthusiastic missionary spirit of the faculty. By and large the faculty consisted of former missionaries to China. Many of them were waiting to be sent back, and looked forward with unrestrained eagerness to that spring day when the assignments from Maryknoll headquarters in Ossining, New York would be released. Whether in class, on all-day hikes, or even when prescribing tasks for daily manual labor, the faculty typically would recount their own personal experiences in the China missions. All in all, the seminary experience was structured in such a way as to enkindle and maintain a living desire to devote and sacrifice oneself totally for God in the mission fields afar. The Venard pulsated with an intense and focused missionary spirit. Because I am essentially a re-ligious missionary activist, I was thrilled and inspired by the life I found and lived there.

It was at the Venard that I was existentially introduced to a regulated disciplined daily life which in many respects was organized around the liturgy. My great appreciation for the structure and enactment of the liturgy, especially the Mass, would later play a significant role in the way I was to conceptualize the structure and enactment of the religion teaching process.

Lakewood, the Catholic Worker, the Lay Apostolate, and Europe

Upon graduating from the Venard, I was sent to Maryknoll Junior College in Lakewood, New Jersey. Some of the priest-professors I had at Lakewood were among the finest teachers under whom I have ever studied. They opened me up to the world of high scholarship, and made this world exciting and relevant. They showed me that meticulous and painstaking scholarship is necessary to locate truth, and to preserve it from corruption on the one hand and from rigidity on the other. They taught me to pore carefully over each word and sentence, mining them for meaning and sifting them for relationships and for inter/intra con-sistency. Though less gung ho than the Venard in explicit missionary focus and atmosphere, Lakewood taught me that no missionary activism can be authentic and effective unless it is born and sustained by that kind of burning love which is pervasively interactive with the processes and products of learned scholarship.

Thanks to James DeFino who was then one of my classmates at Lakewood, I became actively involved in the Catholic Worker move-ment in New York City. The Catholic Worker—or C.W. as we used to fondly call it—is a lay religious movement whose deeply committed members embrace voluntary poverty and seek to bring about a world based on the principles and realities of Christian social justice.

During my vacations from the seminary, I would spend as much time as I could at the C.W. helping to paint the walls, manning the soup line, assisting the full-time members in whatever way I could, talking to the "ambassadors," and attending the Friday night talks by prominent intel-lectual and social leaders. Together with the C.W. members, I picketed

the federal government's office in Manhattan on the anniversary of
Hiroshima. (This was many years before picketing was the "in thing" to
do.) In accordance with one of the C.W.'s basic teachings, I became a
pacifist and refused to register for the draft.

At the center of the Catholic Worker movement lies, not only an all-
giving and highly activist Christian love for one's neighbor, but also a
viable theory of this love. It was a distinct eye-opener for me to discover
that supreme activists like the Catholic Worker members assigned such
a pivotal place to theory in their apostolic ministry. The C.W. members
were deeply aware that unless their many activities were both rooted in
and permeated by theory, there was the distinct probability that these
activities would thereby be rendered chaotic or barren. At the C.W.
there was an abiding awareness that theory is necessary to explain activities and to predict their success or failure. Dorothy Day liked to quote
Lenin to the effect that there can be no genuine or lasting revolution
without a comprehensive theory of revolution.

It was during my time at the C.W. that I became greatly attracted to
the priest-worker movement in France. I read every book and article I
could find on the priest-workers. One of the many things which deeply
impressed me was that the zealous men who joined the ranks of the
priest-workers usually did so, not because of theological reasons, but
because these men discovered in their own personal and religious experience that the French people had become by and large de-Chris-
tianized. As usual, theology was not in the forefront of either the
Church's activity in France or these men's own pastoral ministry. Theology trailed behind. It was only later that theology was invoked by
proponents of the priest-workers to support the movement or by adversaries to condemn the movement.

It was Tom Lilly, another classmate at Lakewood, who got me involved in the lay apostolate. "Lil" was especially interested in that
specific form of the lay apostolate known as Catholic Action, and organized C.A. cells at Lakewood for the purpose of mobilizing the seminarians to establish lay cells after ordination. Through my active
involvement at Lakewood in Catholic Action, I gained familiarity with
the theology and politics of the various forms of the lay apostolate.
Active involvement in Catholic Action had major consequences for my
future personal life and my future religious education apostolate. First,
Catholic Action was consciously based on theory and was permeated
with a clear conceptualization of the structure of action, thus serving as

a potent reinforcer of my Catholic Worker experience. Second, Catholic Action opened up to me on a major scale for the first time in my life the authentic religious validity and tremendous ecclesial worth of the lay state and the lay apostolate.

Toward the end of my second year at Lakewood, the prefect of discipline formally suppressed both the Catholic Worker groups and the Catholic Action cells at the seminary. Some of us continued our involvement in both groups, though in an underground fashion. Through this experience I came to an existential realization that if the Christian church is to fulfill its mission, it must actively promote different and often conflicting apostolic avenues rather than attempting to suppress these avenues. This realization was to grow as the years went on, and to play an important role both in my own approach to religious instruction and in my activities in Religious Education Press.

During the summer which fell between the two academic years at Lakewood, my mother took me to Europe. Though its purpose was primarily to journey to Rome for the Holy Year, the trip soon took on the proportions of the summer-long grand tour so popular in the pre-World War I era. The trip was one magnificent adventure from the time the ship gently slid into the glorious Bay of Naples until we left for home from lovely Lisbon harbor. This trip to Europe was one of the five most momentous and educational experiences of my life. Europe opened up for me the existential fullness and variegated richness of religion and of all life. Henceforeward I could no longer live a religion which was simply one-sided, however important or necessary one or another side might be.

Since that holy summer of that Holy Year, I have returned to Europe as often as I could. I have gone back nearly forty times, including two entire years, almost every summer, and quite a few winter vacations. I have found that I desperately need non-American life and culture and general outlook as expanders and balancers for my personal life as well as for my religious education apostolate.

When Mao Tse-tung came to power in China, Maryknoll was forced to close its missions there. I was deeply saddened at this turn of events, because my whole life had been geared to serving Christ in the China missions. But like many Americans, I had hoped that Mao would be overthrown. When, after a few years, it became evident that Mao's regime was permanent, I left Maryknoll. My adolescence had ended.

LATER ACADEMIC PREPARATION

The Diocesan Major Seminary

The diocesan major seminary proved to be a distinctly different experience from Maryknoll. I was keenly disappointed to find significantly less heart, significantly less unselfish commitment, and significantly less religious gung ho spirit here than either in the Venard or in Lakewood. While a large percentage of the students in the diocesan seminary were fine men with sterling ideals, still it seemed to me that others were already devising ways of securing appointments to plush parishes or were already taking the first measured steps in politically maneuvering themselves into an ascending ecclesiastical spiral which would culminate in a call to the episcopate or at the very least to a high-ranking office in the papal household of the diocese. Since I aspired to be a simple hardworking priest in a slum parish, I quickly moved to disassociate myself from this kind of ecclesiastical politics with its attendant jockeying for personal preferment and position. This seminary experience constituted my first prolonged encounter from the inside of the ecclesiasticalization of the ecclesia. I soon came to despise such ecclesiasticalization, recognizing that it is the source of so much of the evil, corruption, arrogance, narrowness, and lack of prophetic apostolic fervor in the church.

The deplorably low academic level which generally prevailed in the diocesan major seminary came as a distinct letdown from the exciting academic life at Lakewood. More often than not, the diocesan seminary professors were weak both in substantive content and in pedagogical procedure. One professor, who for some unfathomable reason was reverentially called "Pure Intellect" by many seminarians, exclusively conducted his classes by having students one after another read aloud from the textbook. Other professors, a bit more energetic, exclusively ran their classes by reading the textbook aloud themselves. The Reverend Professor "Pure Intellect" taught a full year's course in experimental psychology even though he received his Louvain doctorate in speculative philosophy, and, as far as anyone knew, had never so much as stepped foot into an experimental psychology laboratory. The metaphysics professor, for his part, was trained in dogmatic theology and not in metaphysics. The courses usually did not even attain the level of a purely textbook course. To be sure, only part of the textbook frequently constituted a course. It was only on rare occasions that I saw anyone in the library. My experience of the deplorably low academic standards in the diocesan major seminary taught me never to assume that a cleric automatically possesses that kind of academic background or that level of cultural achievement which the laity have been led to expect of their priests (and ministers). Some clerics are highly educated. However, a great many whom I have met seem to fall short of that level of intellectual and cultural attainment which their ministry perforce presupposes. The discovery and later ongoing reconfirmation of this fact had important ramifications on my later religious education apostolate because it suggested a fundamental reason why so many clerical religious educators naturally expect so little of their learners and co-workers theologically and religiously.

Soon after I arrived at the diocesan seminary, I began to organize small groups of interested seminarians to study Catholic Action for the purpose of implementing this and other forms of the lay apostolate in their future parishes. I was advised by Reverend Professor "Pure Intellect" that activities of this nature were held in official disfavor at the seminary, and that I should desist. I followed his advice.

All these disillusioning experiences at the diocesan major seminary caused me to develop a healthy and wholesome skepticism toward the clergy in general. By this I mean that my experiences at the diocesan major seminary cured me of the exaggerated respect which I previously had for the clergy as clergy. Henceforward I would examine the pronouncements and decisions of the clergy with just as much care and circumspection as I would examine the pronouncements and decisions of anyone else. I would never again accord special weight or undue reverence to clerical pronouncements and decisions simply because they were pronouncements and decisions of the clergy. This newly acquired unwillingness to accord special adulation and submissive respect for clerical pronouncements and decisions on the sole ground of their being clerical, and this newly acquired lack of deference to the clergy, proved to have a pronounced effect on my later religious education apostolate.

However weak they might be, all schools nevertheless have something valuable to teach the students. The most important thing which I learned at the diocesan major seminary in terms of my future religious education apostolate was my encounter with the major world philosophers, men of the caliber of Plato, Aristotle, Aquinas, Kant, Hegel, and so forth. I was especially captivated by the elegance and sweep of comprehensive theoretical systems, that is, of theories which are constructed into overarching cohesive systems explaining all phenomena in an entire field. This encounter with the great philosophers, particularly with Aristotle and Aquinas, not only reinforced the keen appreciation of theory which I had learned so well at the Catholic Worker, but also showed me that the validity and utility of any theoretical assertion can only be adequately tested by inserting that statement into a comprehensive theoretical system. A theoretical system has the inherent power to debug and correct individual assertions within that system; in turn, a theoretical system is itself expanded and refined by each new significant element which interactively becomes a dimension of the system. A person or an enterprise not operating out of a comprehensive theoretical system will most probably end up in all sorts of logical contradictions and, what is worse, in all sorts of failures in the practical order. The whole basis and rationale for my desire to create a comprehensive theoretical system for religious instruction is a direct outcome of what I learned in the diocesan seminary about the necessity and practicality of a theoretical system.

Persons who read my books and then later meet me personally or hear me speak at some popular-type convention frequently tell me that I am quite different in person than the impression about me which they gain from my writings. I always take such statements as great compliments. One thing I have always admired upon reading Aquinas is that it is very difficult to discern the contours and details of his personality from his writings. He took pains to let his theoretical system and its parts stand on their own legs; he did not attempt to buttress his system by the unwarranted intrusion of his own personality. Similarly the gospels do not clearly indicate what the personality of Jesus was really like. In my own scholarly writings, I try hard to emulate Aquinas and the evangelists by not allowing my personality to find its place there. I look with disfavor on those religious educationists who deliberately strive to seduce persons into accepting their views by replacing logic and evidence with personal allusions cleverly crafted to tickle a reader's fancy or to appeal to a reader's deep-seated irrational delights or fears. I also hold in low regard those religious educationists who propose positions primarily to gratify their own egos and needs and ecclesiastical aspirations, rather than utilize their writings as engines for the open exploration of truth.

Persons who read my books frequently ask why I devote so much space to summarizing the viewpoints of opponents, and indeed presenting these summaries before I advance my own position. This is another procedure which I owe directly to Aquinas. In my reading of Aquinas in the seminary, I was deeply impressed by his honesty. The Angelic Doctor was no intellectual bigot. He wished his readers to learn not only the meat of the arguments against his position, but also to become cognizant of the fact that there was a formidable tradition of arguments against his position. Having presented the opponents' viewpoints, Aquinas would then advance his own position, after which he rebutted the arguments of the adversaries. Because Aquinas' procedure is the most intellectually honest scholarly technique of which I am aware, I employ it as frequently as possible in my scholarly writings. I disdain those narrow-minded religious educationists who present their own views without reviewing the finest arguments against their positions, and who implicitly suggest that positions other than their own do not even exist. When situations arise in which I believe that I am not able to do proper justice to positions which are contrary to my own, I will edit a book so as to afford adversaries as well as supporters the opportunity of presenting their views as fully and as forcefully as they wish. I despise those apparently insecure and fearful religious educationists who edit books or sponsor conferences in which only persons who hold views basically similar to their own are represented. Books and conferences of the latter variety enshrine intellectual dishonesty and exalt close-mindedness.

After three years at the diocesan seminary, the members of our class were due to receive the call from the bishop to tonsure. This call is typically a major decision event for every Catholic diocesan seminarian. By the time the bishop's call to tonsure was almost upon our class, I had decided that I would decline and leave the seminary. This decision was an extraordinarily difficult and personally wrenching one for me because I was, as I still am today, living out that primal religious experience with which God blessed me at the age of six. I had always univocally interpreted this religious experience as necessarily meaning that I should be a priest. Because I defined my very selfhood in terms of this religious experience, I therefore defined my selfhood in terms of being a priest. Hence to abandon the priestly life meant to plunge headlong into the realm of nonbeing, nonreality, nonmeaningfulness. It was to commit suicide, for in renouncing the possibility of being a priest I was thereby renouncing the possibility of being my self.

Still, I felt deeply in my heart that I very much wanted to be a priest. How else could I be authentic to my core self, to that self whose very existence is that primal religious experience *en marche?* A major problem I faced in all of this was the priesthood. I had serious doubts about whether it was really possible for me to be a good priest within the confines of that ecclesiastical structure called the priesthood with its suffocating clerical subculture. I was not, after all, what the authorities liked to designate as "a model seminarian." Furthermore, I strongly believed that I lacked the necessary firsthand experience in and of the so-called "world" to make that kind of decision which God had every right to expect from me.

It was on a day in May in the high-vaulted and cool seminary chapel that the name of each seminarian called to tonsure was read from the altar. Most seminarians responded with the centuries-old Latin reply "*Adsum,*" echoing the affirmative reply of Samuel to God's invitation (1 Sm. 3:4). Other seminarians did not respond, thus indicating their decision to decline the bishop's call to tonsure. When the name Jacobus Michael Lee was read, I made no response. A major turning point in my life had occurred, and with it a major turning point in my service to God.

On a densely foggy morning in early June, I returned to the seminary to assemble my belongings and bring them home to Brooklyn. I wanted to say goodbye to the rector, but he was already back home in Ireland for the summer. So I spoke with the man whom the rector had left in charge, the senior canon law professor. I was never in his class; however he had a reputation for being comical. He reportedly had a penchant for doing strange things like writing notes in pencil on his bald pate during class, and then erasing these notes a few minutes later when he thought the notes needed revision. Nicknamed "Porky" because of his short rotund appearance, his common sense was generally regarded as nil. In the course of our conversation I mentioned my grave doubts and severe angst about leaving the seminary. He told me that I should not think at all of the priestly life for five years. At the completion of this period, I should consult a wise priest if my doubts and angst still persisted. I instinctively realized that this man who was so frequently ridiculed by many seminarians gave me the best advice I had received in all three years at this seminary. I scrupulously did what he suggested.

St. John's

In September I enrolled at St. John's University College in Brooklyn because I wanted to become a teacher and needed the proper courses in order to become certified. The seminary had not granted me a bachelor's degree because in my second year there I had elected to spend another entire summer in Europe rather than take a certain required Greek course during the lengthy vacation. Since I have never let my schooling interfere with my education, I decided I could profit far more educationally and apostolically by personally experiencing in depth the architectural and artistic marvels of France rather than wasting my time on what other seminarians told me was a very inferior Greek course.

My year at St. John's was a lovely, blossoming one for me. Over and over again I was forcefully struck at how genuinely nice and kind the St. John's students were, in distinct contrast to the uncharitableness and interpersonal viciousness exhibited by many students at the diocesan major seminary. On the whole, the St. John's students I met seemed to be much more deeply religious in their everyday life than I had previously expected. While the professors I had at St. John's were not of the highest scholarly caliber, they certainly were superior to most of the teachers I had at the seminary. I was particularly impressed at how positively and warmly they reacted to those students who disagreed with their positions, an experience which was in marked contrast to what I had generally experienced at the diocesan seminary. The professors I had at St. John's were all laymen; none was a cleric. I found at St. John's that the lay life was much more open, friendly, natural, honest, and in many ways much more Christian than seminary life. This experience helped me further ease into the lay life and away from the clerical life.

Columbia

The following year I enrolled in the graduate faculty of political science at Columbia University, with a major in American history. This was the first time in my life since kindergarten that I attended a non-Catholic school. It was a deeply exciting intellectual year for me, one which ushered into my life a whole new level of experience in scholarship. The American history program at Columbia was then at the top of its form; possibly this was the finest academic era which that program ever had in its distinguished history. The professors would frequently share with us students the processes and difficulties of writing the book each was painstakingly laboring on at the moment. Often the professors would bring in other scholars from the entire history department to tell us of their own toils in researching and writing the book on which they were currently working. Hearing the firsthand experiences of these great scholars in their arduous scholarly activities made a lasting impression on me. From these illustrious men I learned that high scholarship is very demanding, very meticulous, very difficult, and very time-consuming. High scholarship cannot be done on the run, or in spurts. It is not a task for activists, dilettantes, persons with an axe to grind, or persons who just lust after fame. Rather, high scholarship is only for persons who are deeply committed, greatly disciplined, very hardworking, and basically unafraid to discover data or come to conclusions which might severely modify or even topple their own previous positions. These men taught me that the firstfruit of the painful process of high scholarship is the discovery, confirmation, or rejection of facts or laws or theories which can now be held with confidence because they were discovered in an intellectually honest manner characterized by meticulous methodological care. My firsthand experience with top-drawer scholarship at Columbia exerted an important impact on the contours and direction of my future religious education apostolate.

I supplemented my American history courses with work in other areas, such as ancient history under Elias Bickerman and Jewish history under one of the greatest scholars I have ever met, Salo Baron. My master's thesis was entitled "The Political Genius of A. Oakey Hall," and dealt with the political life and machinations of the man whose greatest fame came from being the mayor of New York City during the Tweed Ring era. When I presented my lengthy master's thesis to the graduate school, the person there believed it was a doctoral dissertation and gave me a Ph.D. card to fill out. I was both honored and spurred on by this.

Political Activity

During the years immediately following my departure from the seminary, I became heavily involved in city politics at the district level. My cousin had run unsuccessfully for the post of state representative and was still president of the political club in the local congressional district. The party boss for the borough of Brooklyn personally urged me to run for office for a variety of reasons which he considered weighty, including the alleged ethnic neutrality of the name James Lee, a neutrality he felt would appeal to the entire range of ethnic groups in the city. My involvement in local political activity taught me that politics is almost inescapably a dirty affair which seems to inevitably lead to a certain sullying and corruption of virtually everyone who participates in it. I found that most persons engage in politics primarily and fundamentally for personal gain of one sort or another. Truth and justice and human betterment tend to be embraced by a political person when these qualities further that individual's self-interest or agree with his view of reality. But truth and justice and human betterment tend to be brushed aside and even trampled upon by a political person when these qualities interfere with the successful pursuit of his self-interest or go counter to his view of reality. The essence of politics of every sort is winning. In order to win, truth and justice and human betterment must at times be violated. When all is said and done, neither truth nor justice nor human betterment is indigenous to politics. In politics there is only self-interest. Politics proceeds by compromise. More often than not, compromise involves the abandonment of people and principles.

During the years in which I participated actively in politics, I found that the persons who were the most vocal on behalf of what they termed "good government" were usually those who secretly believed that the genuine definition of good government is one which advances their own self-interests or which furthers their own views. My subsequent abhorrence for politics both secular and ecclesiastical dates from that time. Virtually all the political activity I have witnessed since those days has amply confirmed my initial judgment. This holds true not only for secular politics, but also (and perhaps even more so) for ecclesiastical politics, religious education politics, and church school politics.

Because of both the essential nature of politics and the constantly recurring antiprincipled incidents which I experienced in the arenas of secular and ecclesiastical politics, I am unalterably opposed to certain contemporary efforts to debase and deform religious education activity by transmogrifying this activity into politics. Religion and politics simply do not mix; their fundamental bases and directions are diametrically opposed.

Teachers College

By the time I finished my master's degree in history, I had decided that I would pursue a doctorate in education at Columbia University's Teachers College. While pursuing my master's degree in history, I noticed in the thesis seminar course that most of the students were engaged in research which I regarded as important to the discipline of history but which I believed was not optimally promotive of restoring the world to Christ. Richard Morris, my master's thesis advisor, was horrified that I planned to attend Teachers College and pursue a doctorate in education. When I told him my intentions, he offered me a doctoral fellowship in history on the spot. His kind offer seemed to be as much motivated by a desire to preserve me from becoming corrupted through the low state of scholarship in education as it was by a desire to keep me within the ranks of history. But I truly believed that I could accomplish more for God and the church in the field of education than in the discipline of history. Put succinctly, I was convinced that God was calling me to make history rather than to write it.

I had, of course, seriously entertained the idea of pursuing a doctorate in theology. Since no Catholic university in the United States at that time allowed a layman to pursue a doctorate in theology, and since theology doctorates in American Catholic universities were of low quality anyway, I gave careful consideration to enrolling for a theology doctorate in Europe. I had tentatively chosen Strasbourg because that university was then reputed to be in the forefront of the *nouvelle théologie*, was very open, was strongly influenced by German as well as by native French scholarly influences, and was ideally situated from a geographical standpoint. But in the end, I elected to pursue a career in education rather than in theology. Though American Catholic theologians of that era were by and large mediocre, the European Catholic theologians were of the highest caliber. This was especially true of those European Catholic theologians who were under the cloud, disparaged, censored, exiled, or otherwise restricted by the official ecclesiastical authorities. The Catholic Church, then, did not have a grave need for another theologian at the international level. By contrast, Catholic education in general, and religious education in particular, were in wretched shape and needed all the help they could get, especially from a layman. Though I would have much preferred to study theology, I chose education because when all is said and done, any person who works in God's service ought not go into a field primarily because he likes it but rather because he is needed.

The academic level of Columbia University's Teachers College during my two years there was very low—even lower than Richard Morris had led me to suspect. Formerly the dominant force in American professional education, Teachers College was in an academic trough when I was there. The professors by and large were not steeped in theory, but operated instead either out of their own unmediated, unreflective experience in some particular school setting or out of some vague, unexamined, naive humanitarian feeling. The professors conducting the teaching process courses were wonderful human beings, but certainly not scholarly or pioneering in the scientific study of the teaching-learning act. Dissertation direction was a farce, since most professors served as the main mentor for as many as thirty dissertations per year. Most of the faculty seemed to be more intent on being "professional nice guys" than serious scholars in education. In such an atmosphere, assumptions replaced scholarship, and statements backed by a toothy grin replaced statements backed by painstaking research. TC's all-too-prevalent lack of rigorous scholarly research, together with that kind of free-floatingness of pedagogical practice which is intrinsically unrelated to theory, reinforced my previously held conviction that if education is to achieve its potential, it must be built on continuous hard-nosed scholarly research and governed by theory to which practice is consciously tethered.

Because in many respects I personified the typical ultraconservative religious mentality of the reactionary Brooklyn Catholicism of that era, I frequently clashed with the explicit or implicit worldviews of many of my TC professors. To the very day I graduated, I staunchly opposed their social-scientific principles of education, even though these persons typically understood and formulated these principles in what I now know to be an unsophisticated and highly watered-down manner.

Though I learned much less at TC than a doctoral student was entitled to, still even a weak educational program has something of value to offer an interested student. I would arrange my program so as to take the courses of those few scholarly professors who brought erudition, insight, and excitement to their courses. From them, and also from the other faculty including the many inferior faculty under whom I studied, I acquired certain basic principles and foci which have since taken their place among the fundaments of my own approach to education. Among these basic principles and foci are the following: education must start with the learner where he is developmentally; learning takes place primarily according to the psychophysiological functioning of the learner and not primarily according to the logical structure of subject matter; content is everything the learner acquires from the teacher, and not just the logical dimensions of the subject matter; the effectiveness of teaching and learning are ascertained by careful empirical research, and not by well-intentioned guesses or speculative opinions; the purpose of education is to foster personal growth in one way or another.

Toward the end of my doctoral studies, I chanced to meet the brilliant young man who for three years had occupied the seat next to me in the diocesan major seminary chapel. Ed had accepted tonsure, stayed on another year at the seminary, and then left. He was pursuing a doctorate in Renaissance philosophy at Columbia. One evening as we were chatting in a cozy neighborhood bar, he told me an incredible story. When he was seriously thinking of leaving the seminary, he sought the advice of his regular spiritual director there. "It's definitely God's will that you remain in the seminary and become a priest, Ed!" said the director emphatically. Shaken at the absoluteness of this advice, Ed sought the counsel of the seminary's official spiritual director, who told him just as categorically: "Ed, it's definitely God's will that you leave the seminary and not become a priest!" Putting down his drink, Ed told me in an exasperated voice: "So what, then, is God's will?"

I have never forgotten Ed's experience. It forced me to reflect often and intensely on the claims of those clerics and religious educators who say they seek proximate explanations of their ministry in God's will or who say they base their immediate activity on the mysterious workings of the Holy Spirit. It seems to me that God's will and the impulses of the Holy Spirit are not mysterious or "out there somewhere," but instead are to be found in the actual workings of personal development, of the natural law, and of societal affairs. The assiduous maneuverings and frequent machinations by the cardinals during papal conclaves surely do not coincide with claims made by many Catholic religious education personnel about the mysterious, free-floating, uncontrollable activity of the Holy Spirit in religious and secular matters. Serious pneumatology seldom if ever concerns itself with one-to-one correlations between the Hold Spirit and specific human activities. Religious educationists and educators make invalid use of pneumatology in their efforts to adduce the Holy Spirit as the primary proximate explanation or the primary proximate mover of religious instruction activity. My reflection over the years of Ed's encounter with the seminary spiritual directors, together with my subsequent investigation of how religious instruction is actually enacted, have led me to vigorously resist the unfortunate spookification with which most religious educationists have endowed the Holy Spirit's activities in the world. I have long since concluded that the Holy Spirit does not capriciously blow where he wills, but rather acts in elegant congruence with the laws of nature which God has made and continuously sustains. The more religious educationists engage in sophisticated theoretical and empirical research on the ways in which religious learning is optimally facilitated, and the more that religious educators base their own efforts on such research, the more they all will be able to cooperate authentically and fruitfully with the Holy Spirit in working with him to renew the face of the world.

The Lay State All the Way

Five years after I left the seminary I still was very much torn between becoming a priest and remaining in the lay state. I was still living out the primal religious experience I had when I was six years old, and I was still univocally translating that experience into the priesthood. At the time I was dating a wonderful girl who was pursuing graduate work in philosophy at Fordham University. She empathized fully with my problem, and suggested that I talk with a Fordham Jesuit professor of psychology for whom she had considerable personal and professional admiration. The interview I had with this man whom I had never previously known and whom I have never seen since turned out to be a major turning point in my life. I walked into his office, and for two short minutes explained my situation and doubts. When I had finished, he asked: "Do you think you can do more good for the church as a priest or as a layman?" I had never thought of my primal religious experience in those terms. All of a sudden, my whole life flashed before me, and the major elements suddenly came together in a new formation. "As a layman," I quickly responded. "Well, I guess that's it," the Jesuit said. "Yes, it is," I responded. I thanked him and left his office. I was walking on luminous clouds. My heart was joyous and was troubled no more. From that moment forward, I clearly recognized that my life with God here on earth was to be spent as a lay apostle. The primal religious experience which I had at six and which I was and still am now living out did not mean that I necessarily should be a priest but rather that I should be an apostle—an apostle in whatever state or condition or profession I could labor most effectively for the church as God's devoted servant. I now was able to embrace the lay life with zest, for I had overwhelming personal proof that it was here that God wished me to serve as his apostle. Though I often think it would be fitting to spend my last years on earth in an austere contemplative monastery, nonetheless since that interview with the Fordham Jesuit I never ever have given even a millisecond's thought to being a priest in the active phase of my apostolate.

My total and unreserved embrace of the lay life had profound effects on my future service for God, especially in the religious education apostolate. I seriously doubt that I could have been simultaneously a good and obedient priest on the one hand and a revolutionary in religious education on the other. One of the two would have to yield substantially—and as is the case with the overwhelming percentage of hyphenated priests, I suspect that my priesthood would get the short end. The priesthood is a total, all-consuming profession of mediating salvation and religiously educating people. Consequently, the priesthood inevitably suffers when it is admixed with any other profession or career.

TEACHING CAREER

Public Secondary School and the Failure of Theology

During my graduate study in history and later in educational studies, I taught full-time in a New York public secondary school. Full-time teaching and full-time graduate study proved quite a demanding combination.

The years I spent teaching in the New York secondary school proved expecially influential for the development of my social-science approach to religious instruction. At the beginning of my secondary-school teaching career, my ideas on how to teach were principally derived from my own theological worldview. But as I taught day in and day out in the secondary school, I discovered that the theological worldview did not seem to be directly generating or explaining effective teaching procedures. The theological worldview was consistently turning out to be useless in helping me to teach effectively. What was worse, I found that the theological worldview was actually hindering me from teaching effectively. The theological approach to teaching was impeding me from searching for fruitful theoretical and empirical sources on which to base my day-to-day pedagogical activities. The theological approach to teaching was obstructing me from locating, using, and verifying the instructional procedures I should have been employing for successful learning.

The pedagogical impotence of the theological view of reality and education was especially marked when I attempted to teach the hoodlum students. The bright students typically would work hard and learn well not primarily as a result of the teacher's pedagogical skill, but because they had a strong personal motivation to get into a good college. Many of the students of average ability had the same personal motivation, or at least the motivation to be good boys and girls. But the hoodlum students, especially the more intelligent among them, had no personal motivation other than to have fun and avoid work. With my hoodlum students, then, I had to be pedagogically "on" at every moment. Any lapse in my pedagogical effectiveness would not just be courting educational disaster, but courting an open riot in the classroom.

I was thoroughly shocked at the total inadequacy of the theological worldview in terms of making me an effective teacher. In every phase of my Catholic education, I had been told that theology is the reigning queen of the sciences. I had been taught that all explanations, all predictions, and all verifications of various kinds of reality are ultimately theological. Yet theology utterly failed to directly generate or explain effective pedagogical practice. Theology utterly failed to tell me how or why my teaching procedures worked or failed. Theology utterly failed to tell me how to predict which of the pedagogical practices I intended to utilize would probably work or flop. Theology utterly failed to tell me the ways I could verify whether or not the students had learned what they were supposed to learn.

The total power of theology to explain and master all areas of reality had been thoroughly part and parcel of my self-system for most of my life. Consequently I completely avoided facing the central fact with which I was daily confronted in the classroom, namely that theology was a dismal failure with respect to my pedagogy. But like many successful survivors whose heartfelt prized guiding theory is consistently proving useless and even ruinous, I abandoned my basic theory without admitting to myself that I was abandoning it. Soon I began to make my own empirical observations on how the students were actually learning as a result of my various teaching practices. Without realizing it, I then devised my own laws for effective teaching, laws derived from my own empirically verified observations. Finally I incognizantly began to formulate an implicit theory to explain and predict and verify my teaching activities. Without admitting it to myself, I had begun to operate on a social-science approach to teaching.

By the time I received my doctorate in educational studies, I had pretty much decided to teach at the college level and devote myself to research in the area of Catholic education. However, I decided to remain teaching for a fourth year because I believed that I needed this additional time to round out my experiential knowledge and skills in the teaching process.

St. Joseph College and the First Book

During my final year in the public secondary school, I was teaching an evening course in the graduate school of Hunter College, and also two courses in the School of Education at Seton Hall University. Though I was offered a full-time position in both institutions, I chose instead to teach at St. Joseph College, then a small all-girls' institution picturesquely situated in Connecticut. I thought that I could exercise my apostolate more effectively at St. Joseph College than at either Hunter or Seton Hall.

St. Joseph turned out to be prototypical of the small provincial Catholic girls' colleges of the 1940s, 1950s, and early 1960s. The nuns' excessive preoccupation with preserving the students' pristine sexual integrity was a constant source of amazement to me.

While the lay faculty were not maltreated by the nuns who ran the college, still they were not at all put on a par with nuns and priests. I always had the uneasy feeling that the nuns regarded lay faculty, and indeed all lay persons, as necessary evils more to be endured than to be valued.

When I came to St. Joseph College, I was in many respects religiously ultraconservative, reflecting to a large extent the reactionary Brooklyn Catholicism in which I grew up. The nuns at St. Joseph pretty much lived out in their own lives this selfsame kind of religion. Furthermore, they had deliberately structured the collegiate educational life there in such a way as to promote an ultraconservative religious consciousness and lifestyle in the students. St. Joseph College therefore provided me with a relatively undiluted milieu in which to observe the existential shape and practical consequences of my ultraconservative religiosity. I was shaken to the foundations of my being at what I discovered. The ultraconservative religiosity of St. Joseph College—a religiosity which I had by and large embraced in my own life—produced intolerance, generated narrow-mindedness, led to an asphyxiation of human affectivity, suppressed authentic emotion, shriveled the personality, and squeezed out the life-juices of religion. I was revulsed. This revulsion led to an intense reconsideration and radical recalculation of my perspective on religion and my enactment of religiosity. After one year at St. Joseph College I renounced my ultraconservative religiosity and took on a liberal progressive religious posture. Of course, it well might be that the St. Joseph College atmosphere served to bring my submerged liberal progressive tendencies to the fore.

My renunciation of ultraconservative religiosity and my espousal of a progressive liberal religious stance proved decisive for my religious education apostolate, and enabled me to see realities and embrace positions which my previous restrictive reactionary religious worldview would have prevented.

My teaching, research, and service activities at St. Joseph College became increasingly imbued with the spirit of liberal Catholicism, a spirit unpopular in the church of that time and especially in St. Joseph College. The nuns cracked down very hard on me for these activities. They endeavored whenever possible to ban my writings, forbid me from speaking, and ostracize me from any discussions of consequence. These suppressive activities on the part of the nuns—suppressive activities which I later received in abundance from the Central Catechetical Establishment and from those diocesan catechetical establishments aligned in fact or in spirit with the Central Catechetical Establishment—taught me the great value of the Gamaliel principle, and showed me that suppression and censorship of differing views not only blocks the emergence of new truths but also does untold damage to the personality of the suppressor and the censor.

I was favorably impressed by the emphasis which the administration and a sizable portion of the faculty at St. Joseph put on educating their students to be scholar-teachers, scholar-homemakers, and the like. Their emphasis was genuine and not mere rhetoric. The insistence at St. Joseph on scholarly-grounded theory actually interpenetrating one's professional activities and one's daily life reinforced and sharpened similar views which I had learned from my Catholic Worker experience. As a result of these beneficial influences, my writings, my classes, and my "outside" speaking engagements have been directed toward the goal of empowering religious educators to vivify their own here-and-now pedagogical practice with the continually fecundating presence of scholarly-grounded theory so as to maximize the effectiveness of their teaching ministry. I am deeply distressed by those denominational religious education administrators and by those national/diocesan catechetical officials who openly disparage the importance of scholarship on the part of the religion teachers under their charge. I hold in particularly low regard those many denominational religious education administrators and those national/diocesan catechetical officials who rob their regular or volunteer religion teachers of personal and professional fulfillment by telling them that all they need to know is some basic doctrines or a few church documents, by failing to put them in touch with serious and scholarly books in religious education, and by condescendingly treating them as mindless pedagogical drones who could neither understand nor profit from an awareness of the operative theoretical framework of their teaching activities.

In January of my second year at St. Joseph I began work on my first book. I devoutly desired that this book make a significant impact on the field of Catholic education. I decided to write a serious textbook for use in Catholic undergraduate and graduate courses in secondary education because I found that by and large Catholics did not read scholarly monographs, especially on the topic of Catholic education.

Writing the Catholic college textbook on secondary-school education proved to be the decisive turning point in my fundamental conceptualization of the teaching-learning dynamic because it was in the process of authoring this book that I consciously abandoned my former theological approach and came to enthusiastically espouse the social-science approach. To be sure, many influences on my life prior to this time actively operated to bring about this molar switch. Nonetheless it was in and through the careful research and intense reflection involved in writing this book that the change did occur. This research and reflection provided the major new *apperatura* which allowed many of my previous experiences to constructively coalesce in a manner which supported and enriched my basic new approach.

When I realized that the reality of the educational process itself dictated my adoption of the social-science approach, I could no longer flee from myself and hide the patent obviousness of this approach as I did in my New York secondary school career. After all, I had to base my book on reality and not on wishfulness or fantasy. As the days and months of writing wore on, I continuously fought bitter battles with myself about the social-science approach. I fiercely resisted this new approach, but inch by inch it inexorably gained ground so that before the book was one-third finished I came to completely adopt the social-science approach, though I must add that my adoption of this new approach was by no means enthusiastic until the volume was nearly finished. In the course of writing this college textbook I found that by embracing a social-science approach to education I was not thereby rejecting theology or a theological approach to divinely revealed realities. I gradually discovered that theology had been itself corrupted by those who were attempting to make it explain/predict/verify education, since such explanation/prediction/verification falls as much outside the legitimate control of theology as does sculpture or literature.

Having become aware that social science constitutes the only proper theoretical grounding for every sort of teaching-learning process, I set about rewriting what I had previously written in the college textbook and preparing myself for the many more chapters yet to be completed. With the exception of my training in history, I had received relatively little solid or sophisticated professional preparation in the social sciences. Indeed, with the exception of historical studies, I had not even read much first-class material in the social sciences. Hence I immediately began to immerse myself in social-scientific empirical and theoretical literature, especially that closely related to the educational process. In terms of social science in general and the social-science approach to religious instruction in particular, I am basically self-taught. Writing the education textbook to be used in Catholic colleges became a personal and professional pilgrimage for me—a personal pilgrimage of journeying deep into myself to search out the relevance of the social-science worldview for my own life, a professional pilgrimage of voyaging into an appreciative awareness of the fundamental shape and flow and content of the educational process itself. I still am on this double pilgrimage, even now.

Every Eastertide I made it a point to attend the annual convention of the National Catholic Educational Association (NCEA) at my own expense because I regarded my presence there as vital for my development as a professional. I was severely disappointed by the antilayperson bias rampant at the conventions. Except for a very few sychophantic and conspicuously fawning lay lackeys which some clerical Catholic college administrators led around in tow, I was virtually the lone lay conventioneer at the NCEA. I felt distinctly out of place and unwanted in such a sea of Roman collars and wimples. I was shocked by the aprofessionalism and antiprofessionalism which was characteristically rife at the NCEA convention. During the official convention sessions, it seemed as though there were more nuns chatting on the boardwalk or browsing in the shops than were in attendance at the meetings. The priests, for their part, appeared so tired after all-night gatherings or parties in smoke-filled hotel suites that they were too weary to show up for the convention sessions, especially those held in the morning. The speakers at the NCEA convention were typically mediocre at best. Only occasionally were renowned scholars invited to address the conventioneers.

My experience at the NCEA conventions taught me two lessons which were particularly useful to me in my successive apostolates of Catholic education and religious education. First, I learned how especially difficult is the task of any layperson who wishes to exercise significant apostolic leadership in Catholic education or in religious education. Being a layperson in a clerical preserve is tantamount to being an unwelcome trespasser violating privileged and reserved territory. Second, I learned from my NCEA experiences that attempts at genuine professionalism in Catholic education and in religious education would more often than not be resisted fiercely by a great many priests and nuns.

When I returned from my Christmas vacation during my third year at St. Joseph, a letter from the chairman of the education department at the University of Notre Dame was waiting for me. This letter invited me to explore the possibility of joining the faculty there. I was surprised by this letter, since I had originally intended to teach at St. Joseph for about ten years, and then to apply for a position at The Catholic University of America with about five scholarly books to my credit. After a few months of pleasant negotiation, I signed a contract to begin teaching at Notre Dame the following autumn.

Notre Dame

The first eight years at Notre Dame were the most exhilarating I have ever spent in academic life. These eight years forcefully demonstrated that there really could exist the Camelot of a genuine university which is also Catholic. These eight years refuted the frequently held view that "Catholic" and "university" are contradictory terms. Under the vice-presidencies of Chester Soleta and especially of John Walsh, Notre Dame emerged as unquestionably the most important and exciting Catholic institution of higher learning in the United States. Soleta and Walsh moved Notre Dame ahead on all fronts. Both Holy Cross priests were especially supportive of the education department. With their encouragement, the education department came to attain the highest peak in its long history.

In early December of 1965 I was invited to Munich to present a paper at a major conference on American Catholicism. A progressive American auxiliary bishop who gave a paper on another topic at the Munich conference urged me to fly to Rome to be present at the historic last week of the Second Vatican Council which was just about to end. I took his suggestion. Being present and well-situated at the momentous events and ceremonies of that final week of the Council made a lasting impression on me. The day after the Council had concluded, I was sitting in a religious community headquarters near Rome's central train station. An elderly European Franciscan missionary bishop who had been an active participant invited me to walk with him on an errand he was about to do. As we gingerly threaded our way across the large square in front of the central railroad station so as to avoid being hit by the cars which were recklessly whizzing around us in what seemed to be an endless variety of directions, I remarked to that saintly old missionary bishop how wonderful the Council had been. Hearing my remark, he stopped right in his tracks, and with cars streaking perilously close to us at breakneck speed, threw his arms around me and exclaimed: "The Council is over! Let's not look behind! Let's now look forward and begin anew!" Seldom in my life have I been as touchingly moved or as significantly influenced by a single short event as I was by that moment. A short while after this occurrence took place in the large square in front of Rome's central railroad station, this remarkable old bishop returned to the African missions and I went back to Notre Dame. But this exquisite moment and its message still burn bright and true in my religious education apostolate. The Council documents are important, of course. But if the church is to move productively forward, then these documents must be looked upon simply as points of departure, not as frozen norms or fossilized directives. I therefore stand staunchly opposed to the aboriginal attitude and pathetic activities of those Catholic religious educators who attempt to use Council documents to validate religious education activity and to constitute the sole basic source of religious education practice. Council documents are productive for religious education when they are judiciously utilized as *one* major point of departure for ecclesial life. Council documents are productive for religious education when they are utilized to illumine from *an* important perspective some religious or theological principle which intersects religious education. To attempt to use Council documents as the validator of religious education activity or as the only source for fruitful religious education practice is not only to shamelessly debase the soul of these documents, but to render religious education endeavor by and large sterile.

The Guidance and Counseling Book

In my first few years at Notre Dame I enjoyed considerable research productivity. The year after I arrived at South Bend, I began work on a major volume on guidance and counseling for use as a basic textbook in Catholic universities and other Christian institutions of higher learning.

Researching and writing this university textbook on counseling exerted a significant and pervasive influence on my later religious education conceptualizations. Viewing the educational process from a perspective complementary but intrinsically related to instruction both confirmed and expanded the social-science approach to education which I had come to espouse during the writing of my textbook in Catholic secondary education. In my research and reflection during the writing of the guidance and counseling book, it became unassailably evident that guidance and counseling practice could be effectively explained and predicted and verified only by social science; theology simply lacked the power to effectively perform this absolutely essential triple task. In the course of researching and writing this book, I came to broaden my involvement with the psychological processes of teaching and learning from my former primary concentration on educational psychology to the broader base of a constellation of psychological perspectives including educational psychology, educational sociology, social psychology, learning psychology, counseling psychology, and clinical psychology. This broadening of my basal psychological viewpoint enabled me to explore the theoretical foundations and existential dynamics of religious instruction more wholly, more perceptively, more accurately, and more authentically.

The Seminary Book

In my research on Catholic education, in the graduate courses I taught to Catholic educators, and in my speeches around the country, I increasingly came to realize that the Catholic clergy in many ways constituted the key to the basic effectiveness of Catholic education all along the line. There could be no substantial improvement of Catholic education without a substantial prior upgrading of the educational attitudes and the educational level of the clergy. Therefore if I wished to be instrumental in bringing about a thoroughgoing renewal of Catholic education, I would have to include in my efforts the reform of the educational attitudes and the educational level of the clergy. Since the clergy's seminary education was largely responsible for determining the later educational attitudes and setting the educational level of its graduates, it was imperative for me to write a book aimed at triggering a major reform in seminary education. Rather than write the book myself, I decided that it would be much better to edit a volume in which I would be able to include original chapters from some of the country's most renowned Catholic scholars, all of whom had a deep interest in seminary education.

The seminary book was an instant sensation. Everybody seemed to be passionately discussing it. Articles about it sprouted up all over the place. Even the secular news media took notice: my photograph and a write-up of the book appeared in the religion section of *Newsweek* magazine, for example. Meetings of seminary officials and faculty dealt with the book at considerable length. Most of the clergy, who in that day and age were quite hidebound, denounced it with a fury usually reserved for issues like birth control and abortion. Theodore Hesburgh told me that quite a few bishops wrote him demanding that he fire me from the faculty of Notre Dame. (Later that year I was promoted to associate professor.) Many seminarians, together with a sizable segment of the progressive elements within the clergy, including some thoughtful Jesuits, responded favorably to the volume.

Of all the books which I have ever authored or edited, the seminary volume had the most rapid and most far-reaching impact. Some persons have claimed that it was this book which triggered the major reforms which subsequently occurred in American seminary education. Such a claim is difficult to document. Besides, correlation is not cause. Nonetheless, many of the proposals made in my four chapters in this lengthy 600-page book, though bitterly denounced at first, were put into action many years later. These proposals, considered dangerous and radical at the time, included the recasting of the seminary into a setting whose axis is the professional education of future priests, establishment of a program providing for a set of progressively scaled pastoral internship experiences for seminarians, abolition of very small seminaries, especially those located in "wilderness" sites, attaching seminaries to major Church-related universities, radical reconceptualization and possible abolition of pretheologate seminaries, formal accreditation of Catholic seminaries by a body external to the sponsoring diocese or religious congregation, implementation of a regular ongoing counseling and psychological services in seminaries, a significant broadening of the tight and rigid seminary curriculum, and the establishment in the seminary of an atmosphere which stressed personal freedom and active decision making to replace the prevalent emphasis on hyperobedience and hyperdocility.

Administration: Leadership and Chore

In the spring of my fourth year at Notre Dame, John Walsh asked me to become chairman of the education department. He believed that the department needed invigoration. I twice declined his gracious offer because of my persistent belief that I am of far greater service to the church as a scholar and researcher than as an administrator. When Walsh asked the third time, I reluctantly accepted under two conditions, namely that I would have total authority with no outside interference in managing the department, and that I would be able to establish a doctoral program in religious education. Walsh agreed, and I accepted his offer. A man of his word, Walsh consistently supported my subsequent efforts as chairman.

Within a month of becoming chairman, I established four major divisions in the department, namely the philosophical and historical foundations of Catholic education, the administration of Catholic educational institutions, guidance and counseling for Christian personnel in a variety of educational settings, and the teaching process including the teaching of religion. It was my dream that such a well-rounded but nonetheless compact program would attract and produce outstanding leaders in Catholic education, leaders who would bring about a dramatic upgrading of Catholic education in all sectors. I wished to make Notre Dame's education department not only the nation's leading intellectual powerhouse in Catholic education, but the principal training ground for its finest leaders as well.

My efforts over the next few years to bring Notre Dame's education department to a position of preeminent leadership in Catholic education consumed all my waking hours and left little time for productive scholarship. During that time I only wrote a few minor articles and a short book, and edited a volume of original essays.

The Book on the Purpose of Catholic Schooling

It was C. Albert Koob who requested that I write a short book on the purpose of Catholic education. Koob headed the National Catholic Education Association at the time. In my opinion, Koob has been the most genuinely open, innovative, intellectually-honest, and dynamic chief administrator the N.C.E.A. has had since the end of World War II. The imaginative Koob had established a series of scholarly books called NCEA Papers in an attempt to bring the fruits of mature scholarly research into the mainstream of Catholic elementary/secondary education and also into the active consciousness of the workaday teacher.

The little book on the purpose of Catholic schooling became widely discussed in Catholic educational circles around the United States. Scholars dealing with Catholic education from the historical, philosophical, or administrational perspectives also devoted considerable attention to the book, with Harold Buetow's *Of Singular Benefit* being a case in point. On the whole, the little book was well received in most Catholic educational circles, including even many conservative groups. Still there was some opposition to the book, probably due to my image as one of the most "dangerous" men in Catholic education.

I was surprised that a less prominent but still very important thesis of *The Purpose of Catholic Schooling* was by and large overlooked by many Catholic educators at the time. This thesis holds that Catholic schooling and Catholic education are distinct. Every Catholic should have a

Catholic education, but Catholic schooling is not always necessary for the attainment of a Catholic education. Indeed there might be situations and circumstances in which Catholic schooling might actually hinder one's attainment of a Catholic education. Though this thesis is now gradually coming to be accepted in Catholic educational circles, nonetheless at the time it was considered very radical and extremely dangerous.

The distinction I drew in *The Purpose of Catholic Schooling* between education and schooling was a relatively new one in those days, even in secular educational circles. It was by and large unheard of in Catholic and many Protestant educational quarters. Some years later this distinction became accepted in the field of Christian religious education. Unfortunately many of those religious educationists who eventually adopted this distinction seem to have been insufficiently steeped in the history of the distinction and in the pedagogical modifications required in implementing this distinction.

The Book on Comparative Catholic Education

During this time I also edited a book entitled *Catholic Education in the Western World*. This was a comparative education volume which presented parallel pictures of Catholic educational activity in six major countries. So as to insure optimal accuracy and national flavor, each essay was written by an important Catholic education scholar living and working in each country treated. This book was primarily a descriptive account of the history, organization, financial support, curriculum, teaching procedures, religious instruction activities, guidance services, and staff of Catholic educational institutions. Each chapter ended with the author's own professionally informed view of the special problems facing Catholic education in his native land. In the concluding section of my chapter, I devoted a few sentences suggesting that though the Catholic school system in the United States must definitely be preserved, still the growing scarcity of personnel and finances indicated that it would become increasingly difficult and eventually impossible to maintain a total Catholic school system which all Catholics would be able to attend. Therefore a redistribution of personnel and financial resources should take place in order to strengthen those school levels such as nursery schools and secondary schools which research has shown to be especially amenable to the formation of deeper attitudes and religious values, and to prune away those school levels such as elementary schools which the research has shown to be generally less influential in terms of significantly affecting deeper attitudes and religious values.

The national press and wire services picked up these few sentences on the realignment of Catholic schools and the eventual abandonment of much of Catholic elementary schooling. *The New York Times*, the *Chicago Sun Times*, and other major newspapers featured this story on their front pages. Additional newspapers around the country also gave prominent attention to my position. So many letters poured into Notre Dame that Paul Beichner, the scholarly graduate dean and leading member of the governing board of the University of Notre Dame Press, jokingly suggested that the Notre Dame post office would have to hire a new employee just to take care of all the mail cascading in about my chapter. Catholic school officials and ecclesiastical leaders—almost all of whom never bothered to read the carefully-phrased passage in my book—heaped denunciation upon denunciation on my head. From the pulpits of all the churches in a major Midwestern archdiocese, the priests had to read a letter from the cardinal specifically condemning my position and its author. The Catholic Educational Establishment in Washington prevailed upon Lyndon Johnson's Commissioner of Education, Harold Howe II, to make a national statement branding my position as gravely detrimental to all American education public as well as private. When I was invited to appear on the *Today* television show to discuss my position, my friend and patron George Shuster urged me to decline because my presence on this national television program would almost certainly result in several bishops canceling contracts they had made or were making with Shuster's research center at Notre Dame.

The strong opposition to some of my books and speeches which I received from certain reactionary Catholic educational and clerical quarters proved to be of great value to me in my later religious education apostolate in that these attacks helped strengthen and fortify me against the national and regional denunciations of a far more virulent and revulsive variety which were to be later directed at me by the Central Catechetical Establishment, by those diocesan catechetical officials who have a constricted view of the pastoral work of the church, and by those individual religious educationists who consider basic disagreements with their pet views as traitorous.

The Religious Education Program

The principal apostolic reason why I eventually accepted John Walsh's offer to assume the chairmanship of Notre Dame's education department was to begin a doctoral program in religious education there. My first and still abiding premier career choice after obtaining my doctorate had been religious education. However, in those days it was virtually impossible for a layperson living in the United States to become either a professor of religious education in an American Catholic university or to become a high-ranking diocesan administrator of religious education. Catholic theologians, even the liberal ones, firmly believed that from a theological standpoint laypersons should not teach religion or otherwise participate in any activity close to the center of the church's sacred activities. Indeed, Catholic theologians were still adamantly asserting that authentic Catholic theology placed the lay state in a position of marked objective and subjective inferiority to the clerical and religious state; hence laypersons should not be permitted to become directly or intimately involved in matters which are axial to the church's teaching or liturgical offices. To be sure, the reason I had originally selected the field of Catholic education as the locus in which to exercise the call God had given me to be his apostle was precisely because my actual first choice, religious education, was barred to me as a direct consequence of the church's theology regarding my lay status. Therefore I chose the locus most closely related to religious education, namely Catholic education. Now as a department chairman in the country's leading Catholic institution of higher learning, an institution which enjoyed tremendous academic freedom and which was not under the control of any bishop, I could realize my dream and begin to build a university-based religious education program capable of exercising major national and international impact. As far as I know, I was the first layperson in this century to head up a religious education program in a Catholic church-controlled institution of higher learning anywhere in the world. I regard this as a great honor.

My preeminent guiding principle in first establishing and then amplifying the Notre Dame graduate program in religious education was quality. If our graduate program was to be of optimum utility to the church, then every phase of it had to be top-drawer. If one is in God's service, nothing less than the best is adequate.

I believe that the Notre Dame graduate program in religious education was indeed characterized by high quality all along the line. Our
faculty was full-time in religious education all year around. I deliberately recruited a faculty with a wide diversity of academic preparation
and theoretical viewpoints.

The faculty in the Notre Dame religious education program were
highly productive. We all spoke regularly at various conventions of
learned societies and at gatherings of Christian educators around the
country. As far as I am aware, no comparable group of faculty members
in any other department at Notre Dame published a greater number of
serious books than did the religious education faculty during the time
span in which the program actively existed. Furthermore, as far as I am
aware, no group of full-time religious education faculty in any other
university or seminary in the United States before or since published a
greater number of serious influential books in a comparable time frame
than did the Notre Dame religious education faculty.

I sharply deemphasized summers-only Master's degrees in religious
education because I have always believed that such degree programs
wittingly or unwittingly promote antiprofessionalism or at least aprofessionalism. Because I wanted the Notre Dame program to have optimal
national and international impact, I concentrated our attention on the
doctoral level.

By and large, Notre Dame's religious education doctoral students
were of superior caliber. Doctoral dissertations generally were superb.
Some of these dissertations were subsequently reworked slightly and
then published as books. For example, Harold Burgess's dissertation was
issued in book form under the title *An Invitation to Religious Education*. This splendid volume soon became the most widely used textbook
in university and seminary introductory courses in religious education.
Ian Knox's top-flight dissertation was published as a scholarly book
entitled *Above or Within?: The Supernatural in Religious Education*.
Other graduates of the Notre Dame religious education program such as
John Welch went on to write books and articles in the field.

As far as I am aware, no single program in the history of the University
of Notre Dame has even produced per capita a greater number of
outstanding leaders for the Christian church than the doctoral program
in religious education at Notre Dame.

The organization, structure, substance, emphasis, and goals of the

Notre Dame program in religious education encapsulated much though by no means all of what I stand for in the field of religious education.

In 1974, James Tunstead Burtchaell, the autocratic and cruel clerical provost of the university, unilaterally suspended and later liquidated Notre Dame's distinguished seventy-five-year-old education department, and with it the graduate program in religious education. Neither he nor his henchmen have ever given a satisfactory reason for this liquidation. I could never understand the murky motives underlying Burtchaell's decision; after all, religious education is central to the church's mission and therefore automatically central to the mission of any university claiming to be Christian or Catholic. The Notre Dame program in religious education was producing more than its share of religious education leaders. Consequently, Burtchaell's heavy-handed despoliation of this program willfully deprived the church of the invigorating services of future religious education leaders. In the final analysis, then, it was the church, and not so much my colleagues or myself who were really hurt by the abolition of the Notre Dame graduate program in religious education.

Ironically, Burtchaell was fired from his position as provost shortly before the education department was finally closed down. Some persons at Notre Dame speculated that his liquidation of the religious education program constituted one proximate reason why the Board of Trustees apparently believed that the despotic Burtchaell was counterproductive to the welfare of Notre Dame.

I was completely crushed by the abolition of the Notre Dame graduate program in religious education. I do not recall any event in my entire life which so totally devastated me as a person and as an apostle as the elimination of the Notre Dame religious education program. For fifteen years I had given myself totally and without reserve to Notre Dame, to the very last drop of my devotion. For me, Notre Dame was not a place to work; it was my very life and apostolate.

The despoliation of the Notre Dame religious education program proved particularly valuable and illuminative to me in my personal and professional life. I learned from this experience to serve God alone, wherever he dwells, and not to place myself fundamentally in the service of any person or of any institution. I will never again give myself totally to any institution, especially if this institution is directly related to or controlled by the *ecclesiasticum*. Ecclesiastical institutions more often than not succumb to the temptation of identifying themselves with the ecclesia and even with God. Without realizing it, I had come precariously close to making an idol of Notre Dame. Furthermore, I had almost made the fatal spiritual mistake of identifying my call to be an apostle with the Notre Dame religious education program, much as I had previously made the major error of identifying my call to be an apostle with the priesthood. Separated from Notre Dame, I was now able to become far more free to be a true apostle, far more directly tuned to God as he meets us in the withinness of all reality, and far more independent to do God's will as I saw it and see it. The destruction of the Notre Dame religious education program proved to be a precious gift apostolically, and had a salubriously purifying effect on me.

Still, in all candor I must confess that scarcely a day in my life has passed since I left Notre Dame that I have not recalled some aspect of the wonderful years I spent there, of the halcyon days of the religious education program, and of the abolition of the education department by Burtchaell and his henchmen.

DEVELOPING THE SOCIAL-SCIENCE APPROACH

Many and diverse are the sources upon which I have drawn in devising the social-science approach to religious instruction. I have indicated some of these influences in previous pages.

I had to work out the social-science approach to religious instruction almost entirely on my own. I never learned it from graduate study in any institution of higher learning.

Goals and Objectives

Religious education has three discrete but highly complementary functions, namely religious instruction, religious counseling, and the administration of religious education activities. I opted to concentrate on religious instruction because religious counseling had already commenced to seriously develop its own full-fledged social-science approach, and the administration of religious education activities was beginning to lean in that direction. An apostle should go where he is needed, and I sensed that the greatest need lay in religious instruction.

Because the teaching of religion is so central to the mission of Jesus and his church, it was with great relish that I embarked on a career specializing in religious instruction. I was shocked, and still am shocked, at how little serious attention the field of religious instruction has given to the teaching-learning act. The teaching-learning act is absolutely central and fundamental to religious instruction. Everything in religious instruction ultimately flows from the teaching-learning act and ultimately flows into the teaching-learning act. Yet the unfortunate thing is that religion teachers and religious education professors have so frequently taken the teaching-learning act for granted, often substituting spooky rationales and untested practices for a theory-based foundation and a corpus of empirically tested procedures. The inevitable result of this dreadful state of affairs is that empty slogans have replaced comprehensive theory, and pedagogical gimmicks have pushed empirically tested practice aside. From the outset of my career in religious instruction, I decided to discover and elaborate the theory and practice of a scientific basis for the art of religion teaching. Such a scientific basis, far from rendering religion teaching antiseptic and inhuman, would instead enable it to become optimally effective and therefore render it as fully human and as fully divine as possible.

The ultimate reason why I developed the social-science approach to religious instruction was to significantly help religion teachers and learners move closer to God by providing a macrotheory which effectively enables religion teachers and learners to be successful in that activity in which they are both cooperatively engaged, namely the teaching-learning of religion. The proximate reason why I developed the social-science approach to religious instruction was to bring into being a field of work and a field of study where only an amorphous and confused mass currently exists. Through the development and implementation of the social-science approach, I have consistently endeavored to make the field of religious instruction intellectually respectable, ecclesially legitimate, and apostolically potent.

My social-science approach to religious instruction, just like my life, is constantly and consciously targeted to basically change fundamental theory and practice in religion teaching.

My principal proximate concern in developing the social-science approach to religious instruction has always been to build a macrotheory which would adequately deal with the wide range of religious instruction theory and practice. A macrotheory is an overall and global form of theory into which are inserted theories and subtheories of lesser scope. A macrotheory lies at the ultimate base of all theory and practice within a given science, discipline, or field. A macrotheory reveals the foundational structure and operations of a particular theory or practice. By centering my attention on macrotheory, I hoped to be able to provide an ultimate workable basis for the field of religious instruction.

The task of developing a clearly stated, conscious, and "up front" macrotheory appears to be wholly new in the entire history of religious instruction. This fact is utterly amazing to me. There has been, of course, a major macrotheory, in various forms and guises, operative in the field of religious instruction down through the centuries. The macrotheory to which I am referring is, of course, the theological macrotheory. But I am not aware of any religious educationist who ever presented the theological macrotheory in a deliberate, systematic, comprehensive, "up front" manner. Instead, religious education writers and practitioners who clung to the theological macrotheory proffered only piecemeal swatches and disconnected fragments of that macrotheory in an irregular, disconnected fashion. Small wonder, then, that religious instruction has been legitimate prey for so many fleeting fads and frothy gimmicks which have so seriously debilitated the authentic progress and growth of religion teaching down the centuries.

Lack of Understanding

Because a conscious and expressly stated systematic macrotheory of religious instruction has always been absent from the field, it is hardly surprising that religious educationists and educators have frequently been unable to grasp the fact that the social-science approach is above all else a macrotheory. For the same reason, religious educationists and educators have frequently been unable to grasp the supreme importance of macrotheory in general and its various enfleshments in particular.

In the early 1970s, the chief administrative officer of the Religious Education Association convened a panel of nationally known religious educators. The task of each panelist was to explain before a large audience the underlying theory and key pedagogical practices of several of the specific models of teaching delineated by a well-known educational textbook of the time, *Models of Teaching*, authored by Bruce Joyce and Marsha Weil. These specific models of teaching included the group investigation model, the concept attainment model, the inquiry training model, the advance organizer model, the developmental model, the nondirective model, and the operant conditioning model. The convenor put me on the panel as a representative of what he believed to be another specific model of teaching, namely the social-science-approach model. When it came my turn to speak, I explained that the social-science approach is not a specific model of teaching, but rather is a macrotheory which lies at the foundation of all specific models of teaching. The social-science approach explains all the specific models summarized in the Joyce and Weil book. Both Joyce and Weil would have immediately understood this fact had they been present. After all, they wrote their book with this undeniable fact at the forefront of their work. But the Religious Education Association official, most of the panelists, and the vast majority of the audience were unable to grasp this elemental point precisely because they simply were unaware of the existence and function of macrotheory.

Almost all the books and articles written in this century have been of the speculative genre rather than of the theoretical type. Speculation, of course, is a way of thinking, and is the contrary of empiric. Theory, on the other hand, is a statement or group of statements organically integrating interrelated concepts, facts, and laws in such a fashion as to offer a comprehensive and systematic view of reality by specifying relations among variables. Herein lies the supreme value and utility of theory. Speculation is one valuable aid in the formation of theory, but it is not theory. Speculation cannot form a valid foundation for religious instruction activity because speculation of itself lacks the three cardinal characteristics of theory, namely explanatory, predictive, and verificational power of the comprehensive and systematic kind. Without theory, everything in religious instruction is necessarily reduced to a hit-or-miss affair. If the religious educator operates without conscious theory, then this individual inevitably becomes ensnared in that which theory would have predicted.

Many religious education writers and convention speakers highlight the centrality of theory. But an examination of their writings and speeches reveals that these persons usually mean either speculation or an intellectual basis rather than theory. Conscious and careful theory-building has not been prevalent in the history of religious instruction. Hence my work in theory construction is often improperly understood.

Macrotheory Construction

Building a theory is very hard work. To construct a theory, one must carefully establish concepts and facts, and then systematically insert these concepts and facts into those kinds of laws and theory which comprehensively explain the interactive variable relations among the concepts and facts. Building a macrotheory is even harder than building a theory, because a macrotheory must perforce be capable of integrating the various theories and sub-theories involved. But if I was to fulfill my apostolate, I had no choice but to plunge in and begin the arduous and painstakingly difficult task of constructing a viable and workable macrotheory for religious instruction.

The first stage of theory construction is to assemble the pertinent facts. But what are the facts? In order to make sure that the facts I used were truly the facts, and not my facts or someone else's facts, I endeavored to erect my macrotheory on the foundation of empirically verified data and on those factual aspects of theory which had been verified. In this way I would steer clear of preoccupations with current fads and personal needs. In gathering my research-based facts, I sometimes would start with my own experience and with the reported experiences of other persons involved in the religious instruction enterprise. Such experiences, I believed, would provide me with valuable clues as to what facts might be important and even more significantly what the parameters of religious instruction might actually be. I then would ransack the empirical research literature to ascertain whether the "facts" derived from my own experience and from the experiences of other religious educationists did indeed have a basis in empirically demonstrated data or whether these "facts" were in one way or another personal projections or distortions. Often I would assiduously comb all the empirical and theoretical literature which I could get my hands on so as to assemble a workable well-rounded corpus of empirically researched data which I believed to be eminently relevant to building a workable macrotheory for religious instruction. I would typewrite, or arrange to have typewritten, all these data on 3 × 5 index cards. When it came time for me to write a chapter or chapter section of a book, or to write an article, I would spread out all the cards on a large table, group the cards according to topic and subtopic, and then let the cards speak to me. Sometimes the cards told me that my previous ideas of "facts" simply were not true.

Sometimes the cards revealed new and hitherto undisclosed ways of looking at the data. I listened carefully and faithfully to the cards. The cards, and the empirically demonstrated data on many of them, have never failed me.

Once I had marshaled those empirically demonstrated data which were relevant to the topic which I was treating, I then endeavored to insert these facts into laws. This was a difficult but exciting process. The next stages of my work, namely inserting the laws systematically into a theory and then inserting various theories systematically into one overall macrotheory, were very strenuous processes, but exhilarating and adventuresome ones. I was always fascinated by the inferences which the facts, laws, and theories yielded in terms of a deeper understanding of the genuine basis and operation of religious instruction activity.

The Trilogy

It was my full and conscious intention that my first book dealing specifically with religious instruction provide an overview of the social-science approach. My explicit purpose was to lay the foundation for the approach, a foundation which would give the field that kind of a comprehensive and workable macrotheory it so desperately needed. My succeeding books would then develop more in detail one or another constituent part of this basic foundational treatise.

The book soon became much longer than I had originally intended. Presenting and interweaving a vast amount of concepts, facts, laws, and theories into one overarching macrotheory was a far more complex and lengthy task than I had previously anticipated. One day, while working in my small tenth floor research office of Notre Dame's huge library building, I suddenly came to the full and startling realization that there was no way in which I could possibly compress all the necessary material into one book. I became alarmed. Anguish followed the alarm. What to do? I chanced to walk up to the eleventh floor of the library building where one of our Notre Dame doctoral students in religious education, Eugene "Gino" Hemrick, was hard at work on an empirical study being conducted by the Notre Dame Office of Educational Research, a correlate of the education department. I explained my problem to Gino. He smiled, and suggested that I break the work up into two separate volumes. I was delighted with the simplicity and eminent good sense of his answer. "Why hadn't I thought of that?" I wondered to myself. Tremendously relieved, I went back to my tenth floor office and began to work out a logical division for the two volumes.

The more I contemplated the matter, the more I discovered that the inner logic of what I was attempting to do demanded there be a trilogy rather than a two-volume set. The first volume would present the overall rationale and foundation for the social-science approach as contrasted to the theological approach. The next two volumes would deal respectively with each of the two major inseparable contents of religious instruction, namely structural content and substantive content. (Structural content is my name for the teaching-learning process itself. Substantive content is my name for the subject matter that is taught-learned. I conceptualize and give the name "content" to both of these to clearly indicate that both the teaching-learning process and the subject-matter product are both full and authentic molar contents in their own right.) Thus the trilogy would comprise a relatively complete and comprehensive overview of the foundation and contours of the social-science approach to religious instruction. I called the first volume *The Shape of Religious Instruction*. The second volume of the trilogy is named *The Flow of Religious Instruction*, a title intended to suggest process. The third volume is *The Content of Religious Instruction*. The book jacket color of the first volume is red, the second volume yellow, and the forthcoming third volume blue—the three primary colors of the spectrum, signifying the primary and fundamental nature of the trilogy.

The Shape of Religious Instruction was published in 1971. *The Flow of Religious Instruction* was issued in 1973. Since that time I have been working on *The Content of Religious Instruction*. I have over 2,500 manuscript pages completed as of the time I am writing this essay. Friends and colleagues have finally persuaded me to shorten the book, and write the remaining three chapters. I think I will at last take their advice.

In writing each of the volumes of the trilogy, I have diligently endeavored to keep two major touchstones ever in mind. These two touchstones are common sense and the natural law.

To my way of thinking, one of the principal strengths of the social-science approach to religious instruction is that it is shot through and through with common sense. I have enormous respect for the common sense of the person in the street, because this common sense typically represents the practical distillation and personal integration of those experiences and hypotheses which the individual has found to be empirically verified as true in his or her own life. I have always subjected my theorizing and my writings to the acid test of common sense. One thing I have found over and over again with the theological approach to religious instruction is that it tends to fly squarely in the face of common sense, offering unreal and even at times spooky explanations in order to cover up its abject lack of common sense.

The natural law plays a vital litmus role in my conceptualization of the social-science approach to religious instruction. From the time I was a young boy growing up on the streets of New York down to the present day, I have always had a deep instinctive respect for the natural law. The natural law, of course, is a description of the basic structure and processive unfolding of a particular reality according to the dynamics of that reality's own exigencies and interactive functioning. In my theorizing and in my writing, I always take great pains to see to it that my hypotheses and my conclusions square as fully and as congruently as possible with the natural law. One of the great abiding strengths of the social-science approach to religious instruction is that it is consciously founded upon and constantly tethered to the natural law. Conversely, one of the greatest of all the weaknesses of the theological approach is that in both its bases and its explanations it flies right in the face of the natural law, operates as if the natural law did not exist, or attempts to suspend the inexorable operations of the natural law.

In developing my macrotheoretical approach, a major and pervasive task has constantly been to directly confront and then integrate into one overarching approach the areas of religion, theology, social science, and the teaching process. Most, and possibly all of the previous books in religious instruction appeared to me to either have naively ignored social science and educational study even as these selfsame books declaimed so very knowingly about teaching, or to have brought in social science by the back door of religious instruction without ever really directly interfacing it with religion and theology and education. Confrontation and integration of religion, theology, social science, and the teaching process was a pivotal task I had to successfully perform if I was to formulate a solid and workable theoretical foundation for religious instruction. In accomplishing this cardinal task, I necessarily had to begin *de novo*, since as far as I was aware there was no previously existing model in the field of religious instruction. I could not adapt any prior macrotheoretical model or formulation; I had to create a totally new macrotheoretical model in the field. I suspect that my sharp break with tradition in this regard, and possibly even more crucially my efforts to boldly confront rather than sidestep the intrinsic relationship between religious instruction on the one hand and religion and theology and social science and education on the other hand are what largely account for the almost hysterical reaction which some religious education quarters directed at me when *The Shape of Religious Instruction* was first published.

One of the major pitfalls which I have assiduously endeavored to avoid while authoring my trilogy as well as my other written works is that of gimmickry. A major axis of my religious education apostolate has always been to provide a thorough and solid basis for the field. To accomplish this crucial task, all sorts of gimmickry necessarily had to be eschewed. Furthermore, every kind of speculative and procedural gimmick had to be forthrightly denounced. Sad to say, gimmickry has long been the bane of religious instruction.

Though I have devoted much of my life to developing a macrotheory for religious instruction, I am definitely not a rationalist. I am an implacable foe of rationalism because I firmly believe that rationalism constitutes one of the most venemous enemies of full-blooded religion. In formulating and verifying a macrotheory I am necessarily engaged in rational work. But my utilization of rationality and my formulation of a rational theory in no way make me a rationalist. By temperament and by daily activity, I am an incurable, red-hot romanticist. Authentic romanticism differs from sham romanticism in many ways, not the least of which is that authentic romanticism is exquisitely interlaced with genuine reality rather than with fantasy or delusion. Authentic romanticism is a way of viewing and loving and acting with reality so as to swing in tune with that sweet essence and those limitless possibilities of reality. Sham romanticism, for its part, attempts to deny or minimize reality in a vain and vainglorious attempt to suck the realistic core out of romanticism and to replace that core with escapism and fancifulness. I do what I do in religious instruction, and indeed in all of life, not for rationality but for love. What I am attempting to accomplish in my social-science macrotheory is not to supplant love with reason, but to help religious educators be more effective in assisting learners and themselves to love and serve God more fully.

Scholarly Writing

Precise and high scholarly writing is among the most difficult, most painstaking, most exhausting, most excruciating, and most frustrating of all human endeavors. This fact largely explains why so few people write scholarly books, especially in religious education.

Scholarly writing is very hard for me. To be sure, scholarly writing is a great burden and ponderous weight which hangs oppressively on my heart and soul all day and night. It is particularly difficult for me to write scholarly books and articles because I love life so very much. To do scholarly work means I have to sacrifice so much of life because genuine scholarship necessarily entails a hard-won combination of theoretical creativity and painstakingly laborious research drudgery. To write is to die to self, and dying is always difficult, especially when it is done in the silence of the library or the quiet of a research laboratory; dying is made a little easier and more consolable when it is surrounded by recognizable pageantry or encased in glory. To write in a scholarly vein is to be engaged in the daily disciplined surrender of one's own impulses to relax and simply enjoy life. To write in a scholarly vein is to exercise great strength to hold one's needs in check when one finds data or laws or constructs which stand in sharp variance with one's own perceptions or convictions. Genuine scholarship is a long and lonely path which few individuals seem to have the patience, endurance, and discipline to tread. Scholarly writing, in short, is hell.

During the long periods in which I write my books and articles, I adhere to a very strenuous schedule. At the end of a research-and-writing day, I am almost always racked with soul-numbing weariness. It is very difficult for me to keep going, knowing that the next day would only bring more of the same. Sometimes the enormous pressure of unrelenting scholarly writing makes me high-strung and irritable. I do not like these lapses into high-strungness or irritability, but I endure them as necessary consequences of the intense and total way in which I am exercising my apostolate.

I take scholarship very seriously. It is through serious and unrelenting scholarship that the true is uncovered and the false discarded. In the final analysis, it is scholarly material which ultimately shapes, refines, and verifies every field of work and every field of study. As far as I can ascertain, there has never been an important popular book, influential popular article, or curriculum textbook series in the field of religious instruction which was not strongly influenced by or even directly derived from someone's prior scholarship.

Because of the centrality and enormous ultimate influence of serious scholarship, I write every word and sentence and paragraph with utmost care. I am, after all, in God's service. When a scholar is in God's service, he must make doubly sure that his words and phrases in the scholarly arena are as pure and as true as he can make them. Anything else constitutes an arrogant affront to the God of purity and truth.

One extremely important reason why I take such great pains in attempting to write accurately and truly is the great damage which can be done by ideas, suggestions, and phraseology which are less than accurate and true.

Quite a few religious educationists and educators who write books and articles fail to do careful research, write imprecisely, and contradict themselves by proposing one course of action now and exactly the opposite later. I am totally incapable of understanding this mentality. I am completely perplexed at how these religious educationists and educators, well-intentioned though they may be, can face themselves and others with honesty. I wonder if these individuals ever have considered the serious damage they can wreak, not just on the field, but far more importantly on persons—persons who trust that what is written in these books and articles is worthy of adherence because the religious educationist or educator who wrote the book or article has supposedly researched with great care and stated with considerable precision the bases and implications of the proposal or idea being advanced. A religious education writer has a tremendous responsibility—souls are at stake.

I take great pains to write in such a way that careful scholars in future generations and in future centuries can meticulously pore over my books and major articles and find no trace of error or inaccuracy. Any scholar who endeavors to offer an enduring and resilient macrotheory must perforce strive to do the same.

To the best of my knowledge, I have never written anything in books or in major scholarly articles about which I did not have overwhelmingly convincing evidence. I take enormous care to let the reader know both the exact sources and the web of reasoning for my key statements and theses. It is a sad and pathetic reflection on the state of the field of religious instruction that some readers view the length and breadth of my footnotes as irrelevant, amusing, or even ridiculous.

If there are points about which I have less than convincing and overwhelming evidence, I will typically qualify my statements with words or phrases like "probably," "possibly," "it seems," "it appears," "tends to be," and so forth. Such qualifications are not mere literary niceties or arcane subtleties of the scholar. Rather, these qualifications are indispensable for accurate and valid communication of the point or thesis under discussion. A scholar, especially a scholar in religious instruction, must have as total a dedication as possible to the Lord of truth. Such dedication is operationalized in writing with consummate care and high precision.

Long ago, when I began writing deep and scholarly material, I found myself necessarily using increasingly nuanced and qualified prose. The reason for this is easy to understand. To be intellectually honest, a writer and most especially a scholar must not make simplistic and sweeping unqualified statements on matters which are themselves heavily nuanced or which entail qualification of one sort or another. To make sweeping unqualified statements is to commit a dishonesty to the readers and a disservice to the field. Yet unfortunately all too many books and articles in the field of religious instruction are characterized by sweeping unsupported statements and by unqualified and unnuanced prose.

In terms of my own macrotheory (namely, how my writing behavior is explained by my own macrotheory), the process content or style of prose must be consonant with the product content or the particular thoughts which are expressed.

I do all my own research, my own crosschecking of sources, and my own writing. I have never had a graduate assistant do my research for me. In fact, I even go to the library stacks myself rather than dispatch a research assistant there. My reasons for doing all my own research and writing are two. First, ransaking libraries by myself reveals to me books, articles, or other sources about which I might well be unaware. Discovery of these hitherto unknown loci of information can become highly useful to me in expanding and correcting my positions. Second, I take my commitment to precision and scholarly accuracy so seriously that I simply do not trust graduate students to be wholly accurate. Students are just that, students; they are not yet mature researchers, and hence lack the critical skill and requisite commitment of a senior researcher. Because I do all my own research and writing, it takes me a very long time to produce a book or a major scholarly article.

My actual writing takes place very, very slowly. When all my 3×5 research cards have been carefully organized and everything is ready to go for writing, it takes me on the average of one hour to compose two hundred words. I spend a long time laboriously poring over each word, consulting the dictionary and books of synonyms to make sure that I have selected precisely the correct word or phrase to convey my meaning with utmost precision. I slave away at paragraphs so that they flow properly and communicate my intent accurately. One of the most difficult aspects for me in writing is that of effecting optimum linkages of word to word, sentence to sentence, paragraph to paragraph, chapter to chapter. The linkages I am referring to are those involving both stylistic content (prose flow) and substantive content (idea flow). In order to mine fully the richness inherent in the complexity and depth of the material with which I am dealing, I do not write in short time frames but instead write in large uninterrupted blocks of time.

I find that the whole matter of consistency constitutes one of the most difficult and most pervasive aspects of writing a scholarly book or major article. I have to constantly be on the lookout for external and internal consistency. In the process of insuring external consistency, I must vigilantly check that what I have written accurately reflects the outside sources which I utilize in my own work. In the process of insuring internal consistency, I must vigilantly check that what I have written in a later part of a book squares with that which is written in an earlier part, and that what I have written in each part of the book is congruent both with that which I wrote in all my earlier writings and that which I will most likely write in my future books. I have to pay supreme attention to consistency, since consistency is at once a hallmark and a test of any valid workable theory. One of the great advantages of constructing a theory is that theory itself helps keep me consistent, since consistency is a major characteristic of theory itself.

My time-consuming and painstaking work in writing scholarly books and major articles is not something I enjoy doing but rather is something I must do if I am to arrive at the truth and serve the field of religious instruction as a scholar. I have repeatedly found that time-consuming meticulous work cannot be avoided if a writer wishes to arrive at what is true and discard what is untrue, if a writer wishes to be more than superficial or trendy. I have little respect for those religious educationists whose books are written in a few weeks or even in a couple of months. Such books characteristically display less-than-requisite scholarly care and precision.

A serious theorist in any field or discipline is typically obsessed at virtually every waking moment with his work, with the inner development and extensions of his theory, and with exploring the connections of his theory with everyday reality. Whether on the beach, at a concert, in an art gallery, photographing wonderful works of religious architecture, poking through the decaying ruins of past civilizations, or simply strolling through the countryside, my mind in one way or another is always consciously or subconsciously considering the further enrichment and application of some aspect of the social-science approach. I have gained some of my most important insights and advances in my macrotheory while interacting with nature and with beautiful human artifacts. I remember, for example, while walking up a snow-covered Austrian mountain on a cold January day in 1974 with twenty pounds of camera equipment on my back, I suddenly got an intuition on totally revising the entire internal construction of the first chapter of *The Content of Religious Instruction*.

A young Protestant religious educationist then teaching in Chicago once wrote me a letter in which he suggested that I should not disagree with other religious educationists either in print or in lectures around the country. I believe that the field of religious instruction would be considerably enfeebled if I or other religious educationists would take his advice. Any respectable field or discipline desperately needs negative critiques as well as positive proposals. Without critiques and disagreement, there is no way in which the field can test the validity and ascertain the worth of its current theory and practice. To be sure, public and open expression of disagreement constitutes one of the very foundations of scholarship. There have been very few major scholars in the history of the world who have abstained from disagreeing publicly with other scholars and with practitioners.

Personal and Religious Benefits

Though my principal and express purpose in developing the social-science approach has consistently been to fundamentally alter and basically enrich the field of religious instruction, nonetheless my own personal life has benefited enormously from my continual work in developing this macrotheory. This is as it should be, since a viable and fruitful macrotheory ought to enrich the personal as well as the professional life of everyone intimately involved in it. As I plunge deeper and deeper into the ocean of the social-science macrotheory, new sights, unexpected sounds, gorgeous revelations, and hidden harmonies in the world as it really is continue to implode in me. The social-science approach is truly a whole worldview, a whole mentality, a whole way of greeting the cosmos and living in it. It is a worldview and a mentality which have enriched my personal life enormously by enabling me to see and touch the world in its own actuality and authenticity. Developing the social-science approach, with its internal web of consistency, has exerted a considerable purifying effect on me: it has helped me contact the world as it really is rather than as I might fantasize it to be, and it has helped keep me from interpreting reality from the perspective of my own hidden personal needs.

Developing and living the social-science approach has also greatly enriched my own spiritual life. I believe that the social-science approach has enlarged and ripened my faith by assisting me to live in a deeper conscious and affective envelope of faith; surely this macrotheory continues to help me shuck the unreal spookiness, the unwarranted magic, and the destructive naiveness which were so very much a part of my faith in bygone days and which still unfortunately remain as debilitating residues in me today. I feel that the social-science approach is constantly opening up new vistas of authentic hope, a hope founded on and permeated with a vision of how the world really is and works rather than on the shallow shoals of false hope and empty wishful thinking. I am alive to the fact that the social-science approach enlarges my still-defective charity so that I am empowered to lovingly embrace the whole world in its trueness rather than futilely grasp the projections of my own needs and fantasies in a base and ultimately blasphemous attempt at love of God.

The Lonely Road

The journey of constructing a complex workable macrotheory for religious instruction takes place on a very lonely road. Few religious educationists or educators appear to appreciate the centrality of theory, much less of macrotheory. Most religious educationists pay lip service to theory, but few of them seem to understand what theory really is, the way it is constructed and validated, and how it differs radically from speculation and tract. Since I am advocating a macrotheory vastly different from the one encapsulated in the theological approach to religious instruction, my journey is all the more lonely. But this loneliness is an indispensable dimension of any life which aims at being truly prophetic. Prophets of yesteryear and of today must necessarily tread the winepress alone. It is lonely for me out there in the field of religious instruction. Still, this long loneliness is at once a high price and a purifying reward, and as such I embrace it warmly and lovingly.

Reaction to the Social-Science Approach

I have been deeply gratified at the growing influence which the social-science approach has thus far exerted on the field of religious instruction. There can be little doubt that the field as a whole is in the process of swinging away from the theological approach and toward the social-science approach. With increasing intensity, religious educators have been consciously making the social-science approach the foundation and rationale of their activities. In some cases, this fundamental swing has been dramatic. In other cases, this basic swing has been slow and almost imperceptible. In short, religious instruction is more and more perceiving itself as an autonomous field with theology playing a supporting role.

Naturally there has been and continues to be considerable opposition to the social-science approach on the part of many religious educators, especially those in the Catholic catechetical sector. Such opposition is readily understandable. The adoption of a social-science approach entails a fundamental reordering of one's own self, a whole turning around in the way one meets and interprets all reality. This basic change in world view is difficult and often soul-searing for persons who by long and hard effort had previously made the theological approach the center of their religious lives and the touchstone of their personal existences. It is quite natural for many of these individuals to strongly oppose and even bitterly lash out at the social-science approach and the persons who advocate it. Since I am the founder of the social-science approach in religious instruction, and since I am one of the few social scientists in general who openly confront theology with social science in a fundamental manner, it is quite understandable that much of the opposition to the social-science approach on the part of religious educators is directed at me and my macrotheory.

Opposition is beneficial to every field of endeavor. More than this, opposition is absolutely necessary for the growth and vitality of every field of human activity. Healthy and high-level opposition provides an indispensable corrective to theory, a corrective which helps refine theory and move it to higher levels. Confrontational opposition is a condition necessary for genuinely creative work such as building a workable macrotheory.

The force and texture of the opposition which has generally been directed toward me thus far is highly revealing since it simultaneously shows the level of much of the field and some of the deep-seated fears operating within much of the field.

The theoretical opposition directed toward the social-science approach has tended to be at a very low level, a fact which itself discloses the level of much of the field of religious instruction. To date, no individual who stands in public opposition to the social-science approach has probed or critiqued the bed-rock basis and fundamental shape of the social-science macrotheory. Rather, those intellectual critiques which have been proffered typically are directed toward some secondary feature of my social-science macrotheory. Yet even these critiques, well-intentioned as many of them are, usually have been either shallow or factually incorrect.

Many of my adversaries have been highly professional, gentlemanly, and open-minded in their opposition. Randolph Crump Miller is a splendid case in point. Though the distinguished Miller disagrees with a great many of my fundamental positions, he has included rather than censored my writings from the professional religious education journal which he once edited, and encouraged rather than banned me from speaking at national or regional meetings in which he had some decisive influence. Some diocesan catechetical establishments of the open-minded type have also treated me fairly and well.

It is with sadness and disappointment that I found some of the opposition which I have encountered has been of a decidedly unprofessional, intolerant, and closed-minded character. This statement holds especially true for the opposition which I have received from the Central Catechetical Establishment and from those diocesan catechetical establishments sharing the same suppressive spirit as the Central Catechetical Establishment. Over and over again, these groups and their apparatchiks have censored my writings, banned me from speaking before conventions or in university settings, and ostracized me in a variety of ways. Dirty tricks have sometimes typified these kinds of odious suppressive activities. Limitations of space prevent me from detailing specific concrete incidents which illustrate the point I am making in this paragraph.

It might well be that some Christian religious educationists and educators, notably within the Catholic sector, possess neither the kind of personal worldview nor the kind of professional macrotheory which allows them to welcome and promote disagreement with their own positions.

In dealing with persons or with institutions which oppose my macrotheory, I have always striven to the best of my ability to base my reaction squarely on the Gamaliel principle. In my professional career, I have never knowingly suppressed or banned the expression of an opponent's idea simply because that person was an opponent or because his viewpoint clashed with my own. This statement holds true both for my own writings and edited works, as well as for my activities as the publisher of Religious Education Press. While I was at Notre Dame, I hired a diverse range of faculty members including some whose views differed substantially from my own. In those national or regional conventions and workshops in which I had influence, I endeavored to the best of my ability to secure a wide variety of speakers including persons who oppose my fundamental position; indeed, whenever appropriate, I deliberately sought out members of the Central Catechetical Establishment and diocesan catechetical establishments to serve as principal speakers. I firmly believe that if an adversary's macrotheory or critiques are indeed sound and correct, then no amount of banning or even dirty tricks on my part would successfully bury such a worthwhile macrotheory or critique. I must emphasize that personally and professionally, banning and other kinds of dirty tricks directed at opponents are abhorrent to me as a human being, as a scholar, and as a Christian. Furthermore, as a Christian and as a scholar, I am strictly required to accord the views of adversaries an open hearing, and if these views are proven to be correct, to modify or even abandon my own position accordingly.

My adherence to the Gamaliel principle does not mean, of course, that I am thereby obliged to abstain from answering my critics or to refrain from showing that they are wrong in those instances in which the evidence suggests that my critics are incorrect. Scholarship such as that involved in constructing, verifying, and critiquing a macrotheory demands that all the evidence be put on the table and rigorously examined.

RELIGIOUS EDUCATION PRESS

The history of how my professional position in religious education was forged would be manifestly incomplete without mention of Religious Education Press.

In the early 1970s, I noticed that major Catholic and Protestant publishers either discontinued or at least sharply curtailed the number of serious and scholarly books they issued in the area of religious education. Several reasons seem to account for this unhappy decision on the part of Catholic and Protestant publishers. The main reason appears to be financial. Religious publishers were losing money on serious and scholarly religious education books because religious educators and educationists simply were not purchasing sufficient quantities of this type of book for the publishers to as much as break even financially. As a religious educationist, I was and still am deeply disappointed at the decision of these important religious publishers because I am convinced that religious education can grow and be vital only if the field is infused every year with a goodly number of serious and scholarly books in religious education.

My deep disappointment at the fact that fewer and fewer scholarly religious education books were issued every year slowly and steadily gave rise to a strong feeling within me that someone should do something about this regrettable turn of events. Since no religious group and no other individual person seemed to be doing anything concretely to invigorate the field by beginning to publish major religious education books, I decided that I should plunge headlong into the breach myself. God's work had to be done, and if no one else was willing to do it, then the task fell to me by default.

Before actually establishing Religious Education Press, however, I put my impulsion to the same severe critical test to which I put any new idea or venture which I might have. The test is this: how does this new idea or venture fit in both with my overall call to serve God and with my specific religious education apostolate? The more I reflected and affected, the more I grew convinced that Religious Education Press could be a legitimate and in some respects a necessary dimension of my call and my apostolate. A publishing venture would be an important element in the galaxy of my religious education endeavor. Religious Education Press, furthermore, could become a major engine for triggering, not simply a dramatic renewal of the field, but even more importantly for laying that kind of solid foundation whereby religious education could become a legitimate field of activity based on a well-constructed theoretical foundation.

From the outset, I knew that Religious Education Press would consistently lose money. After all, the major reason why I founded REP was that major religious publishers had altogether ceased or at least had sharply curtailed issuing serious and scholarly books in religious education chiefly because these books were proven money losers. Because we have always lost money and will continue to lose money for the foreseeable future, Religious Education Press surely is an apostolate and not a business.

From the launching of Religious Education Press until the present, my family and I have directly subsidized this apostolic publishing venture both in cash subventions and in cash-equivalent benefactions. My wife and I work for REP without receiving any salary or income tax write-offs. I do not take royalties for books which I write for Religious Education Press. If my family and I did not continually subsidize Religious Education Press, there is no way in which this apostolate could continue. It goes without saying, of course, that in addition to the financial sacrifices, my family and I make considerable personal sacrifices in order to keep REP going.

From the very beginning, I have attempted to insure that the line of books published by Religious Education Press possesses six major fundamental characteristics. First, Religious Education Press publishes books exclusively in religious education or in areas intimately related to religious education. Second, Religious Education Press publishes books on topics of signal importance to the field of religious education. Third, Religious Education Press publishes only serious and scholarly works. We do not issue popular books or curriculum materials. Fourth, Religious Education Press tries as hard as possible to publish books which are ecumenical in scope. Fifth, Religious Education Press strives to issue books which have high production values, as for example, high-quality paper and large typeface. Sixth, Religious Education Press publishes books representing a wide range of divergent theoretical bases and conflicting points of view; such a catholicity of outlooks is necessary if the field is to be genuinely enriched and enhanced.

Religious educationists and educators by and large have supported Religious Education Press, though not to the extent to which I think genuine professionalism and religious commitment necessitates. Our sales records suggest that as a general rule, Protestant religious educationists and educators on a per capita basis buy more REP books than their Catholic counterparts. This statement holds true at every level, ranging from seminary and university adoption of REP volumes as textbooks to the purchase of REP books by parish religious educators and other kinds of local church workers. It would seem that Protestant religious educationists and educators are more committed to religious education as a serious, focused, and autonomous field than are Catholic religious educationists and educators. Predictably, the Central Catechetical Establishment, and those among diocesan catechetical establishments sharing the same constricted spirit as the Central Catechetical Establishment, has been the religious education sector least receptive to the efforts of Religious Education Press.

In the few years of existence, Religious Education Press has grown quite rapidly. Many contemporary religious educationists have told me at various times that Religious Education Press is now indisputably the most important publisher of serious, significant, and scholarly books in the field. I would like to think that this judgment is true.

What impact is Religious Education Press having on the field? I have no reliable or valid answer to this question. Because Religious Education Press annually publishes more serious, significant, and scholarly books than most other publishers combined, its influence probably will be considerable. It is my fervent prayer that books published by Religious Education Press will give form to what is now an amorphous field, furnish a solid theoretical foundation to what is now a rickety assemblage of pedagogical gimmicks, and offer vitality to what is now a yet-unborn plain of flowers. Whether my prayer will be answered I probably will never know in my lifetime. Given both the nature of prayer and my own many personal failings, such a prayer in itself is its own affirmation.

EXILE IN EGYPT

During my fifteenth year at Notre Dame, I decided to seek a position at another university. I eventually chose not to teach in a church-related university for a variety of reasons. One background factor was that with the exception of the golden pre-Burtchaell days at Notre Dame, I have generally been treated in a more professional way and in a more Christian manner in secular educational institutions than in church-related

schools. Though present, this factor was only adumbrational. The potent factors accounting for my leaving a church-related school setting
were more immediate in nature. Among the most forceful precipitating
factors was Berard Marthaler's banning of a major article of response
which I had submitted to *The Living Light*, the ecclesiastically-approved catechetical organ of which Marthaler serves as executive editor.
In almost every dealing I have had over the years with Marthaler, I have
found him to personify everything I despise about the Central Catechetical Establishment of which he is a prominent leader: closed-mindedness, insularism, a certain underhandedness, obsession with
ecclesiastically-approved catechetical documents, disdainfulness of
laypersons, eagerness to ban and censor the views of persons and groups
whose views differ from the official catechetical party line, and an
especial alacrity to servilely grovel and obsequiously fawn to persons in
positions of ecclesiastical power. Berard Marthaler had published several articles in *The Living Light* written by individuals critical of one or
another of my positions. So, as both to answer the charges of my adversaries and to keep the discussion going, I wrote a lengthy article in which
I responded to the critical points raised by my opponents. Despite the
fact that most editors of serious journals like to promote controversy in
their magazines as a way of providing well-rounded coverage of the issue
under dispute, Marthaler banned my article from appearing in his
catechetical organ. His banning seems to stem from two reasons. First,
he and the Central Catechetical Establishment generally stand opposed
to genuine interchange of divergent ideas or to any viewpoints critical of
positions or interpretations which this Establishment espouses. Second,
my article of response criticized the views of a prominent, eccle-
siastically favored, theological popularizer and some of his proteges;
Marthaler apparently hoped to crawl into that theologian's patronage by
preventing the appearance of an article critical of some of the religious
education views of that cleric and his proteges. At any event, Marthaler's
banning, together with certain occurrences which took place as I was
negotiating for a position in a Catholic institution of higher learning,
forcefully slammed home to me that my apostolate is not likely to
flourish in many church-related institutions of higher learning, especially when such institutions are under Catholic auspices. The Marthaler ban was the final straw in a whole series of difficulties I have had
with that spirit of closed-mindedness and suppression rampant in certain religious education circles.

I selected the University of Alabama in Birmingham (UAB) for a variety of factors, almost all of which were directly related to deliberately enhancing my religious education apostolate. I had never before taught full-time in a university which was Southern, urban, and state-controlled. This new experience, I believed, would help expand my horizons and prevent insularism. Also, the greatly improved salary which I would receive at UAB in contrast to the relatively mediocre salary scale at Notre Dame and at most church-related institutions was also an important factor in my decision since I realized full well that I would need substantially more income in order to financially support Religious Education Press.

My first three years at the University of Alabama in Birmingham were not the happiest for me. There were certain proximate causes accounting for this. However, the basic cause seems to be that I was in a major decompression stage of my life and apostolate, a decompression from the exciting milieu of what was the nation's foremost doctoral program in religious education to a quite different academic environment. Furthermore, I had still not emotionally recovered from the soul-searing shock of the abolition of the Notre Dame graduate program in religious education.

One day I decided to engage in a major reassessment of my situation at UAB. As a result of this reappraisal, I came to the conclusion that I am truly fortunate to be where I am, for surely I am in Egypt with all its material fleshpots and spiritual advantages.

The professional side of my exile here in Egypt brims over with all sorts of opportunities and benefits. Faculty members at UAB enjoy enormous academic freedom. This kind of academic freedom, so requisite for seminal scholarship and stimulating teaching, is of a magnitude as to be unparalleled in any church-related institution of higher learning with which I am personally familiar. I have a great deal of time at UAB for my research and scholarly writing. I have received grants and other forms of assistance from UAB to help me successfully prosecute my research in religious education. Everything considered, the university administration at every level has been especially kind and generous to me. Here at the University of Alabama in Birmingham, I am free of any internal pressure from a clerical administration or from a politically powerful contingent of a theology faculty to interpret religion and religious education in a manner these groups believe to be "correct" or fashionable. Since UAB is not subject to direct or indirect external ecclesiastical control, I am well insulated from any pressures which the *ecclesiasticum* might like to overtly or subtly place on a religious educationist working in those universities or seminaries in which they have some degree of influence. Because I am situated at the University of Alabama in Birmingham, I am out of the clutches of the Central Catechetical Establishment, of diocesan catechetical establishments, and of any ecclesiastical group seeking to restrict, suppress, or otherwise noxiously control my scholarly activities in a university setting.

The personal side of my exile here in Egypt has proved to be enriching and fulfilling. The experience of working in a secular university has been more spiritually envigorating for my soul than I had previously imagined.

The splendid priests who currently staff St. Paul's Cathedral, my parish here in Birmingham, are probably the finest, most pastoral, and most open-minded clerical team of any parish in which I have even been a member. Consequently, I have become more involved in parish and diocesan life in Birmingham than ever in my life before. I was elected to serve on the parish council, and was appointed to membership on the diocesan board of education—two groups which I have found to be notably committed, vigorous, and above all open-minded. (It goes without saying that I have never been invited by the Birmingham diocesan catechetical establishment to work with that group in any way, shape, or form.).

Egypt, despite its bountiful fleshpots, is still Egypt. I do miss interacting with colleagues in a well-defined and ontic religious education program. I do miss teaching graduate courses specifically in religious education. I do miss working closely with doctoral students in helping them hammer out their own theoretical position in religious education, in enabling them to appreciate the theoretical and scientific basis of religious education practice, and in assisting them in writing their dissertations in religious education. I like to think that the face of religious education would have been significantly improved if I were still involved in a top-flight university program of religious education professionally preparing leaders for this field; this thought, by itself, makes me sad that I am not in such a program. Though I am still deeply involved in religious education through my scholarly writings and through Religious Education Press, and though I now work with authors on their books instead of with students on their dissertations, still Egypt does not stand directly in the center of the religious education world. This fact inevitably casts an omnipresent shadow of sadness over me and my apostolate.

Abrupt changes have occasionally happened in the history of the church. In a few rare instances, a church-related institution suddenly emerges which is a Camelot of quality, commitment, and freedom. Consequently, I can never totally rule out the possibility that I will eventually teach and do religious education research at a major Catholic or Protestant institution of higher learning. However, as I see it now, this possibility is extremely remote.

Some years ago, when a prototypical ecclesiastical official ruled imperiously over a major midwestern archdiocese, a number of his priests left the ministry there without his permission. One of these clerics went to Europe on his own to pursue advanced study in theology. A decent and spiritual man, he felt in conscience that he was unable to be an exemplary priest in the kind of repressive atmosphere which the archbishop had created. A few years later, the archbishop was faced with a growing shortage of priests. Biting the bullet, the archbishop wrote all those priests who had left the archdiocese but not the priesthood, inviting them to return. In his letter the archbishop told the priests that all was forgiven, and that they would return in good standing and with his blessing. The priest studying theology in Europe wanted very much to return to his pastoral ministry in the archdiocese, but had serious misgivings about the genuineness of the archbishop's offer of forgiveness or the archbishop's implied hint that he was fostering a more open and ecclesial climate. The priest wrote to a bishop-friend of his who headed a diocese which is in close geographical proximity to that of the archbishop. In his letter, the priest asked his bishop-friend's advice on whether or not he should return to his home archdiocese. Ten days later the priest received a telegram from his friend the bishop. The telegram read: "Herod still lives. Remain in Egypt."

For the foreseeable future, I too will remain in Egypt.

POSTLUDE—VIVACE RINFORZANDO E CON BRIO

A couple of years ago I received a letter from an Australian religious educator. This highly intelligent and altruistic woman had received her doctorate in religious education from Notre Dame. She wrote me reporting that she was fired from her position as director of adult religious education in an Australian diocesan catechetical establishment because she was endeavoring to effect a major renewal in that diocese's adult religious education program. Justifiedly disappointed at the closed-mindedness of Australian catechetical establishments in general, this woman took a teaching position in religious education at a Catholic institution of higher learning in her native country. Commenting on her being sacked from her catechetical position, she wrote: "You set out to professionally prepare what you termed 'leaders for the field,' but did you know that you really trained leaders for a religious education revolution?" I was well aware, of course, that a mainspring of my work has always been that of professionally preparing religious education professors and administrators for that kind of renewal which is revolutionary precisely because this kind of renewal places religious education at center stage rather than in the wings, because it is grounded in a comprehensive systematic macrotheory rather than a rag-bag assemblage of unconnected impressions and gimmicks, and because it is targeted directly at what is apostolically effective rather than what is officially approved by one or another *ecclesiasticum*. Given the pathetic state of religious education throughout much of this century, I would not be true to the vision of quality religious education if I were not a revolutionary.

My scholarly books and articles in religious education have always been revolutionary, and will continue to be so in the future. Religious Education Press is obviously a revolutionary enterprise.

There is a Turkish proverb which states that he who rides the horse of revolution must always have one foot in the stirrup. To me, this proverb means three things. First of all, a dedicated revolutionary must be ready to immediately dismount whenever he finds a situation which holds revolutionary promise. Second, a committed revolutionary must be ready at a moment's notice to leave the place where he is when the revolution beckons, and go immediately to another situation in which the prospects for the success of the revolution seem more probable. Third, an alert revolutionary must be ready to depart immediately when those who would assassinate or wound him gravely are coiled to strike quickly and silently in the night.

Like most apostles and other kinds of revolutionaries, I hope that someone will carry on my work after I die. Perhaps some day God will send me a student or younger scholar whom I can personally prepare for the continuation of my two-pronged apostolate, namely as a theorist-researcher and as a publisher. The birth in 1980 of James V and in 1982 of Michael gave me hope that perhaps my successors will come, fittingly, from the ranks of my own family.

About an hour after James V was born, I proudly carried him from the recovery room to the nursery. On the way, I gazed into his little face, and then-and-there consecrated him to God and to his service with the fervent prayer that God would indeed call him to be his apostle. To the name James which we gave him at birth we added a second name at baptism, the name of the greatest of all God's apostles, Paul. The baptism took place on the feast of the conversion of St. Paul in the Cathedral of St. Paul. The priest who performed the rite is a world-renowned religious educationist who was born and raised in my wife's picturesque home town in the Austrian Alps. The scripture passages which I selected and read during the baptism ceremony were all deliberately targeted to what I prayed would be James Paul's central path in life, namely that of an apostle in religious education.

When Michael was born two years later, I also carried him from the recovery room to the nursery and in the process also consecrated him to God and to God's service. To the name Michael we added that of one of God's most committed and energetic apostles, Francis Xavier. Michael's baptism took place on the feast of St. Francis Xavier in the Church of St. Francis Xavier. The same priest who baptized James V performed the rite on Michael.

While I can consecrate both James V and Michael to God's service, only God can give them the call—the God whom I pray will beckon both James V and Michael from beyond the cosmos through and in the basic being and becoming of all reality. I will do my very best in the remainder of my life to make James V and Michael ready for the call, if and when God gives them the call. I pray that God provides me with the grace and the ability to successfully discharge this awesome duty. If God does not give James V or Michael the call, I shall know of a truth that God has other things planned for them, things in which these two boys can please God more than if they were apostles.

I wish to emphasize strongly that I love all the Christian churches, and most especially my own Catholic Church. I frequently describe myself as a "red-hot Roman Catholic." I also consider myself as intensely loyal to the church, more loyal in fact than those individuals who have made themselves servile sychophants and truckling toadies to the ecclesiastical establishment, possibly in hopes of thereby securing personal privilege or ecclesiastical preferment. To my way of thinking, a groveling attitude toward the *ecclesiasticum* is quite the opposite of genuine loyalty to the church. My view is that lack of rigorous questioning, or a failure to mount opposition when opposition is needed for the church's renewal, constitute grave disloyalty to the ecclesia and even to the *ecclesiasticum*. In those instances in which I criticize the church or in which I press for religious education reform, I do so out of love for the church. I wish this point to be clearly and unambiguously understood. I love the church because the church is the bride of Christ—a much-spotted and oft-ravished bride, a bride whose actions require that she frequently say the *Confiteor*, but all withal, the bride of Christ nonetheless. And did not Christ solemnly promise to be with his church for all time? After all, who can separate Christ from his cross?

Many, many times throughout my life, I have asked myself the question: "Why did God choose me to be his apostle? When there are so many better and more virtuous persons around, why did he select me?" Everytime I ask this question, the same answer returns: silence. I never asked to be an apostle. And most assuredly, I, of all people, am totally unworthy of the call. This statement is not humility; it is stark reality. I have enormous personal failings, as anyone who knows me can amply testify. It is only by God's grace, then, that I am an apostle, and not because of any personal strengths or abilities. It seems to me that because I have so many serious personal failings both glaring and hidden, God's grace and power are thereby made all the more manifest in my apostolate. The failures in my apostolate are a direct result of my own personal defects. The successes in my apostolate are a consequence of the grace of God working through my personal strengths and weaknesses in such a way that these very strengths and weaknesses are felicitously mobilized for the successful accomplishment of an apostolic task.

In calling me to be one of his apostles, God has given me a great honor, an honor which I clearly do not deserve. I hope I have not disappointed God, at least not too much. At any rate, I give the apostolate everything I have.

I have had a marvelous life thus far. A large measure of this is due to the happy and optimistic personality with which I have been endowed. I am an incurable romantic, and everything always works out extraordinarily well for romantics who have a realistic core. The second cause of my marvelous life has been due to the inestimable privilege which God has bestowed upon me in calling me to be an apostle.

I have worked very hard in my adult life, and have been extremely lucky in that I always emerged from every fair wind and from every crisis in better shape than when I entered them. But on careful examination, what seems at first blush to be luck is really not luck at all; instead, it is a consequence which flows inevitably from a living working relationship with God. I have always taken as the official motto of my personal life and of my apostolate the glorious words of St. Paul, words which are as much of an absolute guarantee as any ever written: "For those who love God, all things work together unto good" (Rom. 8:28).

I trust that the sweet and sour grapes of all my past experiences will be beautifully distilled into the rich wine of a continually more capable apostolate.

In any event, I hope that God will go on giving me the grace to energetically gallop into the future in an attempt to hasten it toward Point Omega. And may I always have one foot in the stirrup.

Other Important Books from Religious Education Press

THE THEORY OF CHRISTIAN EDUCATION PRACTICE
by Randolph Crump Miller

An elaboration on the way in which theology affects religious education in a determinative fashion, and on the manner in which religious education enfleshes theology. ISBN 0-89135-049-7

CONSCIENCE: DEVELOPMENT AND SELF-TRANSCENDENCE
by Walter E. Conn

A pioneering new look at the structure and growth of conscience from the interdisciplinary perspectives of ethics, psychology, and theology. Major themes include conscience as the basic form which personal authenticity takes, and conscience as flourishing in self-giving love.
ISBN 0-89135-025-X

DEVELOPMENTAL DISCIPLINE
by Kevin Walsh and Milly Cowles

This volume is the only current major book on discipline which views the discipline process primarily as a task of moral education. The axis of this fine book is that discipline is education in moral and religious discipleship. This volume provides the theoretical background and practical tools necessary for educational ministers to help children and youth to acquire positive discipline. ISBN 0-89135-32-2

CAN CHRISTIANS BE EDUCATED?
by Morton Kelsey

An examination from the standpoint of depth psychology some of the most critical concerns in contemporary religious education, including education for love, education for spiritual wholeness, and education for positive emotional values. This volume integrates religious education with growth in the religion teacher's own personal spirituality.
ISBN 0-89135-008-X

CHRIST THE PLACENTA
by *David A. Bickimer*
The major theme of this scintillating book is that religious education at every level and in every setting must be education for transcendence. Written as a series of letters, this volume is dazzling in the way it integrates religion, poetry, art, modern physics, social science, contemporary theology, and everyday human experience into a spectacular vision of the means and ends of religious education. ISBN 0-89135-034-9

THE FLOW OF RELIGIOUS EDUCATION
by *James Michael Lee*
A serious in-depth look at the nature and structure of the religion teaching process. This volume provides that kind of solid and systematic framework so necessary for the effective *teaching* of religion. A major work. ISBN 0-89135-001-2

WHO ARE WE?: THE QUEST FOR A RELIGIOUS EDUCATION
edited by *John H. Westerhoff III*
An exploration into the identity and special calling of the religious educator as seen by many of the most important religious education leaders of the twentieth century. Many of the most important issues facing religious education are treated in this book. ISBN 0-89135-014-4

AN INVITATION TO RELIGIOUS EDUCATION
by *Harold William Burgess*
A careful examination of the most influential Protestant and Catholic theories of religious education proposed in our time. An essential book for understanding the foundational issues in religious education. ISBN 0-89135-019-5

CREATIVE CONFLICT IN RELIGIOUS EDUCATION AND CHURCH ADMINISTRATION
by *Donald E. Bossart*
A stimulating volume centering around two major themes: the myriad possibilities for growth inherent in all conflict, and the specific procedures which can be used in religious settings to bring out the productive potential in conflict. This interdisciplinary volume deals with the theological dynamics, psychological dynamics, sociological dynamics, and educational dynamics of conflict. ISBN 0-89135-048-9

PROCESS AND RELATIONSHIP
edited by *Iris V. Cully and Kendig Brubaker Cully*
A penetrating examination of how the interactive realities of process and relationship profoundly affect the structure of religious education, theology, and philosophy. Original essays by fourteen of North America's leading Protestant and Catholic thinkers. ISBN 0-89135-012-8

THE SHAPE OF RELIGIOUS EDUCATION
by *James Michael Lee*
No one can discuss contemporary religious education meaningfully unless he or she has read this book. Widely acclaimed as a classic in the field. ISBN 0-89135-000-4

RELIGIOUS EDUCATION AND THEOLOGY
edited by *Norma H. Thompson*
This important book presents a wide variety of diverse and robust points of view on the dynamic relationship between religious education and theology. Original and seminal essays by the most important contemporary religious education scholars. A benchmark book in the sense that it provides the standard against which any future discussion of the relationship of religious education and theology will have to be measured. ISBN 0-89135-029-2

THE RELIGIOUS EDUCATION WE NEED
edited by *James Michael Lee*
A prophetic volume presenting Catholic and Protestant proposals on a viable future for religious education. Exciting chapters by Alfred McBride, Randolph Crump Miller, Carl F. H. Henry, John Westerhoff III, Gloria Durka, and James Michael Lee. This book has as its axis the renewal of Christian education. ISBN 0-89135-005-5

CELEBRATING THE SECOND YEAR OF LIFE: A PARENT'S GUIDE FOR A HAPPY CHILD
by *Lucie W. Barber*
A practical guide for religious parenting and educating. This book is organized around psychologically-proven ways in which parents and members of the helping professions can successfully develop five basic capacities in the child *and* in themselves: trust and faith; a positive self-image; self-confidence and independence; a joy for learning the ability to associate with others happily. ISBN 0-89135-015-2

THE RELIGIOUS EDUCATION OF PRESCHOOL CHILDREN
by *Lucie W. Barber*
A holistic approach embracing all areas of the child's religious life—cognitive, affective, and lifestyle. The most significant work to date on the religious education of preschool children in home and church.
ISBN 0-89135-026-8

RELIGIOUS EDUCATION MINISTRY WITH YOUTH
edited by *D. Campbell Wyckoff and Don Richter*
An insightful in-depth exploration of present concerns and future directions of youth ministry. Informative chapters dealing with the available research of youth ministry, the basic questions the Church needs to answer about youth ministry, the personal and social problems of youth, the ways in which youth can be bonded into a true community which is religious, and other chapters designed to help the religious educator empower youth for religious living and ecclesial service.
ISBN 0-89135-030-6

THE RELIGIOUS EDUCATION OF ADULTS
by *Leon McKenzie*
This superb and comprehensive book has taken its place as the standard treatment of adult religious education. Malcolm Knowles calls it "clearly the most important work to date on adult religious education and one of the most important books on adult education in general."
ISBN 0-89135-031-4

TRADITION AND TRANSFORMATION IN RELIGIOUS EDUCATION
edited by *Padraic O'Hare*
Four important religious education scholars reflect on the urgent but complex issue of how religious education can transform the world while at the same time faithfully hand on the Christian message.
ISBN 0-89135-016-0

RELIGIOUS EDUCATION IN A PSYCHOLOGICAL KEY
by *John H. Peatling*
A perceptive look at religious education from a psychological perspective. This volume shows how psychology can empower religious education to enrich the spiritual lives of learners. A major feature of this book is the penetrating way in which it reveals the religious dimension of psychology and the psychological dimension of religion.
ISBN 0-89135-027-6

MORAL DEVELOPMENT, MORAL EDUCATION, AND KOHLBERG
edited by *Brenda Munsey*
A seminal volume on the interrelated topics of moral development, moral education, and religious education. An interdisciplinary treatment from the perspectives of religious education, philosophy, psychology, and general education. These original essays bring together some of the most important scholars in North America, Europe, and Israel. ISBN 0-89135-020-9

ABOVE OR WITHIN?: THE SUPERNATURAL IN RELIGIOUS EDUCATION
by *Ian P. Knox*
An illuminating survey of the basic theological issue permeating all religious education activity, namely: "How can the religious educator help learners of all ages meet God in their own lives?" A book centering on God's revelation in religious education. ISBN 0-89135-006-3

RELIGIOUS CONVERSION AND PERSONAL IDENTITY
by *V. Bailey Gillespie*
A sensitive treatment of religious conversion as a basic way of achieving personal identity and self-transcendence. This stimulating book integrates psychological findings with both the biblical perspective and theological insights. ISBN 0-89135-018-7

BIBLICAL INTERPRETATION IN RELIGIOUS EDUCATION
by *Mary C. Boys*
An illuminating examination of the way in which the bible and biblical interpretation have affected twentieth century religious education. The first part of this volume is a fine examination and critique of biblical revelation offered by twentieth century biblical scholars. The second part deals with how religious educators brought the bible into the field as salvation history. ISBN 0-89135-022-5

RELIGIOUS EDUCATION, CATECHESIS, AND FREEDOM
by *Kenneth Barker*
A fine examination of the different responses given by religious educationists and catechetical leaders to the call to freedom issued by the church and by the world. A helpful book for educational ministers seriously concerned with providing learners with religious education and with catechesis in and for freedom. ISBN 0-89135-028-4

RESURGENCE OF RELIGIOUS INSTRUCTION
by *Didier-Jacques Piveteau and J. T. Dillon*
A well-developed theoretical foundation for the community and family model of religious education, together with concrete examples of ways in which family and community religious education programs have worked. ISBN 0-89135-007-1

REGARDING RELIGIOUS EDUCATION
by *Mary K. Cove and Mary Louise Mueller*
A helpful volume for parish religious education directors striving to develop an effective program and to enhance the effectiveness of their teaching personnel. Topics include targeting instruction to here-and-now religious living, introducing accountability into all phases of the program, assessment of the learner's religious needs, and coordination of the religious education efforts of various parish and congregation groups. ISBN 0-89135-011-X

CLARITY IN RELIGIOUS EDUCATION
by *Robert Yorke O'Brien*
Clear and practical treatment of some of the most vexing areas in religious education today, such as teaching holiness, teaching biblical miracles, teaching the sacraments, and teaching the church. ISBN 0-89135-013-6

IMPROVING CHURCH EDUCATION
by *H. W. Byrne*
A bible-centered approach to effective Christian education ministry. Written from an evangelical Protestant perspective, this comprehensive book explains practical and workable models for successful total church education, including models for grouping people for effective teaching and learning, models for improved instructional space, models for enriched teaching, and models for improved staffing. ISBN 0-89135-017-9

THE BIG LITTLE SCHOOL, second edition revised and enlarged
by *Robert W. Lynn and Elliott Wright*
This classic history of the American Sunday School in a revised and updated form. A superb and delightful analysis of how the American Protestant Church perceived its educational mission throughout the years, and how it actually went about bringing religion to the hearts and minds of the taught as well as the teachers. ISBN 0-89135-021-7